Passages to Modernity

Passages to Modernity

Motherhood, Childhood, and Social Reform in Early Twentieth Century Japan

Kathleen S. Uno

University of Hawai'i Press • Honolulu

Library of Congress Cataloguing-in-Publication Data

Uno, Kathleen S., 1951
    Passages to modernity : motherhood, childhood, and social reform
in early twentieth century Japan / Kathleen S. Uno.
      p. cm.
    Includes bibliographical references and index.
    ISBN 0–8248–1619–6 (cloth : alk. paper).—ISBN 0–8248–2137–8
(pbk. : alk. paper)
    1. Day care centers—Japan—History—20th century. 2. Child care—
Japan—History—20th century. 3. Mother and child—Japan—
History—20th century. I. Title.
HQ778.7.J3U56 1999
306.874'09520904—dc21   98—47549
                                                                          CIP

University of Hawai'i Press books are printed on acid-
free paper and meet the guidelines for permanence and
durability of the Council on Library Resources.

Printed by Data Reproductions Corporation

To my mother, father, and sister,
and the many other sisters who helped

Contents

Acknowledgments

It is now over a decade since I first began to shape the evidence gleaned from Japanese archives into the arguments and interpretations in this book. I would like to express my gratitude to many fellow researchers on both sides of the Pacific for their willingness to discuss ideas and provide assistance as I worked through documents and secondary works along the long and winding way.

I would like to thank the Japan Foundation, the American Association of University Women, and the Center for Japanese Studies at the University of California, Berkley, for financial awards that made possible the research for the dissertation on which this book is based, and Temple University for a summer research award to research photographs. Warm thanks to Irwin Scheiner, Thomas C. Smith, and Arlie Hochschild for advice, support, and intellectual stimulation. Without the generous assistance of Kyūichi Yoshida, Yasuko Ichibangase, Kazuyo Yamamoto, Kuni Nakajima, Takeo Shishido, Yoshiko Miyake, and Masako Ohtomo, this study would have remained a dream. Kazuo Niimura, director of the Ohara Institute for Social Research, graciously permitted use of the photographs appearing here. Hiroko Hara and Kaoru Tachi also deserve special mention, as do Jun Izumi, Nobuko Ogawa, Eiji Yutani, Miharu Nishimura, Keiko Katoda, Michiko Mabashi, Keiko Kawai, Kiyoko Tani, Ryūtarō Kinoshita, Chizu Teshi, Motoko Ōta, Mitsuru Hashimoto, Sachiko Kaneko, Sako Kawahara, and the faculty of the Social Welfare Department at Japan Women's University. I also wish to thank those who took time out from busy schedules to assist a researcher from afar, including Hiroshi and Takeyo Urabe, Toku Suzuki, Yuriko Kawahara, Masako Arai, Takao Terawaki, Kazuo Jō, Katsuo Takano, Reverend Murayama, Mr. Miyoshi, Tamiko Shimizu, Ken Fukumoto, Ryōsuke Suga, Hideo Kojima, Shōichirō Kami, Masatoshi Okada, and Yoshimori Shibata. Previous work with members of the women's sociology research group, especially Teruko Inoue, Kazuko Tanaka, Mitsue Yoneda, Emiko Kaya, Yōko Shōji, and Aiko Hada, helped establish the foundation for my present achievements. The congeniality and scholarship of Seiichi Andō, Joan

Fujimura, Jeff Hanes, Laura Hein, Linda Angst, Peter Gran, Teshale Tibebu, and Tom Patterson also contributed much to this study. Special thanks to Tsuyoshi Itō for his photographic expertise. Finally, I would like to thank the external reviewers for their comments and Patricia Crosby, executive editor, and Susan Biggs Corrado, copyeditor, of the University of Hawai'i Press for their professionalism and patience in seeing the book through to publication.

Introduction

This book takes up the problem of the growth and expansion of day-care facilities in Japan during the first three decades of the twentieth century. As institutions that educated and nurtured very young children for long hours on a daily basis, day-care centers could have aroused strenuous opposition from parents, families, communities, or government authorities. In addition, the foreign origins of day-care heightened the possibility that Japanese would reject child-care facilities during the nationalistic prewar era. Thus the establishment of day-care facilities, their widespread public acceptance, and their expansion in early twentieth-century Japan are phenomena that call for historical explanation. Exploring justifications for child-care centers and their institutional development sheds light on the genesis of modern[1] Japanese attitudes toward motherhood, childhood, and child-rearing—not only the beliefs of the middle-class founders and lower-class users of day-care centers, but those of private relief specialists and officials in the home and education ministries as well. Above all, tracing the growth of institutional day-care in the prewar era provides insights into the prewar attempts to (re)define female gender and household life in the initial decades of twentieth-century Japan.

This study originated as a desire to explore the history of the *kyōiku mama*, the contemporary Japanese "education mother" who spares no effort to ensure her offspring's success in passing school entrance examinations that for over a century have served as the gateway to prestigious and secure employment in adult life. Reflecting increased interest in Japanese education in the West, the education mother has recently been the object of much attention and predominates among the images of Japanese womanhood both overseas and at home. One writer described the *kyōiku mama* as follows:

No one doubts that behind every high-scoring Japanese student—and they are among the highest scoring in the world—there stands a mother, supportive, aggressive, and completely involved in her child's education. She studies, she packs lunches, she waits for hours in lines to register her child for exams and waits again in the hallways for hours while he takes them. She denies herself TV so her child can study in quiet and she stirs noodles at 11 P.M. for the scholar's snack. She shuttles youngsters from exercise class to . . . calligraphy and piano, to swimming and martial arts. She helps every day with homework, hires tutors and works part-time to pay for *juku* [preparatory, or "cram," schools]. Sometimes she enrolls in 'mother's class' so she can help with the drills at home. . . .

The community's perception of a woman's success as a mother depends in large part on how well her children do in school.[2]

The education mother shuns employment outside the home or other time-consuming activities that would interfere with full-time devotion to the academic success of her child. To the extent that her self-image depends on her child's achievements, her satisfaction in life is vicarious. Acceptance into a top-ranked school brings glory to child, mother, and family, while scholastic failure reflects poorly on herself and the household.

Descriptions of the behavior of the contemporary education mother who dedicates her life to the academic success of her child contrast strikingly with the daily routine of the majority of Japanese mothers of poor to average means who inhabited the rural villages and towns of the pre-World War II era. Accounts of prewar farm women's daily lives report diligent labor contributing to the household's livelihood and barely mention time spent on child care, let alone dedication of long hours to anxious pampering of youngsters who were preparing for entrance examinations. The following translation epitomizes rural esteem for productivity rather than tender mother-child ties in prewar household enterprises:

The young wife was more skilled in weaving than the three young daughters, and she came to be recognized as the best weaver in the village. Her father-in-law and mother-in-law were pleased with her work. But because she was such an excellent weaver, they begrudged her taking any time away from the loom. They would complain, "Our young wife takes a lot of time in the toilet." Or, "She sure takes a long time feeding the baby." "She's so dumb. She's doing the washing again. It's better for the family if she lets the old woman do the washing, and does some weaving instead."[3]

Thus young farm mothers typically rose early in the morning, worked long hours in the fields and at by-employments, and often did much of the cooking, laundry, and housekeeping as well, but had little time for child care. In fact, in three-generation families a young married woman was not referred to as "mother" but as the "young wife" (*yome*), while in two-generation households she immediately became the "housewife," or mistress of the house, without waiting for the senior wife's retirement.[4]

These contrasting images—intensely child-focused contemporary motherhood and the caring but productive motherhood of the previous era—became the point of departure for this study. Initially, the most obvious means of examining attitudes toward modern motherhood seemed to be analysis of the content of the major early twentieth century women's periodicals, *Shufu no tomo* (The housewife's friend), *Fujin no tomo* (The lady's friend), and *Fujin kōron* (Women's central review), but the overabundance of material coupled with the difficulties of access precluded my pursuing changes in conceptions of motherhood in this way. Eventually, I realized that attitudes toward motherhood would emerge in the more readily accessible and compact literature discussing child-care centers. At the time I began research for the dissertation on which this book is based, the major sources, such as annual reports of day-care centers, settlements, and Home Ministry yearbooks, were scattered in university and public libraries as well as at social welfare institutions throughout the country, although the Great Tokyo Earthquake of 1923, the firebombings of the great cities at the end of World War II, as well as floods, fires, typhoons, and bureaucratic housecleanings, have thinned what were once very abundant materials. Thanks to the Shakai Jigyō Shi Kenkyūkai (Social Work History Research Group) centered at Nihon Joshi Daigaku (Japan Women's University), many of these sources have been collected and reprinted since the mid-1980s, when my investigations began. These and other pioneering efforts to make sources more accessible provide a solid foundation for further research in the future.

There are many possible approaches to the study of child-care institutions; however, the ones adopted here were selected to advance an understanding of the central focus of this study—the social history of womanhood and childhood—especially changes in conceptions of motherhood and family life that are embedded in the arguments for and practices of Japan's modern day-care centers. Institutional developments such as the size, curriculum, personnel, and organization of day-care centers and their relationship to the newly developing field of relief work (later, social work) are not ignored, nor are the connections between attitudes toward child-care centers and larger intellectual and social trends, including the nationalism of the era, desire for social or national progress, the rise of feminism, anxiety over the social problems resulting from industrialization, and the search for solutions to such problems that motivated founders and staff members. Nonetheless, challenged by the paucity of works in Western languages treating the social history of modern Japan, especially that of women, children, the household or family, and the urban lower classes, I highlight motherhood and childhood in this study to contribute to the development of these subfields and expand the range of interpretations of modern Japanese history, Japanese society and state, and Japanese modernity.[5]

Inspired by two fine day-care histories by Japanese scholars, the approach of this study nonetheless differs from those works in its concern with changes in conceptions and practices of motherhood, childhood, and family life more than the development of day-care centers as welfare and early childhood educational institutions.[6] In addition, my approach has been influenced by trends in recent scholarship in women's, gender, and children's history beyond the Japan field.

First, while many earlier works in women's history in the West viewed female adults as well as children of both genders as inhabitants of the private world of the home,[7] much recent research, notably that on gender and state—for example, works concerning women and the welfare state, women and political theory, and gender and social policy—has reevaluated women's relationship to the public world.[8] In contrast to previous works on women and the state that emphasized the control exerted by modern states over women, a number of later works have called attention to the impact of women on the state.[9]

Second, recent studies in children's history have considered how the efforts of modern states and private reformers have refashioned, at times unintentionally, children's place at work and at school, which in turn helped reshape attitudes toward children and their positions in households, society, and the nation. As in the case of women's history, studies emphasizing state intentions or the state as an agent of social control have predominated. For example, Jacques Donzelot and Philippe Meyer are suggestive in their respective explorations of the ideological thrust of French "helping" institutions on households, but Donzelot does not fully consider the impact of external institutions or initiatives on processes such as child-rearing within the family.[10] Other works treat reformers' institutions and legislation as middle-class interventions into lower-class life.[11] A handful of very recent studies, however, have stressed lower-class agency, including that of children.[12] These attempts to explore childhood from the perspective of children and the lower classes are noteworthy, although the agency of preschool children, regardless of class or nationality, promises to be still more difficult to research and analyze.

Third, recent trends in women's studies and feminist theory have influenced the conceptual framework and methodology of this study. While historians have traditionally explored continuities and discontinuities in ideas, institutions, and practices, postmodernism has given new impetus to the exploration of opposition or rupture not only in the facts, events, and ideas being studied, but also in the conceptual frameworks scholars employ in analyzing their subject matter.[13] The interrogation of commonly accepted dualisms is another legacy of this new feminist literature; it has produced new insights by questioning dichotomous ways of conceptualizing gender, that is, "public man, private woman," "male subject, female victim," "productive male, reproductive female," and even the dualism "male, female" itself.[14]

My approaches to motherhood, childhood, and social reform draw selectively on the themes, conclusions, and methods of writings in social history and women's studies, including those cited above. Most valuable, in my view, has been methodology that takes discontinuities as a point of departure and questions existing dichotomous conceptualizations. Thus the disjuncture between the images of the productive village woman of the modern era and the education mother of the contemporary era suggests that the study of changes in motherhood and therefore of womanhood in modern Japan might start with a reexamination of "man outside, woman inside" (*otoko wa soto, onna wa uchi*), an aphorism in decline.[15] Rather than regarding this fading contemporary gender dualism that associates Japanese men with outside, or productive, work and Japanese women with inside, or domestic, work as a timeless truth, this study searches for signs of its historicity.

Based on examination of discourses concerning the establishment and operation of day-care centers and on analysis of shifting patterns of child care within households in the opening decades of the twentieth century, this study argues that although household divisions of labor by gender and age existed in early modern Japan, a more rigid female specialization in certain types of domestic work—in housekeeping and child-rearing as opposed to childbearing and expected participation in more varied forms of productive labor—developed during the modern era, especially for young married women. And over time, the activities of children also became more narrowly specialized. Beginning with middle-class children, but later for increasing numbers of lower-class children, participation in housework, child-rearing, and productive labor diminished while time spent at school increased. Children became dependents and consumers rather than income earners and productive workers in their households.

Thus Japanese modernity, a complex series of intertwined changes in society and culture that has been most commonly defined in terms of industrialization, demographic trends, class stratification, and nation-state formation, also involved significant changes in womanhood and childhood, and by extension in gender and household or family life as well.

In exploring how day-care centers (one type of institutional care for preschool children) took root and flourished in pre-World War II Japan, this study emphasizes two major factors: the congruence between nineteenth-century Japanese child-rearing patterns and day-care and the role of nationalism in generating strong, consistent Japanese support for child care. Chapter 1 discusses the approach of this study to the problem of day-care in modern Japan—useful concepts for its analysis, standard explanations for its development of day-care, and above all, the pressing issues of the times when it was introduced into Japan. Chapter 2 discusses late nineteenth-century patterns of child care and how these influenced Japanese responses to the institutional care of young lower-class children in the early twentieth century. It argues that widespread nurturing of infants and toddlers by household members other than mothers at all levels of nineteenth-century society fostered Japanese receptivity to day-care facilities among both their middle-class proponents and lower-class users after the turn of the century. Chapters 3 and 4 introduce the two early centers that became models for later facilites. Futaba Yōchien and Kōbe Seneki Kinen Hoikukai (KSKH; Kobe War Memorial Daycare Association), established in the first decade of the twentieth century, associated day-care with fulfillment of national goals—the political goal of incorporating lower-class children and parents into the Japanese nation-state through moral education and the economic goal of raising national productivity through promoting parental employment and family economic improvement among the urban lower classes. Chapter 5 discusses institutional growth in the next decade that resulted from acceptance of early arguments linking institutional child care with social and national progress at a time when both the Home Ministry (Naimushō) and the imperial institution were encouraging the establishment of private philanthropic and relief works. The KSKH emphasis on economic improvement proved more appealing, although it was not incompatible with the educational aims of Futaba Yōchien. In an era of government and elite preoccupation with the growth of Japan's industry, military power, civilization, and international prestige, this linkage helped marshall broad support for day-care, including from powerful segments of the state bureaucracy. Chapter 6 discusses the founding of the first municipal day-care centers after World War I. Officials hastened to consider means of ameliorating the conditions of the poor after the nationwide 1918 Rice Riots raised the specter of widespread popular uprisings of the needy.

Ironically, the steady expansion of institutional child care in modern Japan took place despite a continuing diffusion of new conceptions of womanhood from the 1870s emphasizing the centrality of the mother's role in nurturing infants and older children. This paradox of prewar day-care—the growing emphasis on mothers' unique role in child-rearing that seemingly contradicted the central purpose of a new institution that cared for young children outside the home—is in part related to the emergence of class variations in prewar Japanese notions of womanhood. While Western notions of educating women for their responsibilities as socializers of a new generation of citizens gained a foothold among the highly educated, nationalist elite at the beginning of the modern era, early modern willingness to harness the productive labor of lower- and middle-class women lingered due to a broad consensus supporting economic development and national strength.[16] Yet as the twentieth century progressed, higher girls' schools and women's magazines reinforced the domestic identity of middle-class women, and advice recommending paid work for married women of the prosperous classes disappeared.[17] Their main calling became the rearing of Japan's future leaders and management of their households according to modern scientific principles. However, lower-class urban and rural women were held to less-stringent standards of maternal and wifely achievement, because their children were destined to become laborers, conscripts, and the mothers of future citizens. Sound physical and moral development were required, but meticulous socialization and careful education of lower-class children were less crucial to the nation's future. Thus private interests and the state encouraged the founding of day-care centers in the cities for lower-class children and their parents from the first decade of the twentieth century.

If there is a gap between images of Japanese women today and their past activities, a second disjuncture can be found between contemporary children who are students and consumers and prewar children of various ages who engaged in important domestic and productive activities for their households. This rupture suggests that it is worthwhile to take a fresh look at age as well as gender in reexamining changes in household and society during the formation of Japan's modern economy and state. To this end, my study will examine changes in childhood as well as motherhood in early twentieth century Japan. To the extent that children's contributions to its maintenance and economy declined, the boundaries between children and adults became firmer, which increasingly differentiated children from adults as the modern era progressed. To the extent that all children, not just those of warriors and rich merchants and peasants, completed compulsory education in the modern era, variations in the early life course of the various classes diminished; over time, increasing uniformity of the life course during childhood became one factor in the emergence of a common national culture. However, as in the case of womanhood, it appears the rate of change proceeded at a faster pace for middle-class than lower-class children.

The rise of day-care centers as well as the reconstruction of womanhood and childhood in modern Japan were linked to a long-term, deep-seated, and at times almost desperate drive for national progress. Insecurity vis-à-vis the powerful industrialized and imperialistic Western states spurred the post-Restoration transformation of Japan. Modern Japanese leaders fully realized that the forging of a strong new nation necessitated the creation of a new people who could meet the varied challenges of modernity as colonists, conscripts, workers, and patriots on the homefront rather than a people whose primary identity derived from membership in a household or local community. That is, national salvation depended on socialization of ordinary Japanese children and the resocialization of ordinary Japanese adults to a new national orientation. And throughout the prewar era, most advocates of Japan's progress expected that private and municipal day-care centers would function as the allies of adult members of households, public schools, and other state-sponsored organizations in shaping children who would loyally serve the needs of national advancement and the imperial state.

1 | Beginnings

In 1868, the opening year of Japan's modern era, socialization and physical care of youngsters took place almost exclusively in the home, but by the third decade of the twentieth century specialized institutions such as public schools, orphanages, reformatories, kindergartens, day nurseries, child consultation centers, and day-care centers[1] assisted increasing numbers of families in bringing up children. Child-care centers were initially established in Japan during the first decade of the twentieth century to educate and care for urban lower-class children under age six. Thus growth of day-care facilities contributed to a modern proliferation of extrafamilial institutions for children that began in the late nineteenth century, an era of unprecedented social change. During the modern era, these and other changes in the methods and content of socialization of preschool- and school-aged children had an impact not only on Japanese youngsters themselves, but on their caretakers—especially mothers and households—and ultimately on the entire society as well.

The Problem and Its Context

Day-care centers appeared in Japan after elementary schools, kindergartens, and day nurseries but before milk depots and mother and child clinics. By 1926, the final year of the Taishō era, social work professionals and educators had come to regard day-care centers as important institutions for children. In the modern era, several types of new facilities for young children developed in Japan. From the late 1870s kindergartens provided special training for a small number of children from elite families, with curricula that sometimes included foreign languages and etiquette. Beginning in the 1890s, a handful of day nurseries (or *crèches*) located at factories and mines provided long hours of custodial care for workers' young children but rarely attempted to develop their intellect or character. In contrast to kindergartens, day-care centers served lower-class children, and in contrast to day nurseries, they combined attention to basic physical well-being with some of the educative functions of kindergartens.[2] Furthermore, in order to improve home life, day-care centers sought to educate not only infants, but their parents and sometimes their older siblings as well. Thus the class of day-care clientele and the combination of physical care and education distinguished these centers from existing early childhood institutions.

Day-care centers attracted a number of influential supporters in the twentieth century, including industrial barons such as Shibusawa Eiichi, Ōhara Magosaburō, and Kobayashi Tomijirō; labor and welfare leaders such as Kagawa Toyohiko and Shiga Shinato; educators such as Naruse Jinzō, Tsuda Umeko, and Shimoda Utako; and most important, bureaucrats in the relief section of the powerful Home Ministry.[3] By 1909, roughly a decade after the first center had opened, the Home Ministry began to encourage the establishment of child-care facilities. That same year, a handful of child-care centers began to receive imperial funding through the Home Ministry. The ministry continued to award financial assistance to a limited number of child-care facilities during the prewar era, but it did not extend such aid to kindergartens.[4]

The rate of increase in the number of day-care centers climbed to twenty to forty facilities per year during the late Taishō era—a rate of expansion that impressed even staunch kindergarten supporters. However, while there were 237 regular child-care centers in Japan in 1926, in contrast to 60 in 1919, they still fell short of the numerical strength of kindergartens, which numbered 1,066 in 1926 and 612 in 1919.[5]

At the First Annual Child Protection Work Conference (Dai Ikkai Zenkoku Jidō Hogo Jigyō Kaigi) in 1925, the chief of the Home Ministry's Social Bureau, Moriya Eifu, summarized the ministry's late-1920s view of the importance of day-care centers in sweeping terms: "The social weaknesses regarding children are the root (*konpon*) of all social problems."[6] Not only for Home Ministry officials but for other supporters as well, the significance of institutional child care lay in its importance to the social order, and implicitly to the nation's future, more than in quantitative increases in the number of facilities and children enrolled. Conceding the popularity and social utility of day-care, in 1926 the Ministry of Education rewrote its regulations to allow kindergartens to operate each day for longer hours and to enroll children under three years of age, like day-care centers.[7]

This study treats day-care and child-rearing in households as part of reproduction,[8] an essential but variable process ensuring the continuity of a society through the creation of a new generation and the physical maintenance, affective support, and training of its future members. Reproduction includes the nurturing and socialization of adults as well as the birth, education, and care of children, because social continuity requires that adults, too, be fed, clothed, and bathed according to culturally variable standards and have important values and knowledge instilled and reinstilled in them. The site of reproductive processes involving children varies. In nineteenth-century Japan, birth occurred principally in households, while care and socialization, central concerns of this study, took place in institutional settings as well as in homes. The establishment and expansion of child-care centers in the early twentieth century provides an opportunity to examine changes in the care and socialization of young children taking place in new institutions outside the home.

If reproduction is cast as the opposite of production of the material goods that ensure human survival, then the history of production, that is, of the economy or political economy, has thus far been studied more extensively than the history of housework, consumption, and child-rearing. However, in the past decade or so many new works illuminating aspects of the history of reproduction have begun to appear.[9] To conceptualize reproduction and production as two distinct processes may reflect the ideologies more than the social realities of the modern world. The dualistic distinction between reproduction and production reflects above all the twin divisions between household and workplace and between household and state that emerged with the development of industrial capitalism. Yet the distinctiveness of these two processes was blurred in preindustrial societies, including Japan. Awareness of the historicity of these terms permits historical analysis of the social changes leading to the separation of various activities that once took place in the household and the genesis of oppositional or dichotomous terms to describe them. It also provides a fresh perspective on many aspects of early modern households and society.[10]

Despite its apparent premise of a dichotomy between paid and unpaid labor in workplace and home, a reproductive approach has advantages for the study of changes in child-rearing, motherhood, and childhood. It facilitates comparison of child-rearing in families with treatment of children in institutional settings and locates these practices and attitudes in a broader social context. Such an approach admits similarities between the public activities of paid employees such as teachers and principals, on the one hand, and the unpaid labor of parents, grandparents, and siblings in the more private world of the home, on the other, in the function of transmitting attitudes and knowledge that children will use later in life. A reproductive approach can also encompass the unpaid or poorly remunerated work of child baby-sitters (*komori,* or nursemaids), apprentices, wet nurses, nannies, or other servants in caring for and training children. In the case of younger children, reproduction involves not only socialization to language, manners and social skills, and academic and vocational learning, but physical care such as feeding, bathing, and nursing during illnesses as well.

One strand of Japanese modernity consisted of the nation-state's challenge to important aspects of reproduction in private households. In particular, the same government officials displayed new ambitions to exercise unprecedented intervention in a household's autonomous authority over its youngest members—its right to raise children as it pleased, to instill in them "proper" values, and freely to deploy their labor. In other words, during the late Meiji and Taishō eras, the nation-state redefined the relationship between family and state (one of the boundaries between the private and public spheres), partly to consolidate its authority over matters important to national life and partly to ensure its own survival by training children to place love of nation above loyalty to family and local community. As part of this process, nationalist interventions also attempted to reformulate norms of womanhood and female conduct, including notions of motherhood and child-care practices. Despite the visions and powers of states and elites, it is unwise to assume that their initiatives were monolithic or invariably successful; pursuit of contradictions and failures can be as illuminating as analyzing positive achievements. In recognizing the common activities, purposes, and attitudes associated with the nominally private act of child-rearing and the nominally public treatment of children in institutions of education and care, a reproductive approach facilitates study of this historical process.[11]

This book focuses on issues related to care and socialization (i.e., reproduction) in early twentieth century Japanese day-care centers for several reasons. First, analysis of arguments for and against institutions minding young children for long hours every day provides invaluable insights into changing perceptions of motherhood, childhood, and child-care practices—insights that cannot be derived from examination of schools, orphanages, reformatories, or other institutions serving older or parentless children. Second, day-care centers promised to socialize urban lower-class children and parents to socially beneficial values at a time when the formation of the character of Japanese citizens, more than the survival of infants, relieved pressing concerns of government leaders and educators.[12] The middle-class staff may have fretted more about the formation of lower-class children's character than did their parents or guardians, but they frequently directed their attention as much to the needs of society and nation as to their lower-class preschool pupils. Third, the institutional features of day-care centers also make them attractive for study. Treatment of young children at day-care centers offers interesting comparisons with child care performed in the family, because both day-care centers and families performed a broad range of activities to nurture and educate young children.[13] Schools were attended by children older than six and consequently focused on learning far more than the physical care of their students.

Finally, the issues raised by studying the prewar expansion of Japanese child-care centers are intertwined with far-reaching and complex transformations taking place in Japanese society during the modern era. These changes include the reformulation of the ideals and conduct of womanhood, childhood, child-rearing, and family life during the transition to an industrial economy, an urban society, and a modern nation-state; the adaptation of borrowed institutions and ideas; the development of social reform and social policy; and the character of broad processes of social change as Japan became an urban, capitalist imperial state.

Interpretations and Explanations

Four explanations for early twentieth century Japanese acceptance of institutional child care come readily to mind: that day-care facilities were simply another instance of Japanese borrowing from the West, that day-care came into being as a humanitarian response to post-Restoration family needs, that child-care centers were created to help working mothers, and that institutional child care served as a means of social control of the urban lower-classes. These earlier interpretations serve as points of departure for this study, although in the end it attempts to move beyond them.

First, it can be said that the day-care center entered Japan from the United States at the turn of the nineteenth century, but by that time it is highly unlikely the establishment of child-care facilities in Japan sprang from a simple impulse to copy Western ways. Receptivity to foreign institutions and ideas had diminished since the enthusiasm of the early Meiji era. Indeed, as early as the mid-1880s the initial wave of importations had brought about an era of reaction against foreign borrowing.[14] By 1900 national pride, which had swelled due to victory in the 1894–1895 Sino-Japanese War (Japan's first modern war), further dampened uncritical admiration for Western values and institutions, and borrowing became less frequent and more cautious.[15]

Second, one might hypothesize that humanitarian motivations such as the desire to help children inspired middle-class reformers to found prewar day-care centers, which often provided preschool education and a broad range of welfare services to lower-class[16] children and their parents. Yet Japanese child-care centers cannot be regarded solely as a response to such sentiments, because impoverished families and neglected children had existed in the hinterlands and great cities before the modern era. Day-care centers would have arisen *before* 1900 had institutional care for young children been no more than a sympathetic response to family distress.[17] Furthermore, although institutions to assist poor children arose in the cities during the Meiji era, the founding of day-care facilities in rural areas lagged despite the presence of ragged, hungry children in the countryside during the prewar era.[18]

To pursue the question of timing, we must ask why humanitarian impulses to succor needy children spurred the establishment of day-care centers—institutions that provided both care and education for lower-class Japanese children at the beginning of the twentieth century. The fact that enrollment policies generally excluded children of the unemployed in part suggests an answer. Modern benevolence toward the poor had its limits; child-care facilities sought to encourage poor parents to work. Thus child care as aid to the needy became linked to economic self-reliance. The values underlying admissions criteria of day-care centers clearly reflect the rise of a modern ethos of self-reliance and industry. No longer should the impoverished expect assistance from their social superiors, employers, or landlords, as they had in the past; in the twentieth century, aid to the unfortunate became less desirable than helping them to achieve economic self-sufficiency. This shift in attitudes toward benevolence, and thus the rise of day-care as well, is related to increasing public concern with urban poverty in the industrial age and the genesis of interest in relief work and social policy on the part of the state at the turn of the century. Not only was there a shift in the character of aid to the needy; there was also a partial shift in the agents of distribution of charity and relief. In the modern era, caring for the poor (as well as children) became more associated with women than it had been in the past.[19]

Third, although the rise of child-care centers after 1900 roughly paralleled the growth of the female factory labor force and the expansion of the modern industrial sector of the Japanese economy, for several reasons it is problematic to argue that the establishment of prewar Japanese day-care centers inevitably accompanied the growth of industry or female employment. First, while the number of day-care centers expanded as the female industrial labor force grew, in the early twentieth century, especially the first two decades, the majority of female operatives were young, unmarried women who did not need child care.[20] Day-care facilities were largely located in neighborhoods rather than at industrial plants, and centers were generally founded not by factory owners but by private philanthropists, educators, relief experts, and later municipal officials. As will be discussed in chapter 3, the lower-class married women who enrolled children in day-care programs were more likely to work at home in family enterprises or outside the home as day laborers or scavengers (e.g., rag pickers) than to hold factory jobs.

Since efforts by factory owners to recruit and hold female workers were not crucial to the establishment of day-care in prewar Japan, rather than focusing exclusively on the relationship between women's industrial employment and the rise of institutional child care, it may be more plausible to posit a link between the rise of day-care and changes in economic organization that reduced the availability of household members to care for young children in the modern era. That is, with the industrial takeoff and rising school enrollment rates at the turn of the century, the separation of workplace and home for the growing ranks of wage workers and the removal of education from the households largely prevented wage earners and students from engaging in child care. From the 1890s these changes in activities beyond the home steadily altered the division of labor in growing numbers of households. In turn, the transformation of division of labor within the household constituted a crucial part of the context surrounding the development of institutional child care in pre-World War II Japan. Thus capitalist industrialization and the nationalist sentiments propelling the development of economy and empire also fueled the founding of prewar day-care centers.

Fourth, it may be argued that prewar day-care centers represented an attempt by the ruling class or the state to exert social control,[21] or some might say to enforce discipline, over the urban lower classes. The persuasiveness of this view hinges on satisfactory explication of the link between the activities and attitudes of private individuals and the state, because the vast majority of prewar day-care centers were private institutions. As we shall see, most of these private Meiji-Taishō child-care centers encouraged household registration and school enrollment and taught the values of thrift, diligence, and hygiene. These actions assisted the implementation of state policies despite the fact that the state had not directly asked day-care professionals to do so. I contend that day-care professionals' broad concern for advancing Japan's civilization, social progress, and national development overlapped with the aims of state officials. Similar concerns resulted in cooperation, often unwitting, between day-care professionals and segments of the state, especially the education and home ministries. However, much evidence also suggests that such private and public early twentieth century attempts at social control were incomplete. Neither state nor private middle-class reform efforts thoroughly transformed the values, homes, or social environment of poor and lower-class city dwellers.

In addition to addressing the inevitable emergence of a disciplinary regime, it is useful also to consider the role of human agency. This perspective then calls for some investigation of individuals and their actions in the creation of modern institutions of reproduction such as day-care centers. In the opening decades of the twentieth century many leading Japanese believed that national and social progress depended not only on policies promoting industrial and military development and transition to constitutional government, but on the resolution of two crucial reproductive issues as well. First was the long-standing desire to create citizens/subjects suited to the needs of the modern state, an issue that statesmen, ideologues, and other nationalist thinkers had confronted since the Meiji Restoration. Second, following the industrial takeoff of the 1890s, new and disturbing social issues emerged. In response, from that decade increasing numbers of policymakers, journalists, academics, and other public-minded Japanese began searching for the means to cope with the undesirable social consequences of industrialization.[22]

The creation of new citizens had been a concern from the earliest years of the modern era. For example, shortly after the Restoration, Fukuzawa Yukichi, who achieved renown as a modern iconoclast and enlightener through his work as a newspaper publisher and educator, encountered a peasant who dismounted from his horse at meeting Fukuzawa, a former samurai, on the road. Fukuzawa fretted

> what fearful weight the old customs had with the people. Here was this poor farmer still living in fear of all persons, never realizing that the new law of the land had liberated him. What could be done with this country of ours when there were so many people as ignorant as this.[23]

Later Fukuzawa and other progressive nationalist thinkers developed gendered visions of education and resocialization that sought to reconstruct Japanese womanhood to meet the needs of the new age. The Western idea of educated motherhood held considerable appeal. By raising children to be patriotic citizens willing to obey the commands of the imperial state, women could contribute to national well-being through their labors in the private world of the home rather than through direct participation in the public world of economy and polity. Fukuzawa proposed more drastic changes, such as granting equal opportunities for women to develop "the body, the intellect, and the emotions" and weightier household responsibilities, including the ownership and management of property. However, Fukuzawa still justified changes in womanhood for the sake of the nation, rather than for the sake of women themselves, and in the end he still defined the domestic world as women's proper place.[24]

Toward Socialization as Social Solution

At the turn of the century anxieties about the social problems of Japan's emerging industrial order heightened, as did the urgency of the search for solutions to reduce the economic and cultural gulf separating the middle and lower classes in the new order.[25] By the end of the nineteenth century social observers noted with alarm the distressing sight of gangs of children roaming city streets. Private observers and government officials feared a rise in crime and economic dependence should large numbers of urban youth grow up without proper moral training and discipline. If idle children grew up to be useless as workers, soldiers, and citizens, economic productivity would fall, and wars would be lost. The nation would face a dismal future. This heightened concern for the character of children as future citizens established a basis for receptivity to day-care centers as institutions instilling useful values in children early in life.

Also, as the prospect of class conflict loomed, many Japanese came to believe that a breakdown of social harmony stemmed from the decline of traditional values such as cooperation and loyalty. They invented new institutions of socialization such as the military reserve organizations, new ethics textbooks, and youth, girls, and women's village associations as means of indoctrination to values approved by state officials.[26]

Furthermore, Japan also faced an economic crisis after the Russo-Japanese War (1904–1905) due to the enormous costs of the conflict and a postwar recession. Officials at the time sought to spur economic productivity in order to increase tax revenues. Prosperous citizens would then be better able to pay increased levies, they reasoned. In the logic of the times, reproductive issues became directly linked to efforts at economic expansion. In addition to economic assistance to local areas for transportation, water, and communications projects, officials in circulars and speeches also waged a moral campaign, urging citizens throughout the country to be diligent and save. The emperor even issued the Boshin Rescript, which carried an identical message.[27] In this context, progress-minded Japanese came to see day-care centers as a means of cultivating habits of industry and economy, which would boost national productivity by resocializing a group of morally deficient citizens.

Finally, urban poverty also constituted a twofold economic problem: first, progress-minded Japanese regarded the poor as unproductive members of society, and second, they viewed relief expenditures as an unproductive diversion of state financial resources. Once more, part of the remedy was training in industry, frugality, and economic self-reliance—a socialization campaign among the poor and the working classes. Japanese leaders welcomed child-care centers as institutions to help lower-class children and adults to develop into productive, obedient citizens. In sum, the turn to new modes of socialization as remedies for the social ills of late Meiji Japan figures prominently in the rise of day-care in the early twentieth century.

2
Child-Rearing in the Nineteenth Century

This chapter explores the care and socialization of children in nineteenth-century Japanese households and extrafamilial institutions in order to assess the implications of preexisting patterns of reproduction for Japanese acceptance of day-care centers in the early twentieth century. In the mid-nineteenth century very few institutions provided care and education for children outside a household setting, although formal schooling had begun to flourish. Within the household, early modern willingness to entrust infants and toddlers to nonmaternal caregivers such as male and female kin and servants persisted after the Meiji Restoration of 1868 despite the introduction of Western notions of motherhood assuming the superiority of infant care by the biological mother. After the Restoration, the number and importance of extrafamilial institutions steadily increased, but important continuities in urban and rural household organization prevented drastic changes in the treatment of children. The elementary school, the most ubiquitous new institution, enrolled youngsters above the age of six, while kindergartens, day nurseries, and later day-care centers took in children under that age.

Because households dominated the care and socialization of children, especially infants, at the beginning of the modern era, this chapter focuses on the treatment of children in late nineteenth century and early twentieth century households more than on reproduction in extrafamilial institutions. In contrast to the norms in Japan today, there is considerable evidence of willingness to resort to multiple caregivers for infants and toddlers in households of all classes in the nineteenth century, which in turn set the stage for the favorable reception of day-care centers—facilities where nonmaternal caregivers provided all-day care and education for young children after their establishment at the dawn of the twentieth century.

Household Child Care in the Nineteenth Century

The development of growing numbers of extrafamilial institutions for children is a hallmark of post-Restoration Japanese society; nonetheless, it would be a

mistake to overemphasize the speed and magnitude of changes in either organizations or individual practices. In pre-1868 Japan the care and socialization of
children took place to a great extent in households, but by the end of the early
modern period increasing numbers of male and female children attended educational institutions. And well into the modern era, despite high nominal rates of
school enrollment, in average and poor rural and urban households, parents and
children often gave higher priority to household or wage-earning activities than
to regular class attendance.

At the beginning of the modern era abolition of the four hereditary class distinctions accorded warriors (samurai), artisans, merchants, and peasants freedom
of occupation and residence, but thereafter the vast majority of Japanese continued to gain a livelihood by means of small farm, retail, or manufacturing enterprises. Their household businesses relied largely on unpaid family labor for both
domestic and productive work, and family survival also required assistance from
local community organizations based on household membership, much as it had
before 1868. Rural areas did not escape progress; the coming of improved roads,
railways, newspapers, telegraph lines, and schools during the modern era linked
villages to the metropole. Yet labor-intensive, unmechanized cultivation by farm
families on tiny plots of land still characterized agriculture, the basic source of
rural livelihood.[1] Those whom the land could not support migrated to find employment in towns and cities, as many had done before the Restoration.

After 1868 most city dwellers continued to live and work in households operating small enterprises, although by the beginning of the twentieth century a
number of traditional trades had fallen into decline.[2] Nonetheless, to assert that
life and labor for ordinary villagers and townspeople retained much of their early
modern character is not to posit timeless, unchanging rural and urban life.[3]
Changes in the household division of labor, attitudes toward formal education, social mobility, and social relations had been occurring throughout the nineteenth
century, but economic and demographic conditions, customary forms of socialization, ideological institutions, and legal codes limited the range of change.

The continued predominance of small-enterprise households in the city and
countryside throughout the modern period accounts for much of the continuity
in the treatment of children. In the early modern period the lion's share of child-
rearing, both care and socialization, occurred in household units, with the education of some children taking place outside the household in various types of
schools. Many children acquired most or all of the vocational training, social
skills, and general knowledge necessary for adult life through socialization
within households. In wealthy households, youngsters might learn from servants

or tutors, while poor or prosperous children placed out as apprentices or domestic servants acquired their trade, manners, and social place from the master, mistress, and other residents of their employer's household. Before the Restoration there were almost no specialized institutions that cared for children, but an expanding network of domain schools, private Confucian academies, and temple schools (*terakoya*) provided a variety of skills ranging from basic or advanced literacy to arithmetic, calligraphy, and moral lessons.[4] However, by the late 1890s, thirty years into the modern period, rising enrollment rates indicate that far more children were being socialized by extrafamilial institutions as they attended the nationwide network of public elementary and higher schools.

In the late nineteenth century household priorities exerted great influence on the internal division of labor, including the task of minding young children. In urban and rural and rich and poor families, young mothers lacked extensive authority over child-rearing if older members were present, and they shared the care and education of even infants and toddlers with other household members. The male household head or senior household members, rather than the mother, generally made important decisions about the care and education of children. The care of young children was regarded as a simple, light task. It was often performed by older children, the elderly, and full-time and part-time servants, freeing mothers for tasks requiring greater skill, strength, or endurance. Rather than devoting most or all of their time to child care, young married women in poor and ordinary households engaged in productive activities such as agriculture, handicrafts, or even wage labor, while in wealthy households they waited on their husband or in-laws, supervised servants, tended family members' wardrobes, and oversaw inventories of household possessions.[5]

The Household Context of Child Care: Structure and Values

The basic setting for reproduction was the household, or *ie*, a form of stem family.[6] Lutz Berkner has defined the stem family as

> a specific type of extended family organization in which only one child marries while remaining at home to inherit the family property and the other children either leave to establish their own families elsewhere or stay in the households as celibates.[7]

Thus a complete stem family consisted of adult couples of two or more generations, the head, wife and children, and the head's parents.[8] In Japan, servants and apprentices were included as *ie* members of inferior status.[9]

The *ie,* however, was more than a coresident kin group. It was a corporate entity that prized its own permanence—the eternal preservation of its status, name, and property. The term "*ie*" therefore carried a range of historical and cultural connotations

> corresponding closely to the varying meanings of our word "house." It may refer to the physical structure, the domicile; to the residents of the domicile, the household; or to the family line, as in the English House of Windsor. . . . It is on this last broader level that it acquires the rich shading of social and ethical value implications important to Japanese society.[10]

Whether translated as "household," "family," or "house" (I prefer the former), the term "*ie*" denotes a corporate unit comprised of past, present, and future generations. Of great importance to the fate of day-care in Japan was the fact that the overriding *ie* goal of household continuity shaped all aspects of reproduction in the family, including procreation, child care, and the education of children.

Children were essential to the achievement of an *ie*'s immortality—the eternal presence of descendants to pay respects to the ancestors, the maintenance of household prosperity, and the preservation of family status in the local community. In most regions during the late Tokugawa and early Meiji periods, parents named the eldest son the successor and sole heir to household property. Alternative practices included assumption of the headship by the youngest son as well as succession by the eldest child and spouse, the latter involving adoption of the husband of a daughter if she were the eldest offspring. Official toleration of variation in succession practices terminated in 1898, when the family section of the newly adopted Civil Code prescribed the succession of the eldest son with rare exceptions.[11] Long-standing local customs did not change overnight; however, after 1898 the birth of a son became more widespread as the goal of procreation.

Emphasis on intergenerational continuity meant that the parent-child relationship, rather than the husband-wife relationship, formed the axis of the Japanese family. The primary aims of marriage were providing the *ie* with an heir, obtaining additional labor for the household, and advancing the household's status or material interests, rather than the uniting of bride and groom in a companionate relationship. Marriage "represented the union of man and woman for the purpose of obtaining a successor to maintain the continuity of Ancestor-worship."[12] Children were precious since they literally embodied the future of the house, but the future successor was far more important than the other offspring in the eyes of adult family members. The heir generally received special treatment ranging from more attention, affection, and praise to better food and clothing than the other children.

In the modern era, parents and grandparents often rejoiced at the birth of a male child, who would in turn grow up to wed and father a successor. A bride who did not soon bear a child could be divorced and sent back to her natal family. If a divorce took place for other reasons, as a rule the household, not the mother, kept the offspring of the marital union. This customary practice was reinforced by law after 1898.[13] Household interests took priority over the bond between mother and child; therefore children belonged to the *ie* rather than to their mothers. Families could hire wet nurses or call on lactating neighbors for assistance in order to raise unweaned infants who were separated from their mothers by divorce.

However, besides the birth of a successor to a mother in the *ie,* adoption also constituted a socially acceptable means of maintaining household continuity. That is, children could be adopted to carry on the household in absence of a natural heir. If an *ie* had daughters but no son, the household head might adopt a daughter's husband as future successor and heir. For childless households, one strategy involved first adopting a girl, then adopting her husband when she married some years later. Alternatively, heirless families could adopt an adult married couple to maintain household continuity. The latter practice indicates greater concern with maintenance of the family as a corporate unit than with continuity of blood lines.[14] In fact, success-oriented merchants sometimes bypassed dull or extravagant natural sons, instead adopting adult employees with greater business acumen as heirs.[15] Households resorted to adoption when natural succession proved impossible or impractical; nonetheless, the birth and rearing of children born into an *ie* was a simpler means of safeguarding the household's vital long-term interests.

If authority over child-rearing and participation in the task of child-rearing itself were not distributed in a way that minimized disputes, discord over child care might jeopardize *ie* continuity. Therefore, in three-generation households the junior wife, a newcomer to her husband's household with questionable loyalties to it, played a limited role in the care and education of the children she bore.[16] Instead, the household head and senior generation—the mother- and father-in-law—had authority over child-rearing, especially the upbringing of the heir.[17] Despite giving birth to new family members, including the heir, a young woman who had married virilocally was not quickly accepted as a household member, and she consequently could exercise little influence over the rearing of over her own children, especially the heir, in an extended household.

The Task of Child Care

Besides household goals, assumptions about how children should be treated and what they needed shaped the distribution of child-rearing work among various household members. Children did not receive elaborate care in ordinary nineteenth-century Japanese households, perhaps because other tasks were often so demanding that family members had little time left over to care for children. When an infant was present, child care, like a multitude of other household chores, had to be performed daily, but the minding of infants and young children was regarded as a fairly simple chore, not as a complex and weighty duty with grave and indelible consequences for future mental, moral, and psychological development. In wealthy families wet nurses provided constant care for infants, while nannies, baby-sitters, or boy apprentices watched toddlers and older children. In poor and ordinary farm families and urban households babies up to age three rode around on the backs of siblings or grandparents, freeing mothers to labor at essential tasks during the day and when necessary into the night. Strapping the infant onto the back of the caregiver, with its head facing forward, also protected the baby from wandering off or hurting itself.[18] The caregivers brought nursing infants to the mother for feeding in average households, while among the rich the wet nurse provided essential nourishment. In short, care focused on the infant's basic physical well-being—its feeding and safety—rather than on painstaking cultivation of its psychological or intellectual development.

Multiple Caregivers in Ordinary Families

Lacking the means to hire caregivers for their children, ordinary families generally depended on their own members to care for young children to free mothers for productive and managerial tasks in the household. Since the senior wife in a three-generation family (the *shufu,* or housewife) wielded authority over household affairs, she typically minded the young children and supervised their upbringing while the junior wife engaged in long hours of handicraft work, strenuous farm labor, or heavy household tasks. Alternatively, other family members such as older children or the retired household head might also tend infants and toddlers.

Women and older children watched over infants and taught their juniors social and vocational skills, but male household heads and fathers[19] were not exempt from reproductive tasks. The fact that boys generally learned occupational skills from older males in the household meant that heads of households, fathers, and grandfathers were largely responsible for the socialization of boys, and above all for the proper rearing of the heir. The household head had a considerable stake in the upbringing of at least one child, since he had the responsibility of finding a suitable successor to take over the heavy responsibilities of continuing the family line, venerating the ancestors, preserving the household occupation and its property, maintaining its status, and representing it to the outside world.

Several early Meiji accounts describe fathers' involvement in child care and their emotional investment in children. First, one intrepid Englishwoman, Isabella Bird, who journeyed through villages in northeast Japan during the 1870s, before the interior was opened to travel by foreigners, reported that

> Both fathers and mothers take pride in their children. It is most amusing about six every morning to see twelve or fourteen men sitting on a low wall, each with a child under two years in his arms, fondling and playing with it, and showing off its physique and intelligence. . . . At night, after the houses are shut up, looking through the long fringe of rope or rattan which conceals the sliding door, you see the father who wears [next to] nothing . . . in the "bosom of his family," bending his ugly, kindly face over a gentle-looking baby, and the mother, who more often than not has dropped the kimono from her shoulders, enfolding two children destitute of clothing in her arms. For some reason they prefer boys, but certainly girls are equally petted and loved.[20]

This description suggests that a father's authority over family affairs did not preclude involvement in child care. In fact, in households with several young children and no older siblings or grandparents to baby-sit, the father's assistance with child care may have been a necessity.

Second, in her autobiography, former textile worker and union activist Takai Toshio (b. 1902) recalled her father's nurturant role during her childhood. She remembered her father as kinder than her mother, and her memoirs record his devoted efforts to ensure the survival of her younger brother. Takai's family was poor; they had migrated from an overpopulated village in central Honshu to live by themselves on forest land where her father made charcoal. They lived in a flimsy hut, with barely adequate food and clothing. Despite their poverty, her father was determined to raise his infant son to become a strong, healthy boy. When his son started eating solid foods at age one, Takai's father began to hunt rabbit, fish, and fowl as dietary supplements. He grilled his daily catches over an open fire and fed them to his son. The father also gave these treats to Takai and her younger sister, but he did not begin to prepare these special foods until after the son was born.[21] Takai's account as well as Bird's observations suggest that even in households without property or an adequate livelihood, fathers could develop an intense emotional attachment to their successors and that such strong paternal sentiments could lead to direct involvement in the care of young children.

Mothers were not the sole caregivers of infants and young children, for a number of reasons. First, although a mother had much authority over child-rearing and household affairs in poorer two-generation households consisting of only the head, wife, and children, her necessary involvement in income-earning activities such as agriculture, by-employments, sales and management, manufacturing, or wage work and in domestic chores left little or no time or energy for child care. As mean household size was about five persons during the prewar era, and slightly over half of the households consisted of only two generations, large numbers of women, particularly those of the lower classes, were likely to experience motherhood in a two-generation household.[22] Yet in two-generation households, the greater authority of a young mother over child care and other household matters was counterbalanced by the disadvantage of not having an older female, that is, a mother- or sister-in-law, to assist with the heavy burdens of housework, child tending, and productive work. Thus in poor and average households children were frequently called on to assist with household chores and productive labor.

Second, when a senior generation was present in the household, the junior wife's work and her relationship with her children were subject to supervision by her in-laws, especially her mother-in-law, who as mistress of the household typically dictated how cleaning, food preparation, laundry, consumption, and servants' labor as well as child-rearing should be done. According to the logic of the *ie*, a newcomer such as the young mother ought not be entrusted with control over its precious children, the embodiment of the household's supreme goal of intergenerational continuity. Therefore, if *ie* members with higher status, such as her husband, parents-in-law or sisters-in-law, chose to make decisions about a child's upbringing, as was often the case, the young wife (*yome*) had to defer to their wishes. And even after a junior wife assumed the position of housewife after her mother-in-law's retirement, force of habit, filial piety, and deference might limit her authority in household management and child-rearing until the death of the senior woman.

Mikiso Hane states about the junior wife in a rural areas during the modern era:

A young wife was treated as an outsider and as the lowliest member of the family until her mother-in-law got too old to run the household. . . . A young wife had to be the first to rise and the last to go to bed. She had to get up at three or four in the morning to cut grass for the horse or ox, work all day, and do the washing late at night after the others had gone to sleep. She had to resign herself to spending little time with her own children, because their care was taken over by her mother-in-law, sister-in-law, or the grandmother of the family."[23]

In metropolitan areas as well, mothers-in-law had more authority over child-rearing than mothers themselves in three-generation households. Reflecting on prewar and early postwar practices, Japan's Dr. Spock, Matsuda Michio, recalled that for the baby's first office visit, "[i]n the past, the mother-in-law commonly carried the newborn baby. The mother herself followed behind."[24]

Hane also notes one of the affective consequences of the young mother's pattern of activities, which reflected the value of her labor and her lack of power in the *ie.* Prolonged daily caregiving by others had great impact on the emotional dynamics of the mother-child relationship in a three-generation household:

All the spare time the young wife had was to be devoted to work. Caring for her children was an indulgence. One young girl recalled that her mother had to be deliberately cool toward her children so that they would go to her mother-in-law or sister-in-law for attention. As a result, the girl came to look upon her mother as a cold, forbidding person. One day, when she was three or four years old, she watched her mother weeping after being tormented by her in-laws. Seeing the child, her mother called her to her side, but the little girl was afraid to go to her. When her mother told her that she loved her, she blurted out, "Do you mean it?" The mother realized that she had turned her daughter into a stranger in her effort to be a good *yome.*[25]

Senior *ie* members, especially the mother-in-law, expected the *yome* to apply herself diligently to housework, agricultural tasks, and by-employments from morning until night with no complaints, a work regimen that left the young wife scant time to devote to child-rearing.

If a grandmother wished to raise the heir or another child, the young wife's duty was to yield to her mother-in-law's wishes. It is likely that grandmothers frequently chose to take charge of their grandchildren. It was part of their duty to the household, and also compensation for not rearing their own children when they had been *yome.* A grandchild also provided companionship if the grandmother lived in a separate residence. Finally, exercising authority over the grandchild and young wife gave the grandmother a chance to assert her hard-won prerogatives as a senior *ie* member. The above story of the young girl treated coldly by her natural mother is one such case. The childhood of Kawakami Hajime, a noted Marxist scholar born in 1879 to a rural samurai household in south-western Japan constitutes another.[26] Although his mother was alive, as the heir Kawakami was brought up from infancy by his grandmother. One biography of Kawakami records:

> A picture . . . taken when Hajime was about three shows him resting against his grandmother's knee, as she sits holding one of his hands in her lap, while his mother, only about twenty at the time stands demurely to one side. The picture symbolizes the relative roles played by these two women in Hajime's early life.
>
> Grandmother Iwa was fifty-two years old when Hajime was born, and with her daughter-in-law to serve her, she now had leisure time and some savings to lavish on her eldest grandson. By dint of hard work, she had managed to acquire enough money to build separate quarters for herself attached to the original family house. Sunao [Hajime's father], his wife, and his second son lived in the old house, while Hajime slept in Iwa's room. This arrangement was a common practice among Japanese families; especially after the birth of a second child, it was not unusual for the first-born to become "grandmother's child." . . .
>
> Iwa doted on her grandchild. She picked him up as soon as he started to cry and walked back and forth in the garden to comfort him. . . . When he was still learning to crawl, she scattered sweet cakes on the floor to encourage him. Wherever Iwa went—to the theater, on picnics, sight-seeing at local shrines or Buddhist temples—she took her grandson along.[27]

In households of modest means, grandmothers such as Kawakami's could devote themselves to child-rearing, leaving the task of running the household to the young wife.

Even grandfathers looked after babies and toddlers. Like fathers and grandmothers, fondness may have motivated some grandfathers to take care of their grandchildren. So, too, might a sense of responsibility for the upbringing of the heir lead grandfathers to tend male grandchildren. On the other hand, a grandfather in a household with few able-bodied adults may have been the only person the household could spare for the relatively light work of baby-sitting.

The renowned ethnographer Miyamoto Tsuneichi, born in Yamaguchi Prefecture in 1907, remembers that even though he was quite young when he used to go to the fields and forest lands with his grandfather, the old man gently began to mold him into a good farmers' son. Miyamoto would ride on his grandfather's back when the old man had no bundles to carry. After arriving at the destination, he was free to wander about while his grandfather worked, but recalled that "when I scampered back from playing in nearby hills, I was relieved to see him there at work. He would encourage me to work too by saying, 'If you pull even one sprig of grass, it helps [my work] by that much.'"[28] The grandfather kept an eye on his grandson while doing other chores, and at the same time taught him wholesome attitudes toward work.

Besides parents and grandparents, older children cared for infants and toddlers in ordinary rural and urban families. Children of both sexes between ages seven and fourteen worked at useful housekeeping and productive tasks such as cutting grass, sweeping, finding firewood, weeding, and plaiting straw cords, and they tended younger brothers and sisters as well. In impoverished families, children might begin to baby-sit siblings at age three or four.[29]

Boys as well as girls minded young children. Katayama Sen, a Meiji socialist born to a prominent family in an Okayama village, recalls that his brother, only four years his senior, as well as his grandmother and aunt, took care of him during his early childhood, while his mother farmed the family lands.[30] A 1900 survey of higher elementary students in a rural hamlet near Yokohama conducted by their teacher revealed that many thirteen-year-old boys helped with both baby tending and housework. The teacher summarized the boys' activities in the following way:

> Boys' daily work [included] 1) cultivating paddies and dry fields, 2) babysitting, 3) indoor and outdoor cleaning, 4) drawing water . . . 5) cleaning lamps, 6) braiding ropes or straw sandals, 7) preparing the bath, 8) doing errands, 9) gathering fertilizer, and 10) reviewing lessons or 11) looking at the newspaper, and 12) other [tasks].[31]

The social acceptability of child-tending by boys is suggested by the praise heaped on one mid-Meiji elementary school student in a novel by Chiba Hisao. Taima Tsuneyoshi, an eleven-year-old fifth son, was praised by school officials in his town for

> being obedient, not quarrelling with others, whether at school or not, and having good character, minding the teachers' instructions well while at

school, and having never been punished for violating school rules. At home, he did not contradict his parents, and had reportedly never angered them or been scolded by them. . . . He always reviewed his lessons after school, but after that, plaited rope to supplement the family finances, and was never lazy. Furthermore, he sometimes babysat his nephew (aged 7) and acted as a scarecrow in the rice fields. . . . Due to the family's financial condition, his parents apprenticed him to a certain shop . . . but the master released him from service because he wore a melancholy look day and night. . . . [H]e was very happy to return home again . . . and his parents sent him to school once more.[32]

School authorities excused Taima's failure as an apprentice, instead lauding his conduct at home and at school, including his work as a baby-sitter. The male writer of the novel's afterword, who grew up in a rural hamlet, also recalls having his baby sister, ten years younger, bound to his back.[33]

Multiple Caregivers in Elite Households

Family members besides mothers cared for infants and toddlers on a daily basis in ordinary rural and urban households; nonmaternal care was also widespread in wealthy households. In rich households, however, the alternate caregivers were hired child baby-sitters, wet nurses, nannies, or apprentices rather than other family members. Despite the introduction of Western conceptions of womanhood emphasizing the critical role of mothers in raising children and the companionate relationship of spouses as the basis for marriage, many aspects of household goals and organization—the aim of household immortality, the junior wife's lack of authority, and work patterns—changed little or not at all in both prosperous and poor families after 1868. These values in turn kept alive many early modern conceptions of child care and motherhood.

In wealthy enterprise households, lingering early modern Confucian family ideals also undermined notions of increased maternal responsibilities for children; authority was vested in the household head and the senior generation, not in the young wife who gave birth to the next generation. Over time new views of womanhood and child-rearing slowly gained greater influence, particularly in the ranks of the new urban middle class, salaried workers, and their families. And as workers leaving the villages gravitated toward freer forms of labor, a growing shortage of domestic servants in the modern era contributed to a slow decline in the practice of employing nonmaternal caregivers.

In rich households, discourses of early modern written culture as well as the logic of the *ie* weakened a mother's authority over her children. By the middle of the early modern period, wealthy urban merchants and prosperous peasants had begun to absorb Japanese Confucian thought, formerly limited to the ruling warrior class, and the influence of these ideas lingered into the modern era. Popular Confucian tracts for women such as Kaibara Ekken's "Onna Daigaku" (Greater learning for women) emphasized female inferiority. According to Kaibara, women were afflicted with seven vices; female moral deficiencies were so extensive that only with considerable difficulty could women conduct themselves well enough to be models of virtuous conduct for children. The advice books admonished young brides to serve their in-laws faithfully, to practice frugality and modesty, and to learn to manage household and servants well, but they scarcely mentioned the responsibilities of motherhood. The lengthy instructions regarding a *yome*'s duty to her husband's parents and siblings suggest that obedience to in-laws in her new household was more important than child care for a young Japanese woman.[34]

Some popular Confucian-influenced writings advised households on how best to educate children. These tracts commonly warned "fathers and elder brother" (*fukei*) or "fathers and mothers" (*fubo*) to take care to choose a suitable tutor for the child. Almost never was advice regarding education and child-rearing addressed to mothers alone.[35] Women did in fact play important roles in child care as wet nurses, nannies, baby-sitters, and mothers, but notions of female inferiority precluded strong female authority over child-rearing and, at least in theory, argued against allowing women the major role caring for children. These tracts delegated ultimate responsibility for children's upbringing to male figures, since Confucian logic dictated that children, especially boys who would assume positions of influence in society, be reared by virtuous men instead of inferior females. In fact, because boys studied under male tutors and learned much about their future occupation from fathers, master craftsmen, or successful merchants, they had much more contact with men than did girls, who were not destined to become leaders in the household or in society and could therefore be relinquished to female mentors. Social norms, then, in theory and in practice placed little emphasis on mothers as autonomous or primary nurturers of infants and young children.

Thus despite the presence of servants, mothers in wealthy households tended to many household tasks, because female idleness was scorned, but child-rearing was not one of their central duties. Unlike lower-class women, mothers in prosperous families did not as a rule participate directly in income-earning activities. Their work for the household, waiting on their husband and in-laws and supervising clothing, household decor, and kitchen supplies as well as servants, left them little time to spend with their offspring.[36]

The lack of extensive daily contact between mother and children, however, caused no anxiety among the adults in the household—neither household head, parents, grandparents, nor servants. Instead, in prosperous households infant care was routinely assigned to child baby-sitters (*komori*) or apprentices for part or all of the day, while as a mark of social distinction, very rich families hired full-time servants such as wet nurses or nannies to specialize in child care.

The *komori* was usually a youngster from a poor family. Instead of helping their own families, studying, or playing, poor children hired out as baby-sitters and spent their daytime hours tending infants in the masters' households. Sugō Hiroshi's historical novel set in the rural Koriyama district of Fukushima Prefecture recounts how boys from impoverished households were hired as live-in baby-sitters: in a lower-class Tokyo district, Sangorō, a sixteen-year-old rickshaw puller's son, sometimes provided unpaid child care for his landlord's infant by strapping the child to his back.[37] In a village in Saitama Prefecture, poor tenant farmers sent out their daughter, Kichi, to work as an unpaid *komori* for the landlord; by doing so, she drained less of the family's meager resources, because she received two out of three daily meals at her employer's house. She continued to work as a nonresident *komori* from age seven to ten, until she grew old enough to do field work.

A description of Kichi's daily routine reveals in some detail the nature of a baby-sitter's duties and the type of care the infant received. Kichi set off for the landlord's residence soon after breakfast seven days a week, then trudged home late at night after finishing a skimpy dinner of leftovers at her employer's. Her work consisted of carrying the landlord's baby on her back all day, except when the child was being fed. The baby pulled her hair, and the young wife criticized Kichi's eating habits. Little Kichi complained, but her mother replied that the family was lucky she was able to baby-sit for the landlord. When Kichi graduated to field work at the age of ten, her younger sister took her place as *komori*.[38] Well into the 1930s, rural households continued to make use of *komori* to care for infants while their mothers worked in the fields.[39]

Some children moved away from home to serve as live-in baby-sitters in nearby towns or distant cities. One woman recalled:

> I was born in 1887 as the oldest daughter in a poor farm family in . . . a village in the watershed of the Yodogawa River in Kochi prefecture. I didn't

go to elementary school. At twelve, I went into service as a *komori* in a paper-maker's household. At eighteen, I became a full-fledged paper-maker . . . and sent home nearly all my wages to help the family finances.[40]

Although hired baby-sitters usually came from poor households, occasionally motives other than poverty led parents to place children in other households. For example, the father of one eight-year-old girl from Niigata Prefecture arranged for her employment as a *komori* for a factory owner's family in neighboring Nagano Prefecture to help her escape mistreatment by her stepmother.[41]

Rather than the joys and satisfactions of nurturing precious infants, baby-sitters' songs reveal the misery and resentment of modern *komori*. Former *komori*, when interviewed in their old age by Mariko Asano Tamanoi, recalled singing, "One, we are all bullied. Two, we are all hated. Three, we are all forced to talk. Four, we are all scolded. Five, we are all forced to carry babies who cry a lot. Six, we are all fed with terrible food. Seven, we are all forced to wash diapers in the cold water of the river. Eight, we are all impregnated and shed our tears. Nine, we are all persuaded to leave, and finally, ten, we all must leave." But baby-sitters could get even with their employers for the unpleasant work and any sexual liberties that might be taken: "Listen, my master and mistress. If you treat me bad, I may exert an evil effect on your kid."[42]

In urban settings the duties of apprentices often included baby-sitting and household chores such as boiling breakfast rice and sweeping floors, as much as productive work. Boys generally became apprenticed to merchants or master tradesmen between the ages of ten and thirteen, although some from poor families might enter service as young as seven or eight. One historian of childhood describes the first stage of an artisan's apprenticeship in the following way:

> When a child was bound out, he lived with the master's family. At first, he began by doing household chores such as drawing water, boiling rice, cleaning the yard, heating the bath, running errands, and baby-sitting. After that he learned the trade, beginning with carrying and arranging tools.[43]

A lacquer craftsman from Wajima on the Japan Sea explained that for the first three years a new apprentice's life consisted of baby-sitting and doing household chores such as drawing water, changing outhouse buckets, and straightening up the workplace. One plasterer from Sagamihara City, Kanagawa Prefecture, who became an apprentice in 1914 at age thirteen, recalled that his early duties included minding the master's child:

I became a plasterer because my father thought that as the oldest son I ought to be prepared to head the family business. . . . Until another junior apprentice entered the household, I had to do miscellaneous chores. I helped prepare meals, babysat, washed the baby's diapers, massaged the master's shoulders, and ran errands for the craftsmen and master. Since the master also farmed, I had to do agricultural work, too. I waited on the master during meals, so it was important to be able to eat faster than he did.[44]

Although not all apprentices engaged in child care, the training of young, unskilled apprentices invariably commenced with easily performed chores. The fact that artisans lumped child care, housework, and errands together, delegating them to neophytes, suggests that they regarded these types of work as menial but necessary tasks in household activities.

Families in the upper ranks of society commonly employed wet nurses (*uba*) to care for infants, a tradition that existed for centuries in Japan.[45] For this reason, very rich families hired full-time servants who specialized in child care as a mark of social distinction. Early modern literary evidence suggests that wet nurses (also called nursemaids) stayed with their charges at least until they reached age three or four.[46] Child-rearing tracts of the day included sections on criteria for selecting *uba* of good character.[47] Authors of these advice books took for granted that caregivers other than the mother would tend young children. Although it was expected that an *uba* or nanny would care for children in rich households,[48] tensions could exist between the pecuniary motivations of lower-class wet nurses and the desire of parents for attentive care for their beloved child or between the nurturing and affection a wet nurse felt she owed to her employer's as well as her own child. Recognizing this gap between expectations of employed and employer, Saikaku, a renowned early modern writer, declared (with some hyperbole), "People say that the three great scoundrels are pack-horse drivers, ship's captains, and wet nurses," since only young women with "the most naive notion of how to raise a child" or gold diggers became wet nurses.[49] The practice of wet-nursing reveals that neither upper- nor lower-class mothers were expected to care for their own infants. Not only did rich mothers largely place their babies in the hands of hired caregivers, but each *uba* had to give up nurturing her own child. A wet nurse had the choice of hiring a foster mother for her own baby, or leaving her infant with the father, who in turn would depend on a live-out, hired wet nurse nearby or the voluntary help of a nursing neighbor to suckle the newborn. Although this form of employment improved the finances of the *uba*'s household, she endured the disadvantages of separation from her husband, the endangerment of her own child's survival, and confinement to the home of her employer.[50]

Wet nurses freed wealthy mothers from the daily toil of feeding, carrying, and bathing young children. Yet the difference in status between child and nanny might be problematic. Early modern advice tracts warned parents to take care in selecting an *uba* in order to avoid improper moral influences on their offspring. Other difficulties might arise for the employer due to status differences between hired nurturer and child. In the opening scene of Chikamatsu Monzaemon's early modern puppet play, "Yosaku of Tamba," the daughter of a feudal lord causes a great stir by refusing to travel north to wed. Her governess, a woman of the warrior class, and other retainers beg her to set forth, but since they are lower ranking, they cannot compel her to begin the journey.[51] Despite disparities in social status, extremely close, lasting bonds might develop between a wet nurse and the child she nursed.[52]

Robert Danly's sketch of the tragic, fleeting life of the renowned Meiji writer, Higuchi Ichiyō, reveals deep affective ties that developed between an *uba* and her charge, but it also shows that the nurturing of the employer's infant came at the expense of the wet nurse's baby. Ichiyō's parents, Noriyoshi and Ayame, descended from wealthy peasants, fled relatively secure lives in their village for a marginal existence in Edo (now Tokyo) in order to marry shortly before the Meiji Restoration. After Ayame bore a child, Noriyoshi's patron, Mashimo, assisted the penniless couple by arranging a prestigious position for Ayame as an *uba* in a prominent samurai family:

Mashimo . . . saw to it that the young bride was properly established in her new home. He sent baby clothes when her daughter Fuji, named for Mashimo's wife, was born on 14 May. And he arranged for Ayame to serve as a wet nurse once she had recuperated from the birth. On 24 June, Ayame left Noriyoshi and the newborn Fuji in Koishikawa for the time being and went off to the Yushima estate of Inaba Daizen, a *hatamoto* [direct shogunal retainer] whose daughter, Ko, Ayame was to nurse. . . .

Taki [Ayame's new name bestowed by Inaba] was constantly reminded of her inferior position. When nursing the Inaba child, deference required her to place a piece of tissue over her mouth, lest she breathe on "the little princess." She paid for the privilege of serving the exalted child by being forced to put her own baby out to nurse and to endure long absences from her new husband.[53]

For seven years, until the family's economic situation improved, Taki lived at the Inaba estate separated from her husband and daughter [Fuji, later known as Ichiyō]. Deep bonds of affection between Taki and Ko survived Taki's departure from the Inaba household. Ko regarded Taki "almost as a mother," and years later nurse and nursling continued to keep track of each other's whereabouts.[54]

In the modern era, elite families in urban and rural regions continued to employ wet nurses. In an 1876 work, one of the first introducing kindergartens to Japan, Kuwada Shingo scathingly remarked that "[t]he *yome* [young wives] in noble and wealthy households always wear makeup and fine garments, but they know nothing about how to rear children. They only give birth, and without ever laying hands on the child, turn it over to an insincere wet nurse."[55] Journalist and educator Fukuzawa Yukichi, who married in 1861, recalled that his wife nursed the first five of her nine children herself, but thereafter hired an *uba*.[56] Writer Dazai Osamu, born in 1909 to a prominent rural family in Aomori Prefecture, was reared by his aunt and hired caregivers because his mother was sickly. He recalls that

> [b]ecause my mother was in poor health, I never drank a drop of her milk, but was given to a wet nurse as soon as I was born. When I was two years old and tottering about on my own, I was taken away from her and put in the care of a nanny—Take. At night I would sleep in my aunt's arms but during the day I was always with Take. For the next five years, until I was about seven, she raised me.
>
> And then one morning I opened my eyes and called for Take, but Take did not come. I was shocked. Instinctively I knew what had happened. I wailed, "Take has gone! Take has gone!" I sobbed, feeling as if my heart would break; and for two or three days all I could do was cry. Even today I have not forgotten the pain of that moment.[57]

A 1913 survey of servants in Tokyo revealed that wealthy households were still hiring wet nurses, mostly country or lower-class city girls, who in turn employed someone else to care for their babies during their term of service. Wet nursing appears not to have been an easy occupation, because the survey also noted that *uba* rarely completed their contracts. One wonders about these women: Did they leave because they were treated badly, or did they want to return to their own children or husbands, or did they leave for other employment in the city?[58]

The Character of Late Nineteenth Century Child Care

In sum, not just mothers, but other household members ranging from grand-parents and fathers to siblings and several types of servants commonly provided daily care for infants and toddlers in nineteenth-century Japanese households. While younger adult males were less likely to provide all-day care for young chil-dren, household heads and retired household heads (grandfathers) had much in-centive to spend time with at least one child, since they were obliged to train a successor. Not only did the presence of a mother-in-law or servants diminish con-tact between mother and child and reduce the authority of a mother over her off-spring, but the father and father-in-law, too, could limit her freedom to raise the children as she wished. Especially in the literate classes, old ideas tended to un-dermine mothers' relationships with their children, because early modern advice tracts held that women's many faults impeded their ability properly to socialize children. Children would become better adults if reared by more virtuous males.

Viewed from a contemporary perspective, this pattern of multiple care-givers may appear to have deprived a Japanese baby of a mother's tender care. In fact, two major advantages of this infant care method are first that it allowed mothers of very young children to participate in productive labor and second that it offered infants a considerable degree of security. The Japanese child un-der three spent most or all of its waking hours strapped to the back of the care-giver, generally the same sibling, grandparent, or servant, each day. The baby was safe and emotionally secure, because it was protected from physical harm, was never alone, and experienced constant, reassuring physical contact with its caregiver. The child was unbound from the baby-sitter's back and brought to nurse at its mother's breast for feeding. The infant was also unstrapped for elim-ination, but mistakes in timing meant that the caregivers not infrequently be-came wet or soiled.

Robert Smith and Ella Lury Wiswell's observations of Suye Village indicate that reliance on multiple caregivers persisted into the mid-1930s in parts of rural Japan, although by this time boys had been largely excluded from infant care. Wiswell's field notes indicate that grandmothers, older sisters, and teenage girl baby-sitters carried infants and young toddlers around on their backs during the day. The baby-sitters watched three- to six-year-olds play together in groups. These older toddlers ran to the caregiver or whoever else was near—sibling, grandparent, mother, father, or neighbor—for comfort or protection. Mothers breast-fed their youngest children, who slept by mother at night, and they also nursed babies of others when the mother was not nearby. Other cosleeping

Women carrying babies in a lower-class district, circa 1920. One infant is held in the caregiver's arms, while the other is strapped on the back with its head facing in the same direction as the carrier's. Courtesy of Ohara Institute for Social Research, Hosei University.

arrangements were also practiced; young children often slept next to fathers, siblings, or grandparents. Thus in addition to mothers, family members or *komori* kept young children reasonably secure and safe.[59]

Post-Restoration Changes

As we have seen, throughout the nineteenth-century nonmaternal caregivers spent as much or more time than mothers in caring for and educating children, including infants, in households of all classes. However, after the 1868 Meiji Restoration, as part of a concerted effort to catch up to the West, the modern Japanese state promoted the creation of new social institutions to consolidate its authority and to strengthen the nation. The new economic and educational institutions—factories, government offices, and schools—made demands on the time and energy of household members that reshaped the household division of labor, including participation in child care. Students attending school and wage-earning members of the family were away for long hours nearly every day, thus preventing them from engaging in baby tending and other domestic activities during working hours.

The new educational institutions affected reproduction in the family in two ways. First, the activities taking place in schools, and to a degree those in kindergartens, replicated some household functions, because they offered children and older youth vocational and moral training for their future roles in society. Second, daily absence from the household for many hours made it impossible for older children attending school to play a major role in child care at home. In founding the public schools and mandating first four, then six, years of education for children of both sexes, the government sought to alter the socialization process to foster state goals. However, the negative impact of compulsory education on the household division of labor and family livelihood stirred resistance to state policy, mainly among ordinary households that depended on children's household or wage-earning labor to survive. The government adopted various strategies such as reducing the duration of compulsory education, lowering tuition rates, and founding special institutions to educate poor children to soothe aggrieved families, but it continued to promote school enrollment and to send out truant officers to compel school attendance. By the early twentieth century enrollment rates suggest that ordinary families throughout the nation had come to accept compulsory schooling.

In the home, care of young children by persons other than mothers was common to all levels of nineteenth-century Japanese society, but with the growth of trade and industry after 1890, a new pattern of child care began to emerge in city households that were no longer productive units. Particularly influential were the family patterns of the new urban middle-class households whose breadwinners filled the expanding ranks of salaried employees, although the new middle class remained a minority of Japan's population during the prewar era. The upper reaches of the new salaried class included influential professionals such as journalists, educators, bureaucrats, technicians, and managers, and in their homes, women and children became dependent consumers as the family shed many of the productive tasks that women and sometimes children continued to perform in rural and urban enterprise households. The old pool of caregivers shrank as cities grew, since urban families on average contained fewer members than rural households.[60]

Children and fathers who went out to schools and workplaces during the day of course were not available to care for infants. In villages, towns, and metropolitan districts where mothers in peasant, merchant, and artisan families still worked, other family members continued to provide care for babies. Thus old family and child-care patterns coexisted with the new; however, as the ranks of new middle-class families continued to swell during the twentieth century, practitioners and advocates of the new patterns increased.

Modern Schools and Child Care

Examination of the impact of modern schools on the process of reproduction in late nineteenth century Japanese households reveals that the policy of universal compulsory education, begun in 1872, worked against the custom of having older children, hired baby-sitters, and apprentices look after the youngest family members. Child-care practices were little affected at first, because families refused to enroll their youngsters, resulting in low school attendance in early Meiji. In 1873, the overall enrollment was a mere 28 percent; twelve years later it had risen only to 49 percent.[61] At the time many average Japanese perceived schools to be detrimental to the interests of their families and localities because schooling was costly, with new local taxes assessed to support public schools. Moreover, children attending schools paid tuition. In fact, education was a double burden for ordinary households because schools drained cash from household coffers and robbed them of the use of older children's labor during prime daylight hours for a period of four to six years. For these reasons, it is not surprising that families of limited means were reluctant to enroll children in schools. Resistance took an active form in some areas during the early Meiji as protestors razed and set fire to schools.[62]

Despite resistance, however, the government maintained its compulsory education policy, because schooling was crucial to shaping the character and talents of future citizens of the new Japan. Through various means educational authorities raised school attendance levels: they threatened with truant officers, they cajoled by offering special schools that allowed children to work—night schools, industrial schools, tuition-free pauper's schools, and baby-sitters' schools (*komori gakkō*). Over time the carrot-and-stick method proved to be fairly effective; by the late Meiji period school enrollment rates had reached 98 percent.[63] Yet registration rates painted a rosier picture than reality. Autobiographies and oral histories reveal that children of all ages were routinely kept home from school when their families required extra labor:

> [M]y family [was] a farm family. I had five brothers and sisters, but one died young. I went to four years of elementary school, but baby-sitting,

baby-sitting. . . . [I]f I calculate it, I actually attended only three full years. I can barely read the syllabary.[64]

Observers were also struck by the low rates of school attendance of urban poor.[65]

Local educational authorities created baby-sitters' schools (*komori gakkō*) as a means of increasing elementary school enrollment. The state was not willing to neglect even lower-class children in its quest to mold loyal, obedient, patriotic citizens through education in state-monitored schools. The nationwide establishment of these schools indicates that large numbers of families could not dispense with children's help in productive and reproductive labor, including the care of infants, by enrolling them in regular public schools. The employment of *komori* in the late 1880s and 1890s was so widespread that it called for special policy measures.[66] *Komori* could bring the infants in their care to baby-sitters' schools, but since the schools' primary aim was to educate children in the elementary grades rather than preschoolers, the facilities for infants were very limited. At the time, the provisions for children under six were as simple as letting *komori* or siblings take turns minding the toddlers in a separate room adjoining the classroom. A few exceptionally well equipped baby-sitters' schools had separate programs and teachers for the preschoolers.[67]

The efforts of the state to mold solid future citizens extended not only to older working children such as *komori,* farm children, and factory operatives; the state encouraged development of new institutions to educate children under age six as well. In creating the modern educational system in 1874 based on Western models, the Meiji government mandated the founding of kindergartens (*yōchien*) as well as elementary schools and higher institutions of learning; and for a similar reason—to improve the quality of the nation's manpower. The first *yōchien* opened in 1876, a few years after the national school system and compulsory education were established early in the Meiji period. It aimed to develop the intellectual abilities of preschool children aged three to six.[68]

The state viewed kindergartens positively, since they fostered early development of the abilities of future citizens. Implicit in the government's endorsement of these schools as well as other educational institutions was the assumption that learning at home from parents or tutors was insufficient to socialize citizens for participation in a modern nation. However, government interest did not extend to funding the construction of kindergartens. Their establishment was left largely to private initiative, as building a nationwide network of elementary and higher schools had higher priority. Public and private kindergartens charged tuition, which tended to limit enrollment to children from wealthy families. The curriculum, which fairly often included foreign languages and Western etiquette, appealed little to lower-class families. The regulations promulgated in 1899 by the Ministry of Education limited kindergarten class-room time to five hours per day, ensuring that operating hours were too limited to permit the schools to care for children while their parents worked.[69]

Attended by a tiny percentage of the nation's preschoolers, kindergartens exerted little influence on the household division of labor or attitudes toward institutional care of children during the late nineteenth century. As these institutions were viewed in the West as training grounds for future mothers, to some extent their diffusion fostered Western conceptions of strong maternal responsibility for the care of young children among the middle-class girls and women who were the mainstays of kindergartens' staff and possibly among the parents of the students as well.

Class Differences in Child-Rearing Change

The separation of workplace and home and compulsory education had an uneven impact on the domestic life of different classes. The practices of the wealthiest families were little affected, since they could still hire private tutors, wet nurses, and governesses to raise their offspring, although criticism of these practices emerged after the 1870s. New middle-class wives' share of housework and child care increased as their children attended school instead of helping with domestic chores and as the supply of domestic servants declined. Supported by their husbands' salaries, these wives of officials, office workers, and teachers became specialists in domestic work, while busy, productive women in the enterprise households of the old middle class—ordinary merchants, middling farmers, and craftsmen or small manufacturers—remained at home to engage in housework and child care as well as income-producing labor according to household needs, much as they had in the early modern era. Families in the lower ranks of rural and urban society generally needed the earnings of women and children to survive. If all able-bodied members worked to support the household, as in the early modern era, it sometimes left neither working adults nor older children with time to spare to tend small children.[70]

Previously, the household had been the locus of productive and reproductive work; now for an increasing number of families child care, consumption, and leisure activities—but not income-earning activities—took place at home. As the modern sector grew, the expansion of employment at large-scale economic organizations refashioned the household division of labor by decreasing the number of family members available for tasks performed at home, including child care. The fact that male wages were nearly always higher than those of married females provided an economic incentive for men rather than women to work at outside occupations.[71] In the middle classes, as school attendance removed older children from the home, mature women and children too young to work or attend school tended to remain at home together.

Among the lower classes, the meager earnings of workers, petty traders, and casual laborers did not permit wives to specialize in housework and child care. Some lower-class women took in piecework at home; others went to work in factories, small businesses, and in certain trades. Young women working outside the home found it difficult to manage child care for infants and toddlers. During the early 1890s a few factory day nurseries, called *kōjō takujisho* (literally, places at factories caring for children), were established to care for the young children of miners and factory operatives.[72] In contrast to *yōchien* and day-care centers (although the latter had not yet appeared in Japan), the factory day nurseries provided custodial care—attending mainly to preschoolers' physical needs such as sleep, food, and safety. The goal of the industrial nurseries was to increase the productivity of married female workers by removing children from work areas, not improving the infants' educational or moral development.[73] Although factory day nursery programs may seem inadequate from a modern point of view, they constituted a little-known early institutional effort to cope with the child-care problems of wage workers during industrialization.[74]

The rise of industry in late nineteenth and early twentieth century Japan expanded the demand for homeworkers as well as factory operatives. Women in lower-middle and lower-class urban families frequently took in piecework (*naishoku*) at low rates to supplement family income.[75] Yet work at home could also interfere with child care. The time regimens of homework and factory labor were more rigid than the work schedules of family enterprises. Factory workers could not take breaks to tend to their children, while homeworkers were subject to the demands of subcontractors, who tended to dump large consignments with tight deadlines on their workers. Female homeworkers sometimes had to work all night and had to enlist their children's help to complete orders on time. When hurrying frantically to finish a consignment, mothers had little, if any, spare time or energy for minding their children.

The rise of new economic and educational institutions after the Restoration inadvertently affected child care in the home. Concerted efforts to change child-rearing attitudes and practices commenced around the turn of the century. The new ideas diffused first among the middle and upper classes through higher education and the mass media. Private educators and education ministry officials took up this cause in the 1890s, displaying marked enthusiasm for the task following the 1894–1895 Sino-Japanese War. The need to mobilize women for national service, especially during wartime, led educators to reevaluate women's nature and capabilities. Women were found best suited to fill supportive roles at home, but they now had to be capable of substituting for men in wars or emergency situations. In 1899 *ryōsai kenbo* (good wife, wise mother), a redefinition of Japanese womanhood, became the cornerstone of the curricula of girls' higher schools attended by daughters of the elite, but it was not explicitly introduced into the curricula of elementary schools until the 1911 revision of the ethics textbooks.[76]

From long before the 1868 Restoration, Japanese families had expected the mistress of the house to be a diligent, shrewd, and dedicated household manager; the new element in *ryōsai kenbo* was its emphasis on motherhood—the married adult woman's indispensable role as the nurturer and above all the socializer of children. No longer was female inferiority grounds for denying women, even young wives, a major role in the education of children. In expecting lower-class mothers to raise industrious and loyal citizens and middle-class women carefully to rear future leaders, the state's new views of womanhood nominally entrusted women with unprecedented responsibility for shaping the destiny of nation and society.[77]

Significantly, the state failed to endorse the child-rearing roles of other household members; by default, it assigned the chief responsibility for the care and training of children to mothers alone. This was in part a response to changing social realities, and in part a reflection of the aims of the state. Children now went out to school, and men, especially urban men, commuted to their workplaces outside the home[78]; neither was expected to be at home during most of the daytime hours. It is likely that parents-in-law were passed over as major providers of child care in recognition of the fact that young women educated under the new regime were more likely than the older generation to train children to give their allegiance to the state rather than household, local community, and province—the key social units of yesteryear. In addition, the fact that new households formed by migrants to the cities often lacked parents-in-law may also have influenced the upgrading of the role of the mother.

However, granting greater authority over child-rearing to mothers as opposed to mothers-in-law, inherent in the "good wife, wise mother" formulation, contradicted another ideological initiative of the Meiji state and the private ideologues who supported it: the family-state (*kazoku kokka*) ideology, formulated in the same era. The values of the family-state stressed filial piety to parents for children and submission to parents-in-law as surrogate parents for women in virilocal marriages as a means of demonstrating loyalty to the emperor. In other words, the more positive evaluation of married women's domestic and public capacities implied by the state's endorsements of "good wife, wise mother" undercut other ideological persuasions instructing a married woman to be subservient to her husband or coresident parents-in-law in the patrilineal stem family established by the 1898 Civil Code.[79]

Although the educational system became the major means for diffusion of a new vision of womanhood associated with novel child-care attitudes and practices, many Japanese women failed to become model *ryōsai kenbo*. The stumbling block was motherhood rather than housewifery. The problem was that the conditions of life in a high proportion of households favored continued reliance on the traditional pool of caregivers, freeing mothers for productive work at home or elsewhere. Busy wives of ordinary laborers, farmers, craftsmen, shopkeepers, and petty manufacturers could not devote more time to their children without undermining their families' precarious economic security.

It is likely that the increasing separation between home and workplace and between home and school from the turn of the century had a more significant impact on lower-class families than did the rise of new conceptions of womanhood. In metropolitan areas diminished control over the deployment of family labor and decreased flexibility in work routines as well as irregular employment, low wages, and long working hours prevented lower-class parents from devoting much effort to child care. And as in the previous era, the physical aspects of the lower-class urban environment, with its lack of open space, its dank, dilapidated, overcrowded housing, and its poor sanitary facilities, created health and safety hazards for children and adults alike. By the middle of the 1880s lower-class children living in the squalor and stench of urban slums began to evoke pity and concern among humanitarians and social reformers. The sight of packs of youngsters roaming the slum streets begging, rummaging through garbage to find food, and engaging in petty theft and rowdy behavior spurred reformers and officials to try to find a means of coping with the issue of unruly lower-class children. The institutional response to the problems posed by neglected or unsupervised lower-class youths began with orphanages and reformatories after the 1870s. Next came special elementary schools and day-care centers after the 1890s, followed by infant and maternal health programs after World War I.

Amid increasing concern about the undesirable social consequences of industrialization at the turn of the century, humanitarians sought to relieve the suffering of poor youngsters. Some of them hoped for general improvement in the home environment of the urban lower classes. Officials worried about the impact of industrialization for different reasons. Their primary concerns were preservation of social order and increasing economic productivity. To attain these ends, they helped create programs and institutions promoting values such as diligence, savings, discipline, and self-reliance in all citizens, especially the urban poor and working classes. Sharing similar concerns, twentieth-century advocates of institutional child care were quick to assert that day-care centers could contribute to the future development and stability of Japanese society and that they could offer two additional benefits—improvement of the urban lower-class household and betterment of the present and future lives of poor children. At the beginning of the twentieth century traditional tolerance for multiple caregivers allayed distrust of day-care centers as institutions nurturing young children outside the home. But in the long run positive support for institutional child care flourished because day-care programs promised benefits not only to poor children, but to their parents, households, and above all, to the entire society and nation.

3

Day-Care and Moral Improvement:

The Case of Futaba Yōchien

On February 2, 1900, in an alley near a notorious Tokyo slum, two young women opened the doors of a tiny pauper's kindergarten to sixteen ragged street urchins. Although a growing number of institutions sought to educate lower-class children of all ages during the late Meiji period, Futaba Yōchien was one of the first institutions in Japan to provide both education and care to poor preschoolers. Reflecting the training and professional experience of its founders, it emphasized both the protection and moral education of youngsters under age six. Futaba Yōchien combined the purposes and features of the kindergarten and the day nursery in a single institution. While its founders, two Christian kindergarten teachers, called it a *hinmin yōchien,* or "pauper's kindergarten," during its early years, it was in fact Japan's first day-care center.[1]

From unassuming beginnings, by the end of the decade recognition by the Home Ministry had helped Futaba Yōchien become known nationwide as a model child-care facility.[2] Prominent Japanese supported the center through monthly subscriptions and special contributions of money and goods. By 1916 the founders had renamed their institution Futaba Hoikuen (Futaba Day-Care Center), a name more appropriate to its dual mission of education and care. Over the years their private child-care facilities received financial support from the Home Ministry, the Tokyo prefectural government, and the Tokyo Prefecture Social Work Association for regular operating expenses and expansion of its program and physical plant.

This institution for young children founded by Noguchi Yuka (1866–1950) and Morishima Mine (1868–1936) reflected late Meiji concerns regarding children. The themes of building moral character through education, achieving universal school enrollment, providing care for poor urban children, and diffusing early childhood education beyond the upper class appear in Futaba Yōchien's purposes and programs. Its program drew on elements of existing institutions, but contained new elements as well. Its educational content was adapted from the curricula of existing Japanese kindergartens; its long hours resembled those of day nurseries. A few aspects of its program, such as support by monthly subscribers, parents' meetings, and the emphasis on instilling proper values in lower-class children and parents, were probably modeled on the practices of the free kindergartens that Morishima had studied in the United States. An institutional hybrid, the Futaba Yōchien goals of physically protecting and educating poor urban preschool children differed from those of existing Japanese early childhood institutions, kindergartens, day nurseries, and baby-sitters' schools.

Beyond the development of children's institutions in Japan, examination of the establishment of Futaba Yōchien and its purposes, organization, and curriculum allows glimpses into shifting notions of womanhood, childhood, and family life in the modern era. Contradictory views of womanhood, especially motherhood, were visible in the social and cultural environment of Futaba Yōchien, where middle-class educators encountered lower-class children and their parents. On the one hand, the holding of parents' rather than mothers' meetings seems to reflect early modern views of motherhood and child-rearing, but on the other, the staff was overwhelmingly comprised of young, single female teachers. Had older conceptions of child-rearing been the sole influence, one would have expected greater reliance on caregivers of both sexes and of diverse ages, or a staff consisting only of male teachers, given early modern beliefs in the moral superiority of men. Furthermore, from the outset one paradox of prewar day-care appeared. In establishing child-care centers, middle-class social reformers such as Noguchi and Morishima assisted women's productive work within and beyond the household. Yet in making it easier for lower-class married women to work outside the home, they seemed to be undermining, if not directly opposing, the education ministry's doctrine of *ryōsai kenbo* (good wife, wise mother), although it could be argued that day-care supported the Home Ministry's emphasis on women's productivity. In any case, day-care and other relief professionals' unwillingness to criticize working mothers contrasts strikingly with the negative views of maternal employment expressed in turn-of-the-century American discourses on day-care. The tacit acceptance of lower-class women's labor force participation by Morishima, Noguchi, and subsequent Japanese advocates of child care may have resulted from lingering influences of Japanese early modern conceptions of womanhood that sanctioned a broad range of female domestic and productive activities to ensure household continuity.

The Female Founders of Futaba Yōchien: Motives and Contexts

The lives of Futaba Yōchien's founders, Noguchi and Morishima, illustrate women's opportunities to act beyond the confines of the household despite increasing constraints imposed by late nineteenth century state policies. Their professional careers and voluntary efforts influenced the development of relief work and early childhood institutions in the first three decades of the twentieth century. Their activities signal that within the confines of emerging state gender ideologies there remained avenues for middle-class women to participate in public affairs. Although the degree of their achievements may seem exceptional, in fact, other women, too, entered long-term, full-time employment and exerted influence on public affairs during the early twentieth century. Yet the founding of Futaba Yōchien was not simply an inevitable result of opportunities for women in education, employment, and charitable work; the experiences and personal qualities of Morishima and Noguchi were crucial.

Although early policies such as equal, compulsory elementary education for boys and girls seemed to promise new opportunities for women in the modern era, by the 1890s state policies had largely eliminated women's direct participation in the public world of politics and the economy. Their main contribution to the public good was to take place indirectly through the rearing of children in the private world of the home, although women were also encouraged to participate in public affairs through voluntary charitable and patriotic work. The Meiji Constitution (1890) and Article 5 of the Peace Security Regulations (1890) denied women suffrage, the right to hold office or join political organizations, or even to hear political speeches. Only by mounting a hasty protest did women retain the right to observe Diet proceedings from the observers' gallery. The 1898 Civil Code barred married women from managing property, choosing their own domicile, initiating a divorce, or testifying as adults in courts of law. During the mid-1880s the enrollment of ambitious girls in rigorous academic programs that served as preparation for university entrance examinations had been shut off, and by 1899 education ministry regulations decreed that study of domestic science in segregated middle and higher schools preparing women for careers as "good wife, wise mother" (*ryōsai kenbo*) would form the cornerstone of women's advanced education. In addition, women were largely excluded from the civil service examinations, although a labor shortage later led to opportunities in lower-level, less prestigious teaching positions.

From the 1890s through the first two decades of the twentieth century, then, the general thrust of state policy was to exclude women from direct participation in the public sphere in the vital areas of state and economy, although the views of ministries, bureaus, and officials were not monolithic. This reversal, following twenty years of greater openness during the first two decades of the modern era, suggests that the earlier efforts of the prewar Japanese state to construct womanhood and gender may be characterized as haphazard, fluid, and at times

contradictory rather than consistently oppressive or tightly integrated and sys-
tematic. But by the end of nineteenth century the Civil Code, educational regulations, civil service rules, and other ordinances enforced a rigorous exclusion
of women from the political world and fashioned a limited, subordinate role for
them in the modern economic world. However, the urgency of the quest to defend Japan from the menace of Western imperialism translated into a perception
that national defense required rapid economic and military progress. To this end,
it was expedient not to perceive ordinary women's traditional income-earning
activities as petty entrepreneurs, family enterprise workers, and pieceworkers in
the confines of the household as transgressions of the state's turn-of-the-century
redefinition of gender boundaries.

And despite *ryōsai kenbo,* which seemed to define women's place as in the
home, as the twentieth century progressed, women increasingly ventured into
the world outside the household. They found employment at factory and low-
level white collar and service occupations, often after completing school and before marriage.[3] Furthermore, the state and nationalist leaders encouraged
women's direct participation in the public sphere *outside* the key areas of government and economy by endorsing, with some equivocation, their participation
in patriotic and philanthropic work.[4] However, in contrast to the West, women
were not to be the main providers of charity. In principle all Japanese men and
women shared the duties of the "family system" (*kazoku seido*), "neighborhood
mutual help" (*rinpo aitasuke*), "shared existence, and shared prosperity" (*kyōson,
kyōei*), all of which could be summarized as the "obligation to assist" (*fuyō gimu*)
needy kin and neighbors.[5] Not until after 1919 did women begin to enter the
state bureaucracies with jurisdiction over relief and social work. Yet they were
eligible only for temporary appointments since they were not allowed to take the
civil service examinations.[6]

Despite the constraints of turn-of-the-century gender policies and norms,
the life experiences of Noguchi and Morishima demonstrate that regulations,
policies, and ideologies of womanhood were unable completely to block women's
opportunities to attain higher education, lifelong employment, and an esteemed,
though limited, role in public affairs. However, the possibilities were brighter
for middle- and upper-class women like Noguchi and Morishima than for
women of the lower classes. Noguchi graduated from the Women's Normal Department of the Tokyo Higher Normal School (Tokyo Kōtō Shihan Gakkō no
Joshi Shihan Gakka) in 1890. Morishima studied English at two schools, one in
Japan and one in the United States, before earning a certificate at Kate Wiggin
Smith's California Kindergarten Training Institute in San Francisco in 1892.

Even more unusual than their high levels of academic achievement was the fact that both maintained lifelong commitments to careers in early childhood education. Noguchi and Morishima entered prestigious positions as full-time teachers at the kindergarten of the Peers' Girls' School (Kazoku Jogakkō Fuzoku Yōchien) when it opened in 1894; by 1907 Noguchi had become the head teacher (*shuji*). Noguchi followed the less-usual path of the single career woman; perhaps it was an economic necessity to remain a full-time professor (*kyōjū*) at the peers' school kindergarten, as she never married. Yet Morishima's professional trajectory also followed an unusual course in that she continued to work at the peers' school kindergarten following marriage and the birth of three children at a time when much social disapproval of full-time employment outside the home for married women existed.[7]

Beyond their educational and career achievements, in an age that denied women equal opportunities to creatively exercise their artistic, academic, political, and administrative talents, Noguchi's and Morishima's founding of Futaba Yōchien demonstrated that women could make useful and innovative contributions to the larger society. Yet in founding Futaba Yōchien, Noguchi and Morishima did not flout the emerging modern conventions of middle-class femininity that encouraged women to engage in charity and social projects.[8]

In starting Futaba Yōchien, Noguchi and Morishima contributed to the development of early childhood education, philanthropy, and social work in Japan by adapting the standard Japanese kindergarten and the American free kindergarten to meet the needs of poor urban children and parents. And by helping strangers rather than only kin and neighbors, they helped further open the way for solutions to poverty based on institutions open to strangers in need instead of on early modern attitudes, benevolence that social superiors owed inferiors due to long-standing personal ties.

Nonetheless, the larger social, political, and institutional contexts do not fully explain why two young women working full-time—one with young children—from Japan's most privileged families would have taken on the extra burden of establishing a charitable institution during their scant leisure hours. Religious factors as well as personal experiences and individual dispositions are important in reconstructing the shared elements that motivated them to create an unprecedented philanthropic project. Work and residence in the heart of Japan's capital city brought to these women an awareness of the dilemmas of urbanization and industrialization. Every day as they walked to and from the Peers' Girls' School, they witnessed the contrast between Japan's most privileged children and the children of its outcasts. In the 1890s they had both become familiar with special institutions designed to provide kindergarten education to lower-class children. In their daily work Noguchi and Morishima confronted issues involving young children and constructed solutions through curricular and institutional innovation. Finally, Christian religious doctrine and the social gospel entering Japan in the 1890s encouraged the two young women to care for not only their relatives and neighbors suffering hardships but to reach out to strangers who were impoverished or ill.

It can also be argued that Noguchi's personal experiences led her to feel sympathy for the poor. During her first year at the normal school, the sudden, and successive deaths of her parents transformed her once-secure family into one in need. At twenty she discovered the thin line between prosperity and poverty in late Meiji and became aware that the latter could result not only from character failings but also from unfortunate circumstances. Religion provided comfort in her misery at the loss of her parents, her economic insecurities, and the burden of providing for her younger siblings. In 1888, two year's after her father's death, Noguchi converted to Christianity.

Noguchi accepted a position at the kindergarten of her alma mater in order to support herself and her brother and sister, and continued there until the principal of the school recommended her for a position as one of two teachers at a new kindergarten at the Peers' Girls' School that would open in 1894. In 1893, while she was still teaching at the normal school kindergarten, a special program—a simplified kindergarten for lower-class children—opened. The establishment of the special kindergarten opened her eyes to efforts to diffuse kindergarten education among the poor. The experimental program was a response to the education ministry's turn-of-the-century policy recommending the diffusion of kindergarten education to the lower classes. This simplified kindergarten was called the annex (*bunshitsu*), and indeed, it was no more than a plain room with two teachers. The quality of the facilities and equipment seemed to reflect assumptions that poor children did not require the more elaborate furnishings and curriculum of the normal school's regular classrooms. The *bunshitsu*'s teachers often complained about the building and their pupils, and had little to say about the successes or failures of their educational mission. They grumbled that their classrooms were too small, too cold in the winter, too hot in the summer, and too prone to odors from nearby privies wafting into the premises. Regarding their pupils, the instructors complained that the childrens' clothes stank from dried sweat during the warmer months because they were rarely washed.[9]

As for Morishima, the little that is known about her life reveals that she, too, had had significant exposure to institutions for poor children before founding Futaba Yōchien. Her parents were involved in an obscure orphanage that apparently cared for children from families who had lost in the brief but intense Restoration Battle of Ueno in Tokyo. Morishima later became acquainted with Tsuda Umeko, one of the first five Japanese women to study overseas, and accompanied Tsuda and Alice Bacon to the United States in 1889, but instead of joining them on the East Coast, she remained in California until August 1892. There, she first studied English, then enrolled in the California Kindergarten Training Institute. Morishima had ample opportunities to learn firsthand about providing kindergarten education to lower-class children, because at her Silver Street Kindergarten, Kate Wiggin Smith was a pioneer in introducing early childhood education to poor children, and the free kindergarten movement was at its peak in San Francisco during the 1890s.[10] After she returned to Japan, she started her own kindergarten, but it quickly failed.

A New Institution for Young Children

A number of institutions for young children existed in late Meiji Japan at the time Futaba Yōchien was founded. As discussed in chapter 2, regular kindergartens were mainly attended by wealthy children, but a few special kindergartens had been established for lower-class children just before the turn of the century. Day nurseries had sprung up at scattered locations to provide simple care for miners' and factory workers' babies. Educational institutions such as child baby-sitters' schools (*komori gakkō*), urban evening schools, and tuition-free pauper's schools had been created to increase the school attendance rates of lower-class children.

As Christians, Noguchi and Morishima undoubtedly heard sermons exhorting them to selfless service of others. They may have drawn inspiration from activities of Katayama Sen and other Christians who founded the Kingsley Hall settlement in Kanda, a working-class district of Tokyo, because Kanda was not far from the district in which the two young women lived and worked. Although detailed evidence regarding Kingsley Hall activities has not survived, clearly Katayama at this time regarded education as crucial to workers' efforts to uplift themselves, and its kindergarten was dear to his heart as one means of workers' self-improvment. Katayama had made a special plea to establish a kindergarten at Kingsley Hall. He opened the kindergarten before beginning the other components of his program, which included public lectures, adult education classes, and his program of advice on emigration to the United States. It is possible that Morishima and Noguchi even visited the settlement—although no record remains—since both the Futaba Yōchien founders and Katayama received advice and encouragement from the missionary Florence Denton.[11]

Noguchi and Morishima knew of secular and Christian efforts to help the poor and educational trends favoring the diffusion of kindergarten education to lower-class children, but according to Noguchi one recurrent set of experiences in their everyday lives spurred them to initate their own philanthropic project. She recalled in her later years why she and Morishima had ventured from educating pampered, wealthy youngsters into day-care work with poor children:

> Morishima and I lived near Kōjimachi and we always commuted to the kindergarten in the Nagata district together. When passing through the Shimorokuban district in Kōjimachi ward, we often saw children drawing letters with sticks in the dirt and eating cheap sweets in the streets. When we returned home from the kindergarten in the evening, they were still playing in the streets. I thought, on the one hand, we have the children of the nobility, raised carefully like butterflies and flowers, and on the other hand, here we have these other children, cast out into the streets. I came to feel that they could not be overlooked and left like this. . . .
>
> As a staff member at the Peers' Girls' School kindergarten, I was very free to do as I pleased. It was an excellent place to work, but the peers' children were raised with wet nurses and under parasols, and we were not permitted to give the children religious instruction. Our young hearts were unexpectedly thrilled by the prospect of assembling these [street] children, so lacking in material goods, and trying to give them day-care education based on true Frobelian ideals.[12]

Compassion for neglected street children as well as religious motives and a desire to implement fully their skills as professional kindergarten educators led to Noguchi's and Morishima's decision to found a private charitable kindergarten. While Friedreich Froebel's[13] methods—which stressed that the kindergarten unlocked the child's inherent potential for union with God, society, and nature—predominated in Japanese kindergartens until mid-Taishō, the religious aspects of his kindergarten method were not emphasized, owing to the taint of disloyalty associated with Christianity following the 1891 *lèse majesté* affair.[14]

As active Christians, Morishima and Noguchi felt constrained by the ban on religious teaching at their place of employment. At their own kindergarten, they would be free to apply the full range of their kindergarten training, a bright opportunity holding the promise of professional and religious satisfaction.

Despite their professional expertise and strong motivation for establishing a new institution for poor children, however, Noguchi and Morishima were by no means certain that their experiment would succeed. The previous failure of Morishima's kindergarten indicated that good intentions alone would not sustain a private charitable endeavor. Noguchi recalled their sentiments as they prepared to open Futaba Yōchien: "We intended to try it for a year, and then to give up if we could not find supporters among our acquaintances and the upper ranks of society."[15]

The two women attempted to adapt the kindergarten to meet the needs of poor Japanese urban children, but they had broader aims as well. The statement of purpose eloquently expresses their objectives:

[T]he benefits [of *yōchien*] do not extend to the poor residing in the lower reaches of society. In addition, because these parents are without education and must strain their bodies and minds in order to make ends meet, they do not have time to pay attention to the children they love. Therefore the children roam the trashy streets from infancy. There they are assailed by the winter winds and are scorched by the summer heat. They become wild and make malicious mischief. Furthermore when they return to their loving parents' side in cramped homes which barely suffice to keep out rain and wind, their food and clothes are unspeakable. Their environment is filled with evil and temptation, which increases their misfortune. When they grow older they fall into crime. This is truly lamentable, for it retards the progress of society and disrupts the social order of the nation. The children don't know that they are in a bad environment, and the fact that they play without evil intentions is quite pitiable. . . .

Is it not our duty as their brethren to take these children and put them in a good environment to make them good citizens before evil influences corrupt them? This work will not only bring happiness to the children receiving care and to their parents, it will raise the level of society and stop crime before it starts. Remember the proverb "An ounce of prevention is worth a pound of cure." This project will be very effective in improving society; it is more fundamental than orphanages, reformatories, and prisons. . . .

We have received the aid and encouragement of other educators and philanthropists, and from January 10 of this year, with the above purposes, we will open a *hinmin yōchien* [paupers' kindergarten] called Futaba Yōchien [Twin Leaves Kindergarten]. These two small leaves will grow, become luxuriant, and shine, and in its shadow, poor children will seek shelter from the wind and rain, and will be able to live with ease. . . . With these aims we ask for public support for Futaba Yōchien.[16]

The statement reveals the founders' main goals. First, they sought to educate poor children by exposing them to a kindergarten curriculum. Second, they aimed to protect them from the rigors of the slum environment, full of physical and moral dangers. The simplified kindergarten *bunshitsu* at Tokyo Higher Girls' School, Noguchi's alma mater, offered kindergarten education to ordinary children; the Kingsley Hall kindergarten provided instruction to working-class preschoolers. Existing factory day nurseries (*kōjō takujisho*) provided physical care for young children while their parents worked.[17] Futaba Yōchien's contribution to the development of children's institutions in Japan was the joining of these two goals in a single institution.

Futaba Yōchien also departed from established goals of children's institutions in planning its institutional program to bring satisfaction to parents. Ordinary kindergartens focused on educating children rather than pleasing parents. Day nurseries tried to give parents peace of mind by keeping infants and toddlers safe, but Noguchi and Morishima anticipated parents would derive satisfaction from watching their children's kindergarten activities. And as we shall see later, they also thought that parents would benefit from the lightened burdens of housework and child-tending that came with placing their children in day-care. Noguchi and Morishima also expected day-care work to improve society in a number of ways. Arguments for other children's institutions also asserted their benefits for Japanese society, but unlike public schools and kindergartens, Futaba Yōchien aimed to accommodate only children of the poor. By transforming slum children into good citizens, day-care would reduce delinquency, contributing to the preservation of the social order and the "progress of society."

It is important to note that nineteenth-century conceptions of child-rearing underlay early Futaba Yōchien documents. In referring to "loving parents" and the "happiness" of parents, the statement of purpose holds fathers as well as mothers responsible for child care. The center regulations also support the contention that Futaba Yōchien's founders did not assume that mothers alone would take charge of child-rearing (or even of housework). They state that day-care would eliminate each father's and mother's worries over child-rearing and would increase the amount of time they had to manage household affairs (*kaji*).[18]

The Pupils' Home Life

By examining the lives of families residing in the slum district near Futaba Yōchien, we may better assess the features of the day-care program and establish a basis for evaluating its strengths and limitations. Although Futaba Yōchien

Tokyo lower-class street scene, circa 1920. Courtesy of Ohara Institute for Social Research, Hosei University.

moved three times within Kōjimachi Ward and neighboring Yotsuya Ward during its first five years of existence, each site was located near or within districts inhabited by poor and working-class families.[19] The Futaba Yōchien annual reports and staff memoirs contain descriptions of the urban lower-class environment and aspects of the pupils' home lives, although one wishes the records were yet richer in detail.

Noguchi described the squalor and density of late Meiji Samegahashi. She assumed a correlation between slum dwellers' physical environment and their moral fiber and viewed day-care work as one means of countering the residents' moral degradation:

When we began our work, Samegahashi, together with Shitaya's Mannenchō and Shinamichō, was one of Tokyo's three largest slums. It was awful in those days. The main streets did not appear out of the ordinary, but as soon as one slipped into the side streets with their rice wine and bean cake shops, the long wooden buildings leaned precariously, the sliding panel doors were ripped, and tenement houses lined the streets. In dirty two- and three-mat rooms, families of five or six lived packed in together.

Of course, sunlight did not penetrate these narrow streets. Foul water accumulated under the floor boards, assailing the nose; the situation literally
stank. The people living there were the lowest of the poor, engaging in day
labor, begging, and collecting scraps to sell. When I thought of raising
children in this corrupt atmosphere, I couldn't help but shudder. . . . Thus
there was value in doing our work. If children came to the *yōchien* and
played all day happily, and if mothers could drop off their children and go
to work without worrying, it was a great help. The *yōchien* filled up. . . .
There were so many prospective entrants that we almost felt burdened by
their numbers.[20]

During late Meiji, lower-class working conditions, characterized by low
wages, long hours, and lack of steady employment, resulted in a haphazard,
sometimes brutal, style of family life. Wages were paid to laborers daily; rents
were also generally paid by the day. Families struggled day by day to obtain food
and shelter. As the earnings of an adult male were often insufficient to support
a household, other members—including mothers, coresident grandparents, and
older children—had to contribute to the family income. Some households could
barely survive despite the wage labor of all able-bodied members, while households burdened by nonproductive members such as nursing mothers, the aged,
invalids, or handicapped or ill members usually failed to make ends meet.

The sixteen pupils who enrolled in Futaba Yōchien the first year (1900)
came from intact families. However, since their fathers earned low or irregular
wages as rickshaw pullers, carpenters, and messengers, in all cases their mothers also contributed to the household income. Most of the mothers worked at
home as pieceworkers rolling cigarettes or as petty entrepreneurs doing tailor-
ing or hair-dressing, although one entrepreneurial mother sold sweet potatoes
on the streets.[21]

In 1906 nearly all of the pupils again came from families with both parents
employed. Again, the fathers were mainly rickshaw pullers, odd-job men, vegetable peddlers, and messengers, while the mothers usually made hemp-soled
sandals or took in laundry at home. However, some mothers were employed outside the home as cigarette rollers at a nearby tobacco factory.[22]

The 1908 annual report described the livelihoods of several families. Their
household budgets reveal the effect of low or irregular wages on homelife; households generally needed more than one income earner to make ends meet. One
child's family consisted of six members in all. The father worked as a craftsman's
helper, earning sixty sen per day. The mother also worked, but her piecework

soling hemp sandals brought in little income. The family lived in one 9 × 12 foot room. Although the father's wages were relatively high, the family's income fell to zero on rainy days, forcing the family members, except the father, to eat "used rice" (*zanpan*) or leftover rice and side dishes from restaurants sold by street vendors.[23]

In another six-member household, the father brought in forty-five sen per day from his work as a carter, while the mother and two older sisters worked in a cigarette factory, the three earning a total of only twenty-one sen per day. A third older sister was gravely ill and unable to work. This family also occupied a single 9 × 12 foot room with no plumbing.[24]

The need for multiple income earners took its toll on child care and other domestic work. Parents and older siblings of Futaba Yōchien preschoolers worked long hours at humble occupations for meager incomes, but they barely managed to sustain their households. The members of these lower-class households had very little time or energy to devote to fundamental child-rearing tasks such as keeping children clean; teaching them proper speech, hygiene, and manners; feeding them nutritious foods; or overseeing their intellectual development. The children were sheltered in dilapidated housing and fed scraps of food or nothing at all on days when the family income was too low. And due to the double burden of tuition and the loss of children's earnings or household labor, many poor urban parents refused to enroll their youngsters in school.[25]

Urban lower-class mothers frequently did piecework in tiny, stuffy apartments, so it was inconvenient to keep energetic preschoolers inside. Letting the children play outside in the streets allowed mothers to concentrate on earning income that was crucial to the household economy. The 1903 Futaba Yōchien annual report observed that

> [t]he children's mothers do nothing but work from morning to night. . . . The children's homes are hot, cramped, and dirty [in the summer]. . . . If they develop a cough, they are just left alone. . . . Since their ailments are usually untreated, the weak ones quickly die, but the children who survive are relatively healthy.[26]

In sum, in urban lower-class households, able-bodied members who were capable of earning income could barely find time to spend with young children. Pressed by economic need, it was impossible for lower-class mothers to devote all their energies to child care and housework. Specialization in domestic labor as a full-time housewife was a luxury they could not afford. And in the opening decade of the twentieth century, there are few, if any, indications that they felt they should do so.

The Children's Program

Noguchi and Morishima intended that Futaba Yōchien's activities improve the lives of slum children and their parents. The curriculum focused on the moral education of lower-class preschoolers; however, the program also made extensive provisions to tend to the youngsters' physical needs, including grooming, bathing, and health care.

The brief set of bylaws governing the daily operation of the center outlined eligibility, registration procedures, operating hours, holidays, curriculum, and fees. Neglected children who could not attend ordinary kindergartens because their parents were too busy were eligible to enroll. Some lower middle-class children with two working parents met these criteria,[27] but the lists of parents' occupations in the early annual reports reveal that in fact only poor children attended Futaba Yōchien. Registration was a simple procedure, requiring only the child's name, address, age, and the parents' occupations. In addition, a staff member generally visited the home in order to gather information regarding the child's family setting.

Futaba Yōchien's hours were longer than those of ordinary late Meiji kindergartens. The children attended six days a week, seven hours a day during the winter and eight hours a day during the summer. Nevertheless, since the workday was about twelve hours, even these extended hours did not fully meet the needs of working parents. Furthermore, the kindergarten was closed on Sundays to observe the Sabbath, but in Tokyo the traditional workers' holidays fell on the first and sixteenth of the month, which meant that children might lack care for up to four days a month while their parents worked.

The kindergarten had two extended holidays: a week-long break at the New Year, the most important national holiday, one that was universally celebrated, and a summer holiday about one month long, one that did not correspond to working parents' days off. The staff members were concerned about the negative consequences of the summer closure on their pupils and their families, but in this instance the needs of staff and children clashed. Since Futaba Yōchien's personnel routinely worked twice as many hours as teachers at other kindergartens, Noguchi and Morishima, and doubtless the teachers themselves, felt they needed a rest during the hottest weeks of the summer to recover from accumulated physical and mental fatigue. The dilemma of conflicting staff and parental needs was solved in the sixth year by inviting student volunteers to teach during the summer.

Futaba Yōchien's program focused above all on the educational, economic, health, religious, and psychological needs of impoverished youngsters. The educational curriculum consisted of the four standard kindergarten subjects prescribed by the 1899 Ministry of Education kindergarten regulations: play, songs, stories, and crafts. Due to the strong influence of Froebel's pedagogy during the late Meiji era emphasizing moral and spiritual training, the pedagogy, kindergarten stories, and songs for children generally had moral themes. And as at most foreign mission and Japanese Christian kindergartens, additional lessons at the optional Sunday school supplemented the moral teachings of the regular curriculum. For the daily lessons, the staff carefully selected materials intended to help their pupils overcome the negative effects of the slum environment in order to become sound adult citizens. But the materials were very simple, as funds to buy supplies were extremely limited. Scraps and items donated by supporters served as materials for the craft periods. Needless to say, the castoffs were no match for the elaborate supplies available to wealthy kindergarten students.

Craft lesson at a day-care center, circa 1920. Courtesy of Ohara Institute for Social Research, Hosei University.

The founders took great pride in one modification of the standard handi-crafts period: instead of folding expensive colored papers into cranes, frogs, and other fantastic shapes, by cutting and pasting the pages of donated magazines, the Futaba Yōchien youngsters made envelopes that were sold to a nearby candy shop. Besides teaching the children to make things, this activity was also de-signed to instill positive attitudes toward work. By demonstrating the rewards of diligent labor, the founders hoped to prevent a "spirit of dependency" from arising in the children. The proceeds from the sale of the envelopes paid the streetcar fares for the graduating class' outing to the zoo in Ueno Park. In this way, the youngsters enjoyed the fruits of their labor as the teachers reinforced the idea that hard work brings rewards.[28]

The curriculum also strongly emphasized savings. In teaching their students to value savings, the Futaba Yōchien staff sought to foster self-reliance, the foun-dation of the children's future economic security. The savings program origi-nated in teachers' fears that their young pupils would become accustomed to re-lying on the charity of others because they did not pay for their lessons. Since laborers were paid by the day, monthly tuition would have constituted an im-possible financial burden for the poor families that Futaba Yōchien sought to serve. Instead, the regulations required children to bring one sen to the kinder-garten every day—for deposit into individual savings accounts. Reporting on the reason for the savings requirement, a visiting writer stated that

> [s]ince this is a charity project, monthly tuition is not assessed, but on the other hand, because giving the services free of charge would cause a spirit of dependency and other harm, the children are asked to bring one sen per day as thanks (*orei*). However, they don't have to save on days when they are absent.[29]

The staff regarded preschool education of lower-class children as a prelude to elementary school. The teachers stressed the primacy of the children's role as students. They set up a liaison with the local elementary school to help the chil-dren obtain fee waivers and to adjust to the school environment. They provided Futaba Yōchien graduates with school supplies and regularly discussed the im-portance of elementary school enrollment during the evening parent meetings, informal contact with parents, and the annual July and Christmas reunions held for former Futaba Yōchien students. The staff constantly urged their young graduates to stay in school and visit their alma mater to serve as positive mod-els for the Futaba Yōchien preschoolers. The teachers sometimes asked their for-mer students to bring report cards and calligraphy samples to show the current students. These return visits also encouraged the graduates to persevere in attending elementary school.

The Futaba Yōchien program included free health care and lessons in hygiene, with the help of a staff nurse, visits by outside doctors, and the assistance of local clinics. Lice, fleas, trachoma, boils, and frostbite were common ailments. Futaba Yōchien also promoted preventive medicine, aiming to improve the children's personal hygiene and to prevent the recurrence of common slum ailments. Lessons teaching nose-blowing and hand-washing were unique to Futaba Yōchien, since upper-class children attending ordinary kindergartens learned the fundamentals of hygiene at home.

The Adult Program

As the Futaba staff became aware of the influence of the home environment on their pupils, they began to complain:

> The older the children become, the less likely they are to attend. This doesn't happen at other kindergartens. Usually children improve over the years as they learn at kindergartens, but our children don't, because their families are bad. No matter how hard we strive, they are only here at the kindergarten for six hours. After that they are free to absorb bad influences [at home]. Under these circumstances, the kindergarten is useless. Parents send their children to the *yōchien* for training, so we can't allow this to happen. If they just stay at home, we can't tell what kind of person they will become.[30]

Since the teachers felt that the home environment exerted a detrimental effect on their students, Noguchi and Morishima decided to extend their educational efforts to other family members as well, beginning with the parents. During the first year Noguchi stated her aspirations for the mothers and fathers of her pupils and how she hoped to realize these hopes:

> The parents will leave the world of poverty behind and rise one step higher if they are made to consider the importance of education, to learn the custom of working hard, and to begin to save. In order to meet the parents and grow closer to them, we have begun parents' meetings and home visits.[31]

The perception that parents as well as children needed education thus led the staff to create programs for adults.[32] In focusing on character development—especially the instilling of thrift and industry—the goals for the parents overlapped greatly with those for the children.

The staff convened what were called "parent meetings" (*oya no kai*) for the first six months. Thereafter, the name was changed to "fathers' and mothers' meetings" (*fubo no kai*).[33] While the annual reports suggest that mostly mothers came to the meetings, the name indicates that both fathers and mothers were expected to attend and by extension that both were responsible for children. The meetings took place once or twice a month in the evening so that working parents could attend[34] and featured performances and demonstrations by the youngsters, hymns, refreshments, religious messages, and advice on nutrition, hygiene, and the role of parents at the day-care center.

The fifth annual report contains a description of one of the meetings and exposes a yawning cultural gap between the middle-class reformers and their clients, and it suggests the enormity of the task the reformers faced in trying to reshape the values of the late Meiji urban lower classes:

> When they come to the kindergarten, [parents] come holding the hand of a toddler with babies strapped to their backs. I'm always surprised that there are so many children. At the last meeting, the room was packed, although it was small and stuffy. First we had the children sing songs. Finally we quieted everyone and spoke for awhile. Speaking at these meetings is really difficult. Words that we think are ordinary they don't understand at all. . . . Once I recommended savings to the parents, explaining its effectiveness. All listened, nodding their heads in agreement, so I thought they'd understood. But the next day our helper [a local resident] said, "What in the world is savings?" She hadn't comprehended any of my talk the previous evening. If the helper didn't understand, I'm sure it's true of all the others, too.[35]

The staff recognized that it was difficult for parents with young children to attend meetings after working all day and preparing the evening meal. Consequently, by the fourth year the content of the meetings became more pleasant with the inclusion of entertainment. The annual report observed that

> The children's mothers do nothing but work from morning until night. They don't even have one day off a year to enjoy themselves. We sympathized with them and couldn't abide this situation. The purpose of these meetings is to speak on useful topics while entertaining them. We always have music. Recently Sakai and his mother came and played a duet for us. At the moment this delicate music played, poverty and pain vanished, and they were overwhelmingly thankful to feel eternal paradise shining in their hearts.[36]

The teachers also made occasional home visits, especially when the children were sick, in order to observe the home environment and to become better acquainted with individual parents. In one teacher's view, home visits helped their work with the children: "Home visits take place from time to time, not at fixed intervals. They are rather beneficial in helping us to understand the family circumstances."[37]

The adult activities focused on the moral, educational, and spiritual needs of the parents, as perceived by the staff members. By talking with parents individually and addressing them collectively at meetings, the reformers sought to persuade them to cooperate with the day-care center's goals. The instructors hoped to counteract the family's supposedly evil influence on their students by reeducating the parents to new values and child-rearing practices.

Middle-Class Teachers' Orientations

The busy staff members, including Noguchi and Morishima, who administered Futaba Yōchien in addition to teaching full-time at the peers' kindergarten, had little free time to exhaustively consider social reform or family ideals. Nevertheless, as relief and educational specialists and as Christians seeking to minister to the weak and to protect lower-class children and improve family life, besides their explicit ideas concerning curriculum and daily activities, they held convictions as well as unarticulated assumptions concerning childhood, motherhood, and desirable family life. Their efforts to improve the home life of their pupils touched on matters ranging from the reform of child-rearing practices to teaching new values and principles of nutrition, hygiene, clothing construction, and household financial management. One can argue that while their assumption that the labor of both parents would support the household and their emphasis on thrift and diligence resonate with early modern values, the teachers' stress on companionate family life, their rather romantic view of motherhood, and their conception of children as dependent students differed from earlier views of the household and its members' roles. However, although it is quite likely that their modern views contrasted greatly with those of their pupils' parents, some traces of early modern views remained in their outlook on family life.

The Futaba Yōchien staff encouraged family togetherness during leisure time, a modern value not universally held in high esteem in Japan at the time.[38] For example, one account of an excursion by teachers, parents, and children to the zoo in Ueno Park in 1901 glowingly stated: "When we saw the limitless joy expressed, when the whole family was together, we thought what a wonderful thing we have done."[39] Whether or not the pupils and parents were as pleased as the description suggests, the teachers' enthusiasm for family companionship in an activity that required expenditures for transportation and admission fees is unmistakable. Yet while the staff praised and encouraged a shared social life at home, they also complained about the influence of parents and siblings on their preschool students. In 1904 the annual report still lamented, "The older this kindergarten's children get, the worse they become. If there's a vacation, too, they get worse, because their families are just no good."[40] Thus Futaba Yōchien staff feared that too much solidarity between children and family members would prevent the preschoolers' from absorbing the content of their day-care lessons.

Examination of stories in the curriculum further illuminate the teachers' values. One Christmas, for example, the teachers praised a neighbor's industrious, self-reliant daughter as an example to the poor children and families served by Futaba:

There's a mother and father, and the father had apparently been a rickshaw puller until he went blind. Since this couldn't be helped, he began vending boiled beans [on the street] during the day and deep-fried sweets in the evening. The daughter isn't yet twelve years old, so she can't carry heavy items. Her father carries the goods, and the daughter leads him, day in and day out for the whole year, with no days off, braving rain and snow. We can hear their voices as they return in the late night cold. For them, every night seems painful. We gave the daughter socks and quilted cotton clothes from items you donated. We thought that a family which makes this type of admirable effort can serve as a model for poor people. We gave them Christmas gifts to encourage their efforts.[41]

The reformers admired the diligence of this young girl, who assisted her father's work every day. They also expressed admiration for the spirit of self-reliance demonstrated by the family, whose members struggled to survive through their own efforts, without expecting others to provide for them. The teachers felt that the qualities of determination, hard work, independence, and patient endurance deserved commendation and aid, so they rewarded the girl with presents and told her story at the day-care center.

A second tale, this time a storybook given to former students at the annual Christmas party, reveals that the teachers saw temperance or abstinence as another desirable feature of family life. The main character of the story is a child who led his parents to stop drinking alcohol. The 1904 yearbook reported that

> [w]e gave the children [who had graduated] one of Tamura Naoshin's children's books for Christmas. It is the story of parents who couldn't [even] buy their darling child *hakama* [culottes] and shoes because they drank. They felt deeply when reproved by their child, and quit drinking. We . . . want one more copy of this book, and are planning to purchase one.[42]

As Christians, the Futaba Yōchien staff believed that avoiding the evils of drink was essential for sound family life, although serving rice wine (*sake*) was such an integral part of weddings, funerals, other rites of passage, and social occasions from ancient times that prohibition was virtually out of the question. Clearly, the teachers chose this story for their former pupils because they believed that parents who drank would not be good providers. At the same time, by selecting this tale they also apparently endorsed the child's role as consumer, since they accepted the child's need or desire for new items of clothing.

The Futaba Yōchien staff's emphasis on temperance and certain forms of companionate family relationships had few, if any, parallels in the early modern Japanese tradition. In early modern productive households there was little need to extol the virtues of family togetherness. Before work and education began to take place outside the family following the 1868 Meiji Restoration, family togetherness was a daily reality. In the early modern period and after, rural parents and children cooperated in farming and by-employments; parents played a major role in their children's education; and both parents and children participated in festivals, work celebrations, and rites of passage that constituted much of villagers' leisure and social life. Shrine festivals and other rituals as a rule organized participation according to male or female age grades rather than mobilizing all household members as a unit. Thus recreation did not necessarily center on family togetherness, nor did leisure necessarily involve expenditures on goods or services. In the modern city, however, work, school, and social life were fragmented, and urbanites were immersed in commodity relations. Togetherness therefore took the form of spending time together after work and school, especially in households whose members were dispersed at schools and workplaces for most of the week. For the lower classes, spending time at home and purchasing sweets or trinkets in the neighborhood were more feasible than expenditures on carfare and admissions to special attractions such as the zoo, which middle-class families could more easily afford.

Temperance, rather than being native value, was an attitude brought to Japan by Christian reformers and missionaries, and it conflicted with customary patterns of social interaction. Yet aside from temperance, in other respects the Futaba Yōchien reformers' views of family life, child-rearing, and mothers' and children's roles may not have been far removed from those of their new middle-class contemporaries. During the twentieth century higher education and printed media exposed large numbers of middle- and upper-class Japanese, especially males but increasingly girls and younger women as well, to new and foreign ideas. Thus many Japanese who were not Christians or who had not studied abroad developed some familiarity with foreign customs, including Western conceptions of love marriages, companionate husband-wife relationships, and affectionate parent-child ties. However, in the first decade of the twentieth century the pupils' urban lower-class parents had had less exposure to new ideas about family life than the middle-class day-care teachers. Thus the gap between the Futaba Yōchien teachers and parents, like the gap between the lower classes and the new middle class in the large cities, was not only a disparity between incomes, but was also a matter of culture.[43]

While hard work and savings constituted the core of Futaba Yōchien's teachings for both children and adults, in retrospect it seems naive or insensitive to try to foster appreciation for hard work in parents who worked from dawn to dusk for a pittance. The parents who worked at casual employment as day laborers were not rewarded for diligence. And no matter how hard they worked, there was no guarantee of future employment. The faster homeworkers labored, the higher their earnings, but in times of recession or overproduction their labor was superfluous. Yet despite these flaws in the prevailing employment system, there is little indication that the day-care center personnel advocated improving wages or working conditions. One can also question the value of promoting frugality among the center parents whose arduous labor, especially that of employed women, did not generate sufficient income to support a household. Nonetheless, throughout the period under study, diligence and frugality remained the watchwords of Futaba Yōchien's approach to the problems of lower-class families. The staff apparently continued to assume that moral virtues would build character and enable families to triumph over economic hardships.

The Values of Lower-Class Parents and Children

Parents' values differed from those of the Futaba Yōchien teachers in several respects. While the staff members idealized a stable, companionate, and economically sound family life with values such as diligence, thrift, cleanliness, and discipline at its core, the family ideals held by the lower-class parents of Futaba Yōchien's pupils are more difficult to discern. In general, efforts somehow to make ends meet and fatigue following long hours of work punctuated by briefer moments of companionship and affection loomed large in the home life of the late Meiji poor, though details of ideals and actual family experiences are elusive. Yet whether or not mothers and fathers longed for a stable, companionate family life free from want, coping with the harsh realities of daily life absorbed most of their energies. Prolonged illness, death, an emergency requiring a sudden cash outlay, or even a succession of rainy days could plunge lower-class families into a desperate situation. In the absence of state institutions, the needy had to rely on relatives, friends, or the thin network of private charitable institutions such as Futaba Yōchien during the early twentieth century. Although gratitude for teachers' assistance and concern as well as respect or deference toward them as members of a higher class sometimes motivated parents to change their ways, lack of time, the precariousness of lower-class life, or a different view of family affairs prevented them from adopting the teachers' values or implementing their suggestions for improving family life.

Regardless of the parents' wishes, instability was a fairly constant feature of their family lives, for several reasons. First, families with low or irregular incomes were generally a mobile lot, because they had to move when jobs disappeared or they could not pay the rent. Second, a relatively high proportion of couples were bound by common-law marriages that tended to be rather less stable than legal unions. Parents disappeared, deserting children and spouse; women walked out on their husbands, taking their children with them, in contrast to the pattern of paternal custody prevailing in the breakup of legal marriages. Third, parents and children might live under separate roofs, because poor parents were more likely to send out children to other households as servants or apprentices, although these practices had begun to decline by the early twentieth century.

As a result of their livelihoods and economic circumstances, it is likely that family survival rather than family improvement was foremost in the minds of the children's parents. The parents had little time to devise strategies to raise the household's income or status and very few financial resources to marshall in order to execute plans. As we have seen, the parents may have been unaware of the idea of saving. Or, they may have found it necessary to spend all their earnings to satisfy immediate needs.

Furthermore, there were reasons for parents, or for that matter the pupils, to reject the teachers' view of children as dependent students. The departure of children from home as apprentices decreased the number of dependents requiring family support and trained the child for an occupation. Sending youngsters out to work in factories did not decrease expenditures on food and shelter, but their wages raised household income. Idle children, those who roamed the streets in gangs, did not earn income; however, they did not incur expenses for tuition, supplies, and clothing as students did. The teachers strove to enroll all the kindergarten graduates in elementary school, and most parents complied at least nominally with their requests. However, surveys of the early Futaba Yōchien graduates show that many children dropped out to go to work after attending school for a year or two. In the lower classes, the older the child, the less likely she or he was to be still attending school.

Yet the economic difficulties of urban lower-class family life did not preclude the development of affective bonds between parents and children. For example, in order to enjoy their children's company on their days off from work, lower-class parents sometimes kept their youngsters home from school. They sided with their own offspring in neighborhood quarrels, and worried when their children fell ill. Furthermore, parents were willing to give small children a generous slice of their meager daily incomes for pocket money. For working mothers, allowing children to buy treats both indulged children and kept them occupied for some time while their mothers toiled at piecework. However, these patterns of parent-child interaction did not correspond precisely to the teachers' conceptions of the companionate family, because lower-class families did not necessarily seek to spend their leisure time engaging in activities or socializing together. Rather than consumption of goods and services or the utilization of leisure time as a family unit, making ends meet and completing basic domestic tasks were focal points of day-to-day household life.

The views of family roles held by the day-care staff and the children's parents provide clues to understanding changing ideas of childhood, motherhood, and family life during the late Meiji period. Apparently changes in conceptions of childhood and motherhood did not take place simultaneously in the various social classes. The middle-class teachers adopted a modern view of children as dependents and students before the lower-class parents did. Parents' and teachers' views of child care and, implicitly, of childhood may have diverged the most regarding the role of sibling baby-sitters. Here, the teachers' emphasis on school attendance clashed with the inclination of poor parents to keep children home to enjoy their company on days off from work and to assign child care, household chores, or remunerative employment—any task they judged necessary for family survival—to their children. In the case of motherhood, the lower-class parents had little reason to turn away from early modern views, while the attitudes of middle-class teachers reveal a fair degree of influence of new conceptions of motherhood and family life.

However, the fact that the adult program was more than just a mothers' meeting, unlike those of early twentieth century U.S. kindergartens, indicates that even the middle-class staff had not yet unequivocally accepted Western views of child-rearing as the calling of women alone, although some passages in the annual reports hint that the teachers regarded mothers as more responsible for raising children than fathers. While it was likely that mothers spent more time with children than did fathers, the teachers were reluctant to jettison completely early modern conceptions of child-rearing that held not only both parents but adults of both genders in a household responsible for child-rearing. Among slum families, child care was still taken up by whoever happened to be free, not just by mothers. If all household members were busy, then no one watched closely over infants and toddlers.

Parents' and Children's Responses to Futaba Yōchien's Program

The yearbooks provide glimpses of the parents' and children's responses to the Futaba Yōchien program. On the whole, the parents appeared grateful for the teachers' efforts to help their children; there are no indications that parents actively resisted the curriculum or resented the teachers' advice.[44] At the evening meetings some parents stated that they were pleased that their children had become better behaved. Others were gratified to have their offspring begin to show them respect by greeting them with *"Tadaima,"* (I'm home) and a bow when they returned from the center or from playing in the neighborhood. There were also economic benefits to families. Mothers working at home at piece rates praised the *yōchien* as a boon to their employment, because their earnings increased. They could work without interruption from or worries about their youngsters. Moreover, children were not around the house to beg for money to buy snacks from passing candy vendors, thereby reducing household expenditures. This was an added economic benefit of child care.[45]

Overall, it seems that the children's responses also were positive. They enjoyed playing in the classrooms and outside; the pupils relished the novelty of regular afternoon snacks, although they were given only the cheapest treats. And despite the teachers' fretting over the bad influence of their home environment, the lessons had some impact on the youngsters' behavior. One kindergarten teacher, for example, reported during the first year that the children's language and manners became less rough and that the little girls' speech became more refined. The youngsters' personal cleanliness and health also improved somewhat. As the children began to bathe a bit more often, some of their eye and skin problems cleared up.[46]

The Larger Impact of Futaba Yōchien

Futaba Yōchien began as two young teachers' year-long social experiment in the education and protection of slum children. By the end of the Meiji period, after operating for a dozen years, it was a thriving, highly respected institution. Noguchi and Morishima's employment at the peeresses' kindergarten enabled them to gain financial support for Futaba Yōchien from members of the upper crust of Meiji society. The roster of monthly subscribers listed leading female educators Tsuda Umeko and Shimoda Utako, businessmen such as Kobayashi Tomijirō, the wealthy founder of the Raion soap and toothpaste company, and one branch of the Mitsui family. In 1905, through the efforts of Futaba Yōchien's highborn neighbor, Count Matsudaira, the center received permission to occupy a small site in back of the Detached Imperial Palace (Akasaka Gosho) grounds free of charge for ten years.[47]

In 1908, in its first published yearbook of permanent relief and charitable works, The Home Ministry recognized Futaba Yōchien, the Kobe War Memorial Day-Care Association centers, and one other institution as model day-care centers.[48] The following year the Home Ministry awarded Futaba Yōchien a stipend to assist its work with children. Thereafter, until the annual reports ceased publication at the end of the Taishō era, the center received an annual grant from the ministry.[49]

As a new type of children's institution, Futaba Yōchien managed to survive and even prosper; however, its success did not quickly inspire the founding of other day-care centers. Despite the fact that patriotic individuals and associations nationwide opened approximately two hundred child-care centers as relief projects during the Russo-Japanese War (1904–1905),[50] apparently no other permanent day-care facilities were founded in Japan between 1900 and 1906. Although Noguchi and Morishima presented day-care centers as a means of mitigating the urban ills of child neglect and poverty, it may be that the Christian elements in Futaba Yōchien's program retarded support for institutional child care outside a small cosmopolitan elite. Since the 1890s, many leading Japanese had come to believe that Christianity was incompatible with the early twentieth century state's cardinal virtue—loyalty to the sovereign. Therefore, despite Noguchi's and Morishima's stated intentions to further the progress of society through day-care work, many Japanese may have doubted that facilities for children patterned after an institution run by Christians could contribute to national progress.

Alternatively, it is possible that lack of awareness and concern about the social problems of the urban poor hampered the establishment of relief and philanthropic institutions for the lower-classes in the cities. The spread of strikes, unionism, anarchism, and socialism during the recession following the Russo-Japanese War heightened worries about the social consequences of industrialization and anxieties about urban social unrest. Perceptions of day-care centers as institutions promoting sound values and increased productivity may have become sufficiently widespread to spur the creation of new facilities by individuals and public-minded organizations.

Moreover, in addition to the above two factors, the expansion of institutional child care may be strongly related to the Home Ministry's campaigns on behalf of reform and relief works (*kanka kyūsai jigyō*) and the appeal of the Kobe War Memorial Day-Care Association centers' rationale for day-care. After 1908, the Home Ministry's endorsements of day-care centers through its relief project yearbooks, its financial assistance to relief institutions, and its nationwide symposia to promote the founding of private relief works undoubtedly spurred the founding of new day-care centers. Visitors inspired by the Home Ministry's publications or lectures could tour Futaba Yōchien, conveniently located in heart of the nation's capital, to learn firsthand about day-care curricula and operations.

Finally, the establishment of a second set of permanent day-care facilities by a secular patriotic organization in Kobe provided another model for institutional child care that was at least as influential as Futaba Yōchien in demonstrating the viability of day-care under Japanese conditions and its merits for children, households, and the nation in the first decade of the twentieth century. The Kobe centers, far to the west of Futaba Yōchien, provided an example of day-care facilities near Japan's second great metropolitan complex, which greatly assisted their diffusion throughout the nation.

4

Day-Care and Economic Improvement:

The Kobe Wartime Service Memorial Day-Care Association

Japan's second set of permanent day-care facilities, founded in the western port city of Kobe by the Kōbe Seneki Kinen Hoikukai (Kobe Wartime Service Memorial Day-Care Association, hereafter KSKH), also contributed much to the development of institutional care for young children in the prewar era.[1] Like Futaba Yōchien, the Kobe centers also instructed and protected lower-class preschool children, but the principal aim of the KSKH program differed from that of Futaba. The KSKH facilities, directed by the male relief expert Namae Takayuki, regarded the financial improvement of poor families as the primary objective of institutional child care. That is, Namae and KSKH emphasized daytime institutional care of children as a means of increasing the earnings of households with two working parents.

In addition, the Kobe centers, which had originally assisted needy veterans' wives and children during the 1904–1905 Russo-Japanese War, linked day-care centers to patriotism and national service. The network of day-care facilities established by the Kobe Women's Service Association (Kōbe Fujin Hōkōkai) had proven the utility of day-care centers during wartime mobilization. Operated by KSKH after the war, the Kobe centers established assistance for veterans and their families and the boosting of national productivity through diligent labor of the poor as peacetime rationales for institutional child care. The link that the KSKH facilities forged between day-care and national progress became a key factor in maintaining state and public support for day-care in Japan during the strongly nationalistic prewar era. While the founding of the KSKH centers did not immediately stimulate the construction of facilities in other regions, except possibly the Aizenen Hoikujo in Osaka in 1908, they were commended as model centers in the 1908 and 1909 Home Ministry relief project yearbooks, as was Futaba Yōchien. Following publication of the yearbooks, the number of day-care centers in Japan began to increase, a trend I discuss in chapter 5.

Infants, toddlers, and teachers with indoor play equipment at a Kobe War Memorial Day-Care Association (Kobe Seneki Kinen Hoikukai or KSKH) child-care center, circa 1920. Courtesy of Ohara Institute for Social Research, Hosei University.

Japan's Second Day-Care Model

In 1906 KSKH established Japan's second major late Meiji day-care facility by reopening three day-care centers that a local women's patriotic association had operated during the Russo-Japanese War.[2] The wartime centers, called *hokanjo,*[3] had provided day-care and employment assistance to impoverished families of soldiers on duty overseas. KSKH's postwar vision of the mission of institutional child care continued to emphasize above all stabilization of families' economic situation, while demonstrating increased concern for the children's health and education.

The leading figure at both the wartime and postwar Kobe centers was Namae Takayuki, a Christian who had spent three years in the United States studying relief and philanthropic works. Namae directed the day-care centers until 1909, when he left Kobe to assist in development of relief projects in the Home Ministry.[4] By the 1910s Namae had become a nationally recognized authority on the practical aspects of relief work, especially child welfare programs. In later years, long after he had stepped down from the KSKH directorship, Namae continued to commend KSKH facilities as model Japanese day-care centers.[5]

The first article of KSKH's organizational bylaws set forth its aims:

The purpose of this organization is to care for the children of well, disabled, or deceased veterans, and other children, in order to assist the livelihood (*seigyō*) of the head or family and to carry out both employment introductions and encouragement of savings.[6]

The aims of the postwar centers, called *hoikujo,* were nearly identical to those of wartime *hokanjo,* which had sought to gather and care for the young children of soldiers at the front during the day, in order to help the families gain a livelihood.[7] The efforts of both the earlier wartime day-care centers and the later war memorial centers were directed primarily at improving the economic well-being of the children's households.

Although both the KSKH centers and their predecessors aimed to assist veterans' families and to improve household finances, one significant difference between the old and new centers was the range of intended clients. The wartime facilities had given first priority to veterans' families, but the postwar centers enrolled children of poor nonveterans' households. The deprivations of soldiers' families during the Russo-Japanese War increased awareness of poverty as the result of social conditions rather than the perceived moral deficiencies of the poor. The broader eligibility criteria of the postwar KSKH centers suggest that during the severe recession following the Russo-Japanese War, perceptions of poverty as resulting from unfortunate circumstances rather than individual moral weakness began to extend beyond the families of former soldiers. Yet this new awareness had limitations. KSKH admissions policies continued to exclude the children of unemployed parents, even though the occupations of the poor and working-class were very insecure.

KSKH regulations outlined the methods by which the day-care centers would accomplish its objective of providing economic assistance to needy families. The four basic program areas were: 1) day-care, 2) employment introductions, 3) encouragement of savings, and 4) health care for children. Three of the four areas—day-care, employment introductions, and savings—were related to economic concerns, reflecting KSKH's orientation toward economic improvement of family life. The fact that two of the four programs served adults demonstrated the KSKH centers' commitment to helping the entire family rather than just preschool children.

The operations of the KSKH day-care program better suited the needs of working parents than did Futaba Yōchien's schedule. The center holidays corresponded very closely to those of late Meiji workers in the Kobe area. The *hoikujo* closed only twice a month, on the first and sixteenth, and for five days at New Year's, a holiday observed by everyone, including laborers and the poor. The centers were open from dawn to dusk, approximating the length of the standard work day for most regular wage workers. The long hours of operation allowed parents to maximize their earnings by working a full day. Parents with unusual working hours could arrange special drop-off and pickup times. Thus many children regularly stayed at the centers as late as 8:00 P.M. In addition, the centers provided the noon meal and morning and afternoon snacks, sparing parents the trouble of preparing children's lunches. Children who stayed late received an evening meal in addition to the usual snacks and lunch. The devotion of some of the staff members as well as the grueling work schedules of some of the parents are revealed in the recollection of one teacher who suffered from lack of sleep because a parent who worked in the distant harbor regularly brought a child at two in the morning.[8]

Employment introductions were another key aspect of the KSKH day-care program. The KSKH organizational history describes its late Meiji employment assistance as follows:

> The true mission of social projects is to give a foundation for living, which employment assistance does. Monetary assistance is only a temporary method. The day-care centers have made extreme efforts [with employment assistance] and have had fairly good results. Unfortunately, we have no statistics for the Meiji era, but at that time, when there were no employment exchanges, it is not hard to imagine that these introductions took a lot of effort. There was no way [to proceed] except through the good will of entrepreneurs who understood social projects. In addition, we could make small loans of capital [to the children's families]. We would like the public to know how our day-care centers made efforts on a one-to-one basis to help wretched families get back on their feet again.[9]

Although the wartime *hokanjo* had served primarily the working wives of soldiers and the postwar *hoikujo* helped many war widows and wives of disabled veterans, condemnations of employed mothers or suggestions of a conflict between working and being a good mother are entirely absent in descriptions of the Kobe day center programs. Instead, the centers actively helped jobless women and men find gainful employment.

Helping guardians find work constituted one means of assisting poor families, but a second method of livelihood assistance, the encouragement of saving, occupied a central place in the KSKH program as well. KSKH considered saving to be essential to the improvement of family life. One writer explained why KSKH decided to emphasize savings: "Needless to say, it is unnecessary to repeat that explaining frugality and diffusing [the idea of] savings was the key to success in home improvement (*katei kaizen*)."[10] The staff members believed that even their impoverished clients could put away money for a rainy day, and regretted that the center users' attitudes impeded formation of regular saving habits. One teacher explained:

Of course, it couldn't be expected that these needy (*saimin*) families would have much surplus money, since they had many unsatisfied basic needs. Yet there are always unnecessary expenses . . . in the life of any class. Poor people say, "If you don't eat food when it's on the table, you can't save much," and "Tomorrow, tomorrow's wind will blow." They, who are content to make ends meet even for one day, recite proverbs such as "You can't use today's money again."[11]

Concrete advice offered to KSKH center parents included encouragement to save "the allowance they don't give out because they have enrolled a child in the *hoikujo*" and "the money left over after all expenses for that day's living are paid out."[12] Although clients could save only "tiny amounts, 1 or 2 sen" per day, the Kobe child-care reformers reported that

we encourage them to bring the money to the day-care center when they can for the purpose of saving for the children's future educational fees. We put this money into postal savings stamps, and keep the passbook at the day-care center. In this way, they can see how useful savings can be—even if not for the child's education, for family emergencies like illness or for investment as capital in their occupations.[13]

The centers' efforts aimed at teaching the guardians to save more than the children, in order for parents to accumulate money to spend on their children and other family expenditures.

The centers also stressed health care and nutrition, believing them to be pre-requisites for the sound physical development of children. The thirty-year KSKH history stated that "[t]he children's health was the aspect that needed the centers' attention the most."[14] The regulations stipulated that children would receive weekly eye, ear, nose, and throat checkups and periodic internal exami-nations as well. Health professionals carried out these preventive examinations and provided treatment for the children's numerous ailments.

Although KSKH did not specify education as one of its four basic program areas, the KSKH staff nevertheless introduced kindergarten activities in their classroom routines[15] and actively promoted school attendance for children after graduation. As discussed above, parents were encouraged to save for their chil-dren's elementary school expenses—tuition, supplies, and new clothing. Day-care teachers sometimes obtained tuition waivers and furnished six-year-olds with school supplies. When the reformers discovered that many of their gradu-ates stayed home from school on stormy days because the children lacked proper rain gear, they gave the children umbrellas. Finally, many poor children could not enroll in school because their births had not been recorded in family regis-ters as required by law. The staff helped parents register their children, and this process often entailed correspondence with households and offices in distant places, since many parents had migrated to Kobe from other regions.[16] Clearly, these activities demonstrate that KSKH center personnel believed formal edu-cation was important for their pupils.

The Significance of the KSKH Centers

The KSKH program contributed much to the development of the Japanese day-care tradition, perhaps more than Futaba Yōchien. Nonetheless, leading studies of Japanese day-care history have tended to overlook KSKH contributions. In my view, there are three major reasons for this neglect. First, Futaba Yōchien opened prior to the Kobe centers. As Japan's earliest institution providing edu-cation and care to lower-class preschoolers, it is inevitably the first day-care in-stitution noticed by researchers. Second, many KSKH documents, including the annual reports, were destroyed in the firebombings of World War II. In contrast, a thirty-year series of Futaba annual reports have survived to the present. Third, Futaba Yōchien is more visible to scholars and the public than are the KSKH fa-cilities since it is located in Tokyo, the center of Japan's political, educational, and economic systems in the postwar era. However, in the early twentieth cen-tury the economic, cultural, and political importance of Kobe-Osaka-Kyoto (or

Kansai region) rivaled that of Tokyo. The relative decline of Kansai due to the loss of the colonies following Japan's defeat in World War II has fostered scholarly neglect of history of this region, including the many innovations in day-care and other relief institutions that developed there during the prewar era.[17]

Although KSKH's contributions to the development of institutional child care in Japan have been overlooked, it is nevertheless true that many later centers adopted KSKH practices of long operating hours, employment introductions, and attention to hygiene and medical treatment—positive aspects of the Kobe centers' legacy. And not a few followed the KSKH centers in making household economic improvement their primary aim. Yet three other KSKH legacies are more difficult to assess—the link it forged between day-care, patriotism, imperialism, and admissions policies that excluded the unemployed, and heavy emphasis on the economic aspects of family improvement.

First, the Kobe centers tied day-care to patriotism, a crucial factor in establishing the legitimacy of institutional child care in the strongly nationalistic climate of turn-of-the-century Japan. The KSKH centers' forerunners, the *hokanjo,* had served wartime national goals by helping poor soldier's wives and children, while KSKH itself gave priority to veterans' families and operated under an organizational name that reminded all of the facilities' patriotic origins. Despite the foreign roots of day-care, even during spikes of nationalist sentiment, when foreign institutions and ideas came under attack, criticism of day-care centers by the general public and welfare professionals is strikingly absent. The patriotic content of day-care programs may have contributed to bureaucratic and elite acceptance of institutional child care. Although the exact titles of songs sung in day-care centers are unknown, like late nineteenth and early twentieth century kindergarten curricula, they must have included military songs and the national anthem. Indeed, during the 1930s, as Japan turned again to militaristic expansion to ameliorate prolonged domestic crisis, the number of day-care centers rose dramatically.[18] They were justified as contributing to healthy population growth by reducing infant mortality rates. In all likelihood, the long-standing association of institutional child care with advancement of the national good, which began during the Russo-Japanese War, as well as continued popular acceptance of nonmaternal caregivers' role in child-rearing, shielded day-care centers from censure as foreign institutions even during the increasingly xenophobic 1930s.

Second, the Kobe war memorial centers established a tradition of exclusionary enrollment. During the war, only children from impoverished veterans' families were admitted. After the war, although poor children from nonveteran households became eligible for care, children of unemployed parents could not enroll at the center. Futaba Yōchien's admissions policy, on the other hand, was more liberal. Combined with its emphasis on moral training for parents as well as children, it is likely that Futaba Yōchien's open policy gave more families a chance to achieve economic recovery. In contrast, by assuming that the unemployed did not deserve to use day-care facilities, the Kobe centers may have excluded some genuinely needy families and eliminated entirely the possibility of improving their finances, shaping the character of their children, or influencing their breadwinners.

Third, KSKH regarded day-care as one of several means of assisting the livelihoods of poor families, which was an economic goal. Its program relied heavily on such economic measures as employment introductions, loans, and savings to attain its ultimate goal of family improvement, although instilling values such as industry, savings, and planning were as important as the types of economic assistance offered. The regulations and statements of purpose of many day-care centers founded during the Taishō period, particularly the numerous city-operated day-care centers established after the 1918 Rice Riots, reveal a similar emphasis on the economic aspects of family improvement.

Comparing Futaba Yōchien and the KSKH Centers

While the primary goals of the Futaba Yōchien and KSKH programs differed, it is important not to overstate the differences. The Futaba Yōchien program placed more emphasis on serving children, but it also provided education, recreation, and at times employment introductions for parents. The KSKH program devoted a greater proportion of its activities to adults. Nonetheless, two of its four basic program areas were aimed at children. The Kobe centers' stated purpose was to care for children and to assist adults in achieving financial stability in order to help poor families improve their livelihoods. The KSKH conception of reforming home life strongly emphasized the financial aspects of family improvement, although the KSKH centers also provided educational and health programs for children. Futaba Yōchien tended to stress that the moral improvement resulting from kindergarten education would benefit the individual and society. Economic benefits received less emphasis than in the KSKH program, but the Futaba Yōchien teachers were fully aware of the positive impact of day-care on household finances and approved of the economic stability that moral improvement would bring to poor urban children and parents.

In part the differences in goals and program emphasis may stem from differences in the specializations of the centers' founders. Noguchi and Morishima were trained as early childhood educators and held full-time appointments at a regular kindergarten, while Namae specialized in relief and charity work. It is reasonable to assume that professional training would affect conceptions of what day-care center aims and activities should be. Thus Futaba Yōchien was more child-oriented and placed greater emphasis on educational activities than the KSKH centers. Because the major long-term goal of relief work was achievement of self-reliance—that is, a stable livelihood—a task that *adults* could best accomplish, the program of the KSKH centers emphasized activities for adults and stressed children's hygiene and nutrition to a greater extent than did Futaba Yōchien. However, it is likely that, like Futaba Yōchien, the KSKH children's curriculum included stories and activities that encouraged the development of industry, frugality, and savings, in order to prepare poor children to grow up to be self-supporting adults.

Conversely, the shared American background of the reformers also helps to account for the similarities of Japan's two great early day-care institutions. Morishima and Namae had both studied and visited American charitable organizations. Morishima had trained at a U.S. free kindergarten in the 1890s, and Namae had spent three years just before the Russo-Japanese War touring American relief and philanthropic projects, including charity kindergartens. In the late nineteenth and early twentieth centuries, the character of the American kindergarten was ambiguous. It was viewed by some as an agent of assimilation teaching immigrant children and mothers American ways of life, while others perceived it as an educational institution functioning primarily to prepare young children for elementary school. In addition, charitable, or free, kindergartens for immigrants were often part of settlements located in U.S. urban slums. Thus Morishima and Namae took their experiences back to Japan, and, despite the differences in emphasis, both Futaba Yōchien and KSKH consequently sought to instill the virtues of diligence, thrift, cleanliness, and respect for education in poor Japanese children and adults and to provide them with social services as well as education.

However, Japanese founders adapted the child-care center to the native environment. The establishment of parent and guardian clubs at Futaba Yōchien and the KSKH centers—unlike mothers' clubs in the United States—very likely reflects nineteenth-century Japanese family practices that granted ultimate authority over child-rearing to household heads and senior household members rather than mothers.[19] Also, the high priority awarded to household economic improvement at the KSKH centers contrasts with the primary emphasis on education and cultural assimilation in the U.S. centers, whereas the Futaba

Yōchien program seems closer to its American counterpart in this respect. While in part KSKH's focus on livelihood stemmed from a desire to help war veterans' families attain financial security, it was also undoubtedly related to the general public concern about the nation's economic and military shortcomings in the years immediately following the Russo-Japanese War. In my view, the prevailing perceptions of Japan's weaknesses set the stage for Namae first to discover and then to assert publicly that institutional child care could make a significant contribution to national weal by increasing the productivity of the poor and reducing their dependence on private charity or state relief. Association of the economic benefits of day-care for the poor with the public good subsequently proved to have enduring appeal in late-developing pre-World War II Japan.

The available sources suggest that Futaba Yōchien and KSKH staff members held similar views of childhood and responsibility for child-rearing. Both sets of teachers firmly believed in the value of formal education, although they must have realized that school attendance severely limited (without completely eliminating) children's opportunities to engage in income-earning activities or to help with domestic chores at home. Thus they implicitly endorsed the modern view of the child as student, dependent, and consumer rather than the older view of the child as a worker at productive or reproductive household tasks. In contrast to their modern views of childhood, however, both sets of directors and teachers seemed to embrace the early modern views of child-rearing. Their policies and programs generally assumed that responsibility for raising children and earning income belonged to both parents, rather than assigning child-rearing exclusively to mothers and wage-earning exclusively to fathers. There was no discernible criticism of working mothers from day-care professionals; in fact, they directed little attention specifically to the difficulties of working mothers or to social problems caused by mothers' employment. Thus Futaba Yōchien and KSKH staff members seem to have organized the adult activities at their facilities based on the conviction that poor mothers needed to work. In particular, they conducted meetings for adults in the evenings, which allowed employed fathers and mothers to attend. With their dawn-to-dusk operating hours and their employment assistance and loans for mothers as well as fathers, the KSKH centers unequivocally supported mothers as workers.

To what extent did the views of urban lower-class parents concur with those of the Futaba Yōchien and KSKH staffs? Lower-class parents' conceptions of children's roles appear to diverge from those of the middle-class teachers to a greater extent than did their views of responsibility for child-rearing. Center families' reluctance to enroll children in schools and their difficulties in sustaining children's attendance suggest strongly that these families did not view a child's primary role as that of a student. However, because the financial resources of late Meiji lower-class families could rarely sustain a prolonged period of childhood dependency, it is difficult to determine whether the resistance to enrolling children in school was a conscious choice.

The same constraint applies to reconstructing lower-class views of motherhood as well, because again economic resources limited the options of poor and working-class women. The nineteenth-century division of labor by age and gender had developed in a household economy of scarcity. According to custom and household need, children and women worked at a variety of productive and reproductive activities considered appropriate to their strength and experience. Intensive care of young children by a full-time mother was an unaffordable, perhaps inconceivable, luxury for the families of day-care users and other families of poor to middling means in the first decade of the twentieth century.[20]

While economic factors tended to limit the range of choice for lower-class children and parents, it is difficult to argue that they were the only factors shaping views of home life and family improvement. If, out of gratitude or deference to their social betters, needy parents attempted to understand and implement the reformers' suggestions, the cultural gap between the poor and the higher classes in the modern cities as well as the meager conditions of life of the needy meant that parents could not invariably heed center advice.

The Significance of the Early Day-Care Centers

Day-care centers were first established at the end of the Meiji era, when Japanese grew increasingly aware of problems in the "complicated society"[21] resulting from three decades of rapid political and economic change following the Meiji Restoration. Alarmed by the twin specters of urban poverty and the growth of labor and social movements, officials, intellectuals, and public-minded citizens attempted to invent ideologies and institutions to check these unforeseen, undesirable consequences of industrial growth.[22] Around the turn of the century the Japanese began to establish study groups and new types of private relief institutions such as the Shakai Seisaku Gakkai (Social Policy Association), the Shakaishugi Kenkyūkai (Socialism Study Group), the Christian social settlement Kingsley Hall, and Futaba Yōchien, Japan's first day-care center.[23]

From the first, day-care advocates had viewed child-care centers as a remedy for social ills afflicting late Meiji society. After the depression and social unrest following the Russo-Japanese War, Japanese leaders sought to mitigate the problems of the emerging urban, industrial order to ensure the nation's steady economic and military progress. At this time local and national administrators began to show increased interest in campaigns, institutions, and social projects that promised to increase productivity and quell potential social discontent. Concern for the negative consequences of industrialization deepened following the war, prompting the Meiji emperor to issue the Boshin Rescript calling on Japanese to work hard, be frugal, and serve their nation loyally.[24] If the Japanese did so, then (theoretically) the evils of the modern age—labor unrest including strikes, tenants' discontent, socialism, female quests for greater personal autonomy, and politics based on self-interest—would quietly disappear.

The initial exuberance over victory in the Russo-Japanese War was followed by introspection and doubt. Government officials feared that the decline of diligence, loyalty, and national unity boded ill for sustained progress. However, they did not simply brood; they acted. In response to a postwar sense of impending social crisis and moral disintegration as well as long-standing desires to mobilize village residents for loyal service to the nation, between 1905 and 1925 army officials, led by Tanaka Giichi, created a series of organizations—Imperial Military Reserve Association (Teikoku Zaigo Gunjinkai) and Greater Japan Youth Association (Dainippon Seinendan)—to nurture a spirit of dedicated, patriotic service in rural men and boys.[25] After 1909, the Home Ministry also instituted a series of measures intended to promote national development and national unity by shoring up traditional values such as diligence, loyalty, and obedience in the villages. These measures, called the local improvement movement (chihō kairyō undō), included the establishment of youth groups, girls' associations, women's associations, as well as financial assistance for various rural projects.[26]

Previous scholarship has treated the local improvement movement as a conservative, bureaucratic response to an alleged decline of "good manners and beautiful customs" (junpū bizoku) in the rural areas; however, little attention has been directed toward understanding the development of urban "purveyors of ideology."[27] Carol Gluck characterizes the late Meiji–early Taishō "patriotic and hortatory sermons" (kokumin kuniku) aimed at the common people of the cities as one such ideological initiative, but she argues that "absence of a readily available stratum of local urban leaders who could serve as community custodians of ideology" and the "fickleness of its concern for the cities" led the government to abandon its commitment to ideological efforts in the cities when in 1914 it ceased funding its lectures for commoners.[28]

In contrast, I contend that sustained Home Ministry efforts to promote the establishment of private urban relief projects such as day-care centers represent the government's attempt to create urban ideological institutions. The thrust of the state's efforts after 1909 may have been directed at villagers, because in the early twentieth century Japan's population was overwhelmingly rural, but this did not mean that government policies neglected urban commoners. Japan's educated, forward-looking bureaucrats understood that successful industrialization would swell the ranks of city dwellers, requiring urban as well as rural ideological initiatives to engage the Japanese masses in the march to national progress. Examination of late Meiji–Taishō Home Ministry conference proceedings as well as of welfare journals, organizational records, and biographies of prewar relief experts indicate that the Home Ministry encouraged the founding of day-care centers and other urban relief projects (*kyūsai jigyō*) by influential individuals and local associations to promote national values in urban society after 1909.

Properly socialized to diligence, cleanliness, and the value of education, the urban poor could contribute to Japan's economic and social development. Failing that, if individual thrift and industry improved, welfare expenditures could be minimized, allowing increased investment in infrastructure or military projects. While the Home Ministry itself did not operate relief institutions, in addition to holding regional seminars on relief works, it disbursed funds on a yearly basis to various projects in the cities after 1909.[29]

It is not a coincidence that the timing of Home Ministry support for child-care centers and other urban relief works commenced in 1909, the year that the local improvement movement began. Furthermore, both the local improvement and urban relief programs fell under the jurisdiction of the Local Affairs Bureau of the Home Ministry (Naimushō chihōkyoku). Ministry officials employed similar means to promote rural improvement and urban relief projects—symposia lasting several days featuring lectures by local and national experts and Home Ministry personnel. Home Ministry staff members (generally from the Local Affairs Bureau in the early years) as well as regional experts lectured at both types of symposia. Finally, the goals of the local improvement movement and the purposes of urban relief projects such day-care centers, as well as the values these programs attempted to foster, were strikingly similar. The local improvement movement had four major components: the founding of local associations to support sound values and customs, including diligence, frugality, savings, harmony, loyalty, and rural productivity; the reorganization of local administration and shrine mergers to reduce the independence of local associations in order to support sound values and customs including those immediately preceding; the funding of local public works to increase rural productivity; and the reorganization of local administration and shrine mergers to reduce the independence of village communities. Two of these four aims—moral education and increased productivity—resonate with the goals of Japan's first two day-care centers. And the next chapter will demonstrate that the new facilities modeled on Futaba Yōchien and KSKH that were established in the second decade of the twentieth century continued to stress the twin goals of moral cultivation and improved family livelihood.

Thus after the turn of the century, when government leaders came to view the results of the existing socialization taking place within households, schools, and local communities as insufficient to meet the needs of the emerging urban, industrial society, the Japanese state began to encourage the construction of a new network of ideological institutions to ensure that children and adults would practice the virtues of industry, thrift, hygiene, and patriotism. While some of the new institutions were directly supported by the state, others were created through private initiatives and thus were not directly controlled by the state. Nonetheless, through financial incentives and official commendations, the government encouraged the formation of private institutions nurturing values conducive to its vision of national progress. Because the goals of day-care centers coincided with the nationalist aims of promoting national strength, imperialism, and progress through moral improvement and increased productivity, prominent Japanese were willing to cooperate with state initiatives by supporting these novel institutions for poor urban children and their parents.

5

Nationalism, Motherhood, and the Early Taishō Expansion of Day-Care

During the first decade of the twentieth century Futaba Yōchien and the KSKH centers established fundamental standards for day-care in pre–World War II Japan. During the 1910s (the first half of the Taishō period) the rising number of child-care institutions, the appearance of networks of centers, and the continued support of the Home Ministry and the throne indicate that day-care centers were becoming firmly rooted in Japan. During this era, despite minor regional differences, a broad, informal, yet durable consensus concerning day-care purposes and programs emerged, one that lasted beyond formation of the Ministry of Health and Welfare (Kōseishō) in 1938.

In previous chapters I contended that Futaba Yōchien and the KSKH centers, especially the latter, articulated a link between child care and national progress. Day-care proponents thereafter held that instilling the values of hard work, frugality, discipline, and self-reliance in urban lower-class parents and children would advance the development of Japanese industry, empire, and civilization. Accordingly, the more day-care centers multiplied, the more state and society would benefit.

This logic appealed to progress-minded bureaucrats and public-minded citizens, who began to support day-care endeavors after the Russo-Japanese War. During the 1910s municipal officials, civic organizations, philanthropists, and community leaders began to take interest in day-care centers as a practical means of ameliorating urban poverty and assisting recovery from natural disasters. In support of these ends, key government organs such as the Home Ministry, the throne, and newly founded municipal relief departments continued to commend day-care facilities and provide financial assistance during that era and beyond.

This chapter explores the consensus regarding the goals and features of child care that developed in Japan as day-care centers proliferated during the second decade of the twentieth century.[1] In general, economic objectives were foremost during the early 1910s, when nearly all day-care facilities were located in the two great metropolitan zones surrounding Tokyo and Osaka, but the vast

majority of centers also gave high priority to education as a means of cultural assimilation of the poor. During the Taishō era the appeal of programs centered on
these two major aims was so great that alternative views, even those of a leading
relief expert such as Ogawa Shigejirō, who advocated institutional child care of
children under three as a means of reducing infant mortality, were virtually ignored. The ideas of social and national progress held by center founders, staff
members, and day-care supporters, particularly the relationship between desires
for national advancement and support for child-care facilities, are crucial in explaining the strong emphasis on the economic benefits of Taishō day-care.

Yet despite the expansion and growing appeal of institutional child care, the
diffusion of new attitudes toward motherhood threatened to diminish the appeal
of day-care centers during this decade. Although much of the positive regard for
day-care stemmed from its promise to improve society and nation, acceptance of
day-care also depended on tolerance of multiple caregivers for young children,
notions that derived from lingering early modern Japanese attitudes and practices tolerating infant and child care by persons besides the natural mother.[2]
Thus this chapter also examines the influence of mother-centered views of child-
rearing on Japanese day-care practices and their justifications during the second
decade of the twentieth century.

Development and Diffusion of Day-Care Centers

Following the establishment of Japan's first permanent day-care facility—
Futaba Yōchien in Tokyo—additional child-care centers were slowly founded in
poor and working-class districts in other metropolitan areas. The reopening of
three of the Kobe wartime centers in 1906 brought the total to four nationwide,
but thereafter the pace of establishment quickened. By 1912, three years after
the Home Ministry began to hold symposia throughout the nation encouraging
the founding of relief projects (*kyūsai jigyō kōshūkai*), fifteen day-care facilities
were in operation. Two-thirds of these were located in Osaka, Kobe, and Tokyo,
three of Japan's "six great cities" (*roku daitoshi*).[3] As the Taishō era progressed,
the pace of expansion increased. During 1917, the year before nationwide riots
over rice prices spurred development of a host of new social programs,[4] the number of day-care centers climbed to sixty, with the yearly rates of increase ranging
between five and ten centers per year from 1918 to 1921.[5]

Individuals and private organizations founded child-care institutions in
Japan's two great prewar metropolitan regions, the Kansai and Kanto areas.[6] Individuals tended to found single centers, although they not infrequently orga-

nized associations of supporters to contribute to operating costs. Dōjoen Yōji Hoikujo (1913) in Tokyo and Izumio Aijien (1914) in Osaka are two examples of individually founded centers. Organizations also established single facilities, including Osaka Hokuin (1912), Ōfūkai Takujisho (1913), Dōbō Hoikujo (1914), and Taishō Fujinkai Takujisho (1918). A handful of large organizations, such as the Kōsaikai and the Tokyo-shi Tokushu Shōgakkō Kōenkai (Tokyo City Special Elementary School Booster Club), private organizations receiving funding from municipal administrations of their respective metropolitan areas, established networks of centers during the early Taishō era.[7]

Two principal goals appear in late Meiji–early Taishō day-care statements of purpose. The first, following KSKH, stressed that day-care could be a means to family economic improvement, while the second, following Futaba Yōchien, emphasized the educational functions of day-care centers. During the first half of the Taishō era centers favoring family financial gains were more popular than those giving top priority to the mental and moral development of lower-class children and their parents. However, as at Futaba Yōchien and the KSKH centers themselves, the two purposes were not mutually exclusive. Rather, most centers acknowledged both aims, but tended to emphasize one over the other. While these differences in emphasis led to minor differences in center programs, on the whole, similarities in center purposes and features were more striking than differences during early Taishō.

During the 1910s the emphases of statements of purpose varied by region, although the goals of centers in the Kansai region displayed more uniformity than those of the Kanto area. All of the early Taishō day-care facilities in Osaka— Aizenbashi Hoikujo, Ōsaka Hoikuin, Fudōji Hoikuen, Izumio Aijien, Minami Ōji Hoikujo, and the seven (later nine) Kōsaikai day-care centers—followed the pattern of the KSKH centers in emphasizing the economic aspects of family improvement. In the Kanto region day-care centers such as the four Tokushu Shōgakkō Takujiba, established between 1912 and 1919 by a private philanthropic association, also gave top priority to household economic gains, while two leading Tokyo centers, Dōjōen Yōji Hoikujo and Ōfūkai Takujisho, both established in June 1913, followed Futaba Yōchien's lead in stressing the moral and intellectual development of preschoolers to a greater extent than economic aid.

Despite the widespread appeal of the economic orientation of the KSKH centers and the establishment of Japan's first networks of day-care centers by local philanthropic organizations such as KSKH in Kobe and Kōsaikai in Osaka, the significance of the Kansai area to the development of institutional child-care in prewar Japan has been underestimated in previous research. While the KSKH and Kōsaikai centers are extensively treated in local day-care histories such as *Kōbe no hoikuenshi* (History of Kobe Day-Care Centers), published by the Kobe League of Private Day-Care Centers, and *Hoikujo no Ayumi 1909–1945* (Footsteps of Day-Care Centers, 1909–1945), published by the city of Osaka, the fact that Kōsaikai (a private association receiving Osaka city funds) operated seven day-care facilities before the 1918 Rice Riots spurred the creation of networks of municipal facilities in the 1920s has largely been ignored in studies treating child-care history at the national level. Yet the influence of the KSKH and Kōsaikai goals and facilities and the fact that Osaka was the first city to establish municipally funded, municipally operated day-care centers after the 1918 Rice Riots, indicate the critical importance of the Kansai region to the development and diffusion of institutional child care in pre–World War II Japan.

Economic Aims in the Kansai Region

The purpose of Aizenbashi Hoikujo, Osaka's first day-care center, established in 1909,[8] was to help "laborers having family financial difficulties" by providing daytime care (*chūkan hoiku*) for their children. Since Ishii Jūji, the founder of Aizenbashi Hoikujo, admired the work of KSKH and had studied its day-care facilities before founding his center, it is not surprising that its principal aim, ameliorating lower-class families' economic difficulties, resembled that of the KSKH centers.[9] Like the KSKH centers and Futaba Yōchien, Aizenbashi Hoikujo regulations took for granted that institutional child care would assist working parents of both sexes; they did not assume that working mothers in particular needed help with child-rearing, nor were mothers excluded from the category of "laborer."[10]

The aims of the Kōsaikai day-care division also emphasized economic improvement. In December 1913 Kōsaikai, a private relief organization formed in Osaka early in 1913, established a number of projects, including day-care for poor children, a simplified kindergarten for poor children, an evening *komori gakkō*, employment introductions, writing of documents for illiterates, and work projects for veterans. By February 1914 Kōsaikai had established five child-care centers in lower-class Osaka districts, and by 1919 it operated nine facilities—Japan's most extensive early day-care network.[11] The first Kōsaikai yearbook revealed the organization's goals in founding the child-care division as

> taking in during the daytime children of the lowly (*kasōmin*), whose activity is hindered by having young children; providing the children with play,

songs, and other elements of kindergarten education; and finally, through the children, diffusing the idea of savings to improve homes and reform community customs.[12]

The yearbook indicates that Kōsaikai day-care aims included the familiar themes of livelihood assistance, savings, and reforming family life, as well as a new one, community betterment. In 1920 the goals remained unchanged:

> to take in children who prevent full development of work ability of labor-ers or the poor . . . to give these children a kindergarten education, to in-culcate in them the idea of savings, to uplift family life and to improve the neighborhoods.[13]

Similarly, Ōsaka Hoikuin, founded in November 1912 by Kyūgokai, a Shizuoka Prefecture relief association, aimed to upgrade the lives of poor fami-lies by relieving their economic difficulties.[14] According to the regulations, Kyūgokai's day-care center aimed to care for "children between ages 1 and 5 . . . of persons who cannot work or whose work is hindered by their children," in or-der to promote "life improvement (seikatsu kōjō) through children."[15]

Izumio Aijien, established in Osaka during the early Taishō period, also aimed primarily at relieving poor families' economic difficulties.[16] The first ar-ticle of the regulations clearly sets forth the Izumio day-care center's goals: "This center is to take in children of persons whose occupation is hindered by young children in order to allow them to engage in their occupations with ease and to care for and educate their children."[17]

Despite the predominance of KSKH aims in the Kansai region, a handful of centers pursued other goals. In Kyoto, Shinai Hoikuen, founded in 1914 in a working-class district by a Christian nurse, stressed child care (hoiku) itself, rather than learning or family financial betterment.[18] Dōbō Hoikujo, established by a Buddhist women's association (Bukkyō Dōbō Fujinkai) in Kobe, operated a child-care program to facilitate fellowship among members. The group con-sisted of "women who had received Buddha's spirit (kokoro), which moves friends to give each other mutual aid in order to advance." The association's members collected money, rented a house, and began to care for about forty children in 1914. The users of this center included not only wage workers and the poor, but many petty shopkeepers who obtained economic benefits from day-care; how-ever, the center's goals also included fostering cooperation, religious fulfillment, and female fellowship.[19]

Economic and Educational Aims in the Kanto Area

The objectives of the newly founded day-care centers in the Kanto area were more diverse than those of the Kansai region. Some, like the KSKH centers, emphasized economic improvement, while others, like Futaba Yōchien, gave priority to educational goals. The fact that some Kanto child-care centers emulated KSKH aims, while no centers in the Kansai area adopted Futaba Yōchien's emphasis on education as a primary goal, suggests that the KSKH aims had a wider appeal than those of Futaba Yōchien. However, in the Kanto area there were a few day-care facilities like the Jidō Chūkan Azukarijo, which seemed to have followed neither the KSKH nor the Futaba Yōchien pattern.

Tokyo's first day-care network followed the lead of Kansai centers in assigning top priority to family economic aid. Despite their association with paupers' schools, the principal aim of the four Tokyo City Special Elementary School Boosters' Association day-care centers (founded in 1912, 1914, 1916, and 1919)[20] seems to have been the economic well-being of poor families rather than education. During mid-Taishō, housing projects, work projects, and child-care centers (*takujiba*) were established in the vicinity of the paupers' schools in order to assist the pupils' families. The main aim of the day-care program was clearly economic: "[T]o care for preschool children of guardians with children enrolled in special schools who cannot engage in their work due to child-care difficulties."[21] Parents participating in booster club work projects as well as parents holding other jobs were eligible to send their children to Tamahime Day-Care Center or one of the other facilities. Parental employment was primary, while education of the youngsters was secondary.

In contrast, Sakamaki Kenzō's Dōjōen Yōji Hoikujo,[22] established in Tokyo in June 1913, followed Futaba Yōchien in giving precedence to the moral training of preschool children and their parents. Dōjōen's emphasis on educaiton doubtless stemmed from the fact that Sakamaki's child-care project evolved from the founder's earlier philanthropic works, two educational programs aimed at adults and school-aged children residing in a slum district in Asakusa Ward:

> The origins of this center are that its founder Sakamaki Kenzō lived for many years in lower-class society (*saimin shakai*). He felt overwhelming sympathy (*dōjō*) for the poor, so from January 1905, he began a postal savings club called the Diligence, Savings and Scrap-Collecting Club (Kinben Chōchiku Sekijinkai), or Clink Club [apparently named after the sound made by jingling coins]. . . . In March 1910, he established an evening

school in Hashibanchō for poor children in the area, baby-sitters and apprentices, who could not attend school during the day. As a related project, in June 1913, he started a day-care center (*hoikujo*). At first, only 18 children enrolled, but local circumstances favored use of this facility. It developed quickly, and continues to this day [1920].[23]

The Dōjōen educational program, like that of Futaba Yōchien, stressed character development through means Sakamaki considered appropriate for young children. A 1917 description characterized the Dōjōen program as follows:

It employs group care for the children in its care, and places emphasis on family-like upbringing and the fostering of good customs and the development of self-reliance (*jichi no seishin*). . . . However, the educational method emphasizes physical education. Play and songs are part of the curriculum, which strives to develop knowledge and virtue (*chitoku*).

The center provided these services tuition-free, although one sen per day was assessed to offset the cost of daily snacks.[24]

Furthermore, the Dōjōen staff created additional programs for their pupils' guardians and siblings:

Once a month, the Parents' Club (*oya no kai*) and Lantern Slide Club (*gentō kai*) meet. The guardians assemble so that the center has contact with the home. In addition, on holidays, mothers and older sisters are encouraged to come to the center. Assistant teachers are dispatched to homes or flyers are sent seeking their replies to plan for the contact with the home regarding the children's education (*kyōyō*).

Through these three types of meetings, as well as the home visits, there were frequent opportunities for contact between parents and teachers.[25]

In contrast to the other Kanto facilities, the program of one Tokyo center provided academic as well as ethical education to its preschoolers. According to a 1920 description, the primary aim of the Jidō Chūkan Azukarijo, a Buddhist-operated facility established in a charity lodging located in Wakamiya district, Honjo Ward, in May 1917, offered day-care to

poor children aged three to seven from the area where the Free Lodging is located and cares for them free of charge from dawn to dusk every day. The method is according to Buddhism, so the children worship Amida Buddha once a day with their teacher. In addition to play, songs, and stories, the children above age four are taught the syllabary and numbers. When children are sick, the center finds a way to have them treated. The staff members sometimes visit the children's homes and caution parents regarding child-rearing.[26]

Thus the curriculum at this facility differed from the norm by including reading, writing, and simple religious instruction in addition to the usual attention to children's health needs, kindergarten subjects, and moral education.

The Taishō Women's Club (Taishō Fujinkai) established a child-care project in Tokyo in October 1917 for secular reasons, seeking to promote middle-class women's involvement in social reform through the creation of programs for the urban underclass by "researching and operating a project appropriate for women." It envisioned day-care as a means to offer "guidance and comfort" to the lower classes. In addition to the day-care center (*takujisho*), it also engaged a visiting nurse (*junkaishi*) who primarily offered health care advice in the neighborhood.[27]

Programs Fit Center Aims

Statements of purpose, descriptions, and regulations indicate that most early Taishō day-care institutions sought to achieve twin goals—the improvement of family life, especially its finances, and the education of preschool children. While a greater number of centers emphasized the former more than the latter, general acceptance of both objectives resulted in similar programs. In order to improve family life, most child-care centers tried to educate parents by providing moral training aimed at increasing household income and fostering hard work and self-reliance; the centers also gave advice regarding new methods of child-rearing and household management. For the youngsters, virtually all child-care facilities included in their daily routines educational activities drawn from kindergarten curricula. These fundamental features of day-care programs predominated from the turn of the century well into the 1930s; thereafter, the objectives of day-care centers shifted to reduction of infant mortality under the pronatalist policies of the Ministry of Health and Welfare during World War II.

A major feature of pre-World War II day-care centers was the attention devoted to the pupil's physical well-being. Staff members spent around two hours each day keeping children clean. At many centers teachers regularly gave the children baths and trimmed their fingernails and, when necessary, picked lice from the children's heads, combed their hair, and laundered their clothes. The curricula included instruction in personal hygiene, and most centers provided medical treatment for the children's ailments. In addition, staff members generally sought to educate parents in hygiene, nutrition, simple medical treatment, child-rearing, and child-development principles through informal conversations and evening meetings at the centers and through home visits.

Common goals led to similar daily operations as well. Like their late Meiji predecessors—particularly the KSKH centers—long operating hours, holidays corresponding to those of working guardians, attention to the children's mental, moral, and physical development, and efforts to improve various aspects of the children's home life characterized their programs. A few institutions offered only child care, but most provided services beyond education and health care for preschoolers. As the decade progressed, in addition to meetings and outings to provide educational and recreational opportunities for the parents, many centers began additional services such as employment introductions, loans, reading and scribe services, afterschool clubs for older children, free evening clinics, or lectures open to the general community. Large organizations such the Kōsaikai in Osaka and Tokyo City Special Elementary School Boosters' Association established other social projects—housing, orphanages, and work projects—as well as day-care centers for the urban poor. The expansion of services in the 1910s reflected rising concern with the problem of urban poverty and foreshadowed the establishment of private and municipal social settlements with day-care programs at the core after the 1918 Rice Riots.[28]

Due to the size of their rented quarters and the logistics of working with lively preschoolers, centers tended to be rather small, commonly taking in from 40 to 70 children. For example, each Kōsaikai center had an enrollment limit of 50, although total enrollment at the seven Kōsaikai centers in 1916 totaled 231.[29] Some centers founded by individuals were quite small, caring for only about 20 children. With respective enrollments of 300 and 138 children at a single facility, Futaba Yōchien and Dōjōen Yōji Hoikujo ranked as institutional giants in the day-care world. The centers generally took in children between the ages of two or three and school age (six to seven years old).[30]

Rejection of Ogawa Shigejirō's Aims

The aims of improving family life and educating preschool children predominated in the statements of purpose and programs of early Taishō Japanese day-care centers. As we have seen, a handful of day-care centers pursued goals different from those of Futaba Yōchien and the KSKH centers; however, the alternative views of these local organizations did not achieve regional or national

influence. Nonetheless, Ogawa Shigejirō, an Osaka City relief specialist and former Home Ministry official, unsuccessfully championed other aims for Japanese
daytime child care. Ogawa insisted that the saving of infants' lives should be the
primary concern of Japanese day-care facilities; however, the articles he published in relief journals with nationwide circulation had little impact on the
practices, aims, and policies of the day-care world. Until the formation of the
Welfare Ministry during the Pacific War, the Futaba Yōchien and KSKH models continued to attract the greatest number of supporters among the philanthropists and professional relief workers who established child-care centers.

Ogawa[31] argued strongly that the principal aim of day-care should be reduction of infant mortality—a conviction gleaned from European relief institutions for young children, particularly those of Germany. To achieve this end, facilities should gather children under age three rather than three- to six-year-olds.
In contrast to Morishima, Noguchi, and Namae (see chapters 3 and 4), who had
been influenced by American institutions for children, Ogawa's perceptions of
child-care goals and programs reflected the influence of and his admiration for
these European views, and as such diverged markedly from those of Futaba
Yōchien and the KSKH centers. Although Ogawa moved to Osaka at a time
when only three child-care facilities existed there, his advice was largely ignored
by local individuals and organizations establishing new day-care centers, and it
had even less impact on other areas of Japan.

Ogawa's early views on institutional child care appeared in "On Daytime
Child-care Work," the lead article in the October 1913 *Kyūsai kenkyū* (Research
on relief), journal of the Kyūsai Jigyō Kenkyūkai, an association studying relief
projects that he had helped found in Osaka three months earlier. The article revealed that Ogawa regarded German rather than U.S. institutions for young
children as models for Japanese child protection facilities. In early twentieth century Germany, he wrote, there existed two major institutions for preschool children—day nurseries for infants under three and infant schools for children above
three. Ogawa focused his attention on day nurseries (*kripen* in German, *crèche* in
French).[32]

In his article Ogawa stressed that true day-care projects (*chūkan hoiku jigyō*)
cared for children under two or three in order to reduce infant mortality rates.
The primary goal should be to protect the lives of infants, as German day nurseries did. He argued:

> Of course it is necessary to have various sorts of care and educational facil-
> ities for lower-class preschool children which substitute for the home. . . .

Infant day-care at Hyogo Day-Care Center, Kobe, circa 1920. Courtesy of Ohara Institute for Social Research, Hosei University.

First, one must find a way to succor (*kyūsai*) those most in need of protection. Lower-class infants under age one fall into the unfortunate circumstances of illness and death more easily than other young children, and many of them are also subject to abuse and infanticide. Some are neglected due to ignorance, laziness, or carelessness on the part of their families, and many become foster children or are given away by their parents to be raised by others. Therefore it is natural for child protection institutions to give priority to infants.[33]

Thus for Ogawa, saving infant lives was more important than educating preschool children.

Since infants were susceptible to disease, Ogawa warned that adequate sanitary precautions were of utmost importance to day-care facilities. The number of children under care ideally ranged between twenty and thirty. He recommended that the day-care center be located in a new building equipped with an entry room, kitchen, toilets, a washroom, a bath, a feeding room, separate rooms for infants and toddlers, and a play area, located as close to the parent's work-place as possible. The overall atmosphere should be "clean, orderly, and calm."[34]

Ogawa roundly criticized existing Japanese day-care facilities, charging that they incorrectly mixed the functions of educational institutions such as kinder-gartens and baby-sitters' schools with day-care work. He further complained that child-care centers in Japan ignored infants, the group most in need of care, either by lumping together children between ages one and seven at a single fa-cility or by taking in only children between three and seven.[35] To Ogawa, con-temporary Japanese centers that aimed to improve family finances and the val-ues of poor children and their parents—the goals of most existing Japanese centers—missed the point. He wrote that in Japan at the time

> relief of working women results from child protection. This not only has
> the direct effect of rendering some assistance to the lower classes; it also has
> an indirect, favorable effect on their spiritual life. However, day-care is not
> offered to rescue them from economic difficulties; the improvement of fam-
> ily finances is secondary.[36]

Ogawa listed numerous benefits that would accrue to children, lower-class families, and Japanese society from establishment of day-care centers. The "blessings of paradise" for children headed his list. Next came "relief for the eco-nomic difficulties of the working class," suggesting that Ogawa dared not com-pletely ignore the great popularity of economic improvement as a justification for day-care. The remaining four benefits were "prevention of the tragic events of abortion, infanticide, abandonment, cruelty, and placing children with foster parents"; "reduction of the infant mortality rate"; "assimilation of lower-class families"; and "adjustment of the evil of class enmity," two assisting children and two aiding society.[37] It is likely that Ogawa listed many advantages in order to broaden the appeal of day-care; however, the arguments in the body of the arti-cle stressing the critical need for care of children under three and his scornful la-beling of current Japanese facilities as day-care centers in name only make it clear that he viewed the saving of infants' lives as the primary aim of day-care.

Although Ogawa found fault with the current goals of Japanese day-care, he approved of a handful of current Japanese day-care practices. He supported re-strictive enrollment, believing that institutional care for children of employed guardians would promote hard work:

> Parents who entrust a child, especially the mother, should be diligently
> working at their current occupation and be unable to care for the child at

home for economic or work-related reasons, or they should be in a situation in which it is really inconvenient to provide care. The children of unemployed, lazy persons or persons whose conduct is improper should be refused care even if they meet the admission criterion of having child-care difficulties.[38]

As with his ideas on day-care, Ogawa's views on women's roles were heavily influenced by European conceptions. Thus he criticized adoption, a practice most Japanese believed necessary for household continuity, and called for Japanese women of prominent families to become more active in relief work, following the example of German women. His assumption that mothers are the primary caregivers for young children also seems to reflect German rather than Japanese conceptions of womanhood.

Ogawa also felt that a day-care fee should be charged, for reasons similar to those of his contemporaries. It would "preserve the parents' natural sense of the obligation to assist (*fuyō gimu*)."[39] That is, because parents were bound to succor their legally recognized offspring, they should pay for day-care, which substituted for parental child-rearing.

In October 1913 only three day-care institutions—Aizenbashi Hoikujo (1909),[40] Ōsaka Hoikuin (1912), and Fudōji Hoikuen (1913)—existed in Osaka. At the close of "On Daytime Child-care Work," Ogawa called for the immediate establishment of additional day-care facilities in Osaka and addressed specific advice to the city's largest relief organization, Kōsaikai. Ogawa urged this affluent, powerful organization not to repeat the mistakes of existing Japanese institutions in planning their new day-care project.[41] Nonetheless, the Kōsaikai day-care centers, founded successively after December 1913, excluded infants, offering care only to children between the ages of two and six. Only in cases of extreme poverty (when the family could not provide proper nourishment) could guardians obtain special permission to enroll younger children.[42] Furthermore, another early Taishō day-care center, Izumio Aijien, founded by a private philanthropist near Osaka in March 1914, also rejected Ogawa's child-care ideals.[43]

The complete absence of Ogawa's influence is conspicuous in a November 1915 article by Kōsaikai president and Osaka city relief official Inada Jō discussing the main and secondary purposes of his organization's day-care division. Inada explained that positive relief projects were required in order to prevent poverty, and that "[d]ay-care is the only positive project our organization currently operates; therefore, we do not hesitate to spend a relatively large amount of money on it."[44] He then stated the principal aim of Kōsaikai day-care: "[o]ur organization [uses] day-care as a means of promoting work, and cares for children who get underfoot in place of laborers [their parents]. The secondary purposes are community reform, improvement of customs, encouragement of savings, and improvement of work."[45] Inada's statements reveal that Kōsaikai day-care aims differed sharply from Ogawa's hopes for the program. Spurning Ogawa's advice, the Kōsaikai followed the lead of KSKH and most existing Japanese child-care facilities in emphasizing education, family economic improvement, the amelioration of poverty, and the care of children between the ages of three and six as its primary objectives.

Several factors account for the resounding rejection of Ogawa's views by the Kōsaikai and other day-care centers founded subsequently in Osaka and the rest of Japan in the 1910s and 1920s. First, Ogawa was a newcomer to Osaka, and his area of greatest expertise was prison and reformatory work rather than daytime child care. In seeking to shape Kansai day-care aims and practices, he had to compete with Namae Takayuki, former director of the renowned KSKH *hoikujo*. As consultant to the KSKH centers and their wartime predecessors between 1904 and 1909, Namae had already established a widely known model for day-care in the Kansai region seven years before Ogawa arrived in Osaka. During those years, many persons interested in relief and charitable work in Kansai and other regions had visited the KSKH centers. KSKH was supported by wealthy and powerful Kobe citizens and had been commended by the Home Ministry. KSKH's reputation as a model day-care organization was further enhanced by Namae's appointment to the Relief Section (Kyūsaika) of the Home Ministry's Local Affairs Bureau (Chihōkyoku) in 1909 and its inclusion in the ministry's 1909 relief project yearbook. After assuming his post in Tokyo, Namae continued to praise the KSKH *hoikujo* as exemplary day-care facilities at yearly Home Ministry regional symposia (*kōshūkai*) on relief works. Thus Namae's vigorous activity at the Home Ministry facilitated nationwide diffusion of livelihood assistance as a rationale for day-care.[46]

Given the long tradition of KSKH influence in Kansai and Namae's later prestige as a Home Ministry official, it is not surprising that Osaka day-care reformers rejected newcomer Ogawa's ideas. In addition, Ogawa's forthright criticism of existing day-care facilities may have alienated potential supporters.

Second, cost may also have undermined support for Ogawa's conception of child care. Ogawa himself recognized that facilities for infants required special equipment, very low staff-to-child ratios, and extensive cooperation with doctors and nurses. The individuals and small organizations that operated day-care centers in Japan could not easily pay for the additional staff and equipment to implement infant care. Ogawa had had high expectations for Kōsaikai due to its solid financial base; nevertheless, as a rationale for its day-care division, Kōsaikai found economic improvement to be more appealing than reduction of infant mortality.

The final, and perhaps decisive, reason for the rejection of Ogawa's day-care policies lies in Japanese motivations for founding and sustaining day-care during the opening decades of the twentieth century. The impulse to found day-care centers was part of a drive for national integration, which generated new bureaucratic initiatives following the Russo-Japanese War, including the Local Improvement Movement (*chihō kairyō undō*), mainly aimed at rural areas, and relief projects (*kyūsai jigyō*), mainly aimed at urban areas. These programs emphasized productivity, savings, and moral improvement of ordinary Japanese citizens. Increased productivity would benefit the individual by raising living standards and benefit the nation by enabling citizens to bear the increased taxes that policymakers felt necessary for national development. Inculcation of proper values promised to keep welfare expenditures at low levels by reducing reliance on government relief and retarding the emergence of undesirable social movements.

However, Ogawa's conceptions of child protection emphasized saving the lives of infants, reflecting the goals of European day-care programs, especially those of France (where the day nursery originated) and Germany, where national policies promoted population growth. Such concerns were largely absent from the concerns of bureaucrats and other proponents of national progress in Japan in the decade following the Russo-Japanese War. Therefore, they preferred that child-care facilities nurture values that would promote the economic well-being of ordinary citizens and the nation or minimize social unrest.

Day-care centers that incorporated the kindergarten's aspiration to better society by improving the character of the rising generation appealed to Japanese leaders of the 1910s in a way that the pronatalist orientation of the continental European day nursery could not. Late nineteenth century American kindergartens sought to instill the native middle-class values of thrift, industry, cleanliness, discipline, and respect for education in immigrant children and their parents through charity (or free) kindergartens, an aim that paralleled that of early twentieth century Japanese state policies seeking to instill conservative values in the rural and urban masses. Thus Futaba Yōchien's justification for day-care had considerable appeal in early Taishō Japan, because its emphasis on moral training, as well as its cultivation of hard work, savings, and respect for education, matched prevailing state and elite desires to forge national unity and advance economic development.

The aim of European day-care centers, to increase population, contributed little to the easing of a second major late Meiji state concern—increasing the prosperity of ordinary citizens. Although Meiji nationalists realized that depopulation would shrink the pool of potential laborers and soldiers, Japan's population had increased steadily after the Restoration. Their country did not need to raise its population growth rate, especially given its straitened economic circumstances following the Russo-Japanese War. On the contrary, an increasing rate would undermine state efforts to raise general standards of living by placing additional pressure on the country's limited economic resources. Thus KSKH's day-care model, which promoted lower-class employment and sought to improve urban lower-class families' financial situations, was of considerable interest not only to Taishō businessmen and officials preoccupied with raising productivity, but to social reformers seeking to alleviate poverty as well.

Although Ogawa's views did not become a main current of Japanese day-care thought in the Taishō era, they were not completely ignored. When Aizenbashi Hoikujo was reorganized as Ishii Kinen Aizenen in 1917, it opened one day-care program to care for children under three and another at the same site to provide both care and education to children between three and seven. Ogawa's membership on the Aizenen board of directors undoubtedly influenced the decision to start separate infant and preschool programs. However, on the whole Ogawa's emphasis on day-care as a means of reducing infant mortality was at odds with current Japanese conceptions of prequisites for individual and national progress. Therefore, his ideas found few adherents during the 1910s and 1920s.

The Impact of New Views of Motherhood

In general, the goals and programs of early Taishō day-care facilities followed models established at the dawn of the twentieth century; however, by the middle of the Taishō period changes in the adult evening programs began to take place. The fact that parent's meetings began to be called mothers' and mother-older sisters' meetings suggests increased acceptance of new notions of motherhood and child-rearing by day-care professionals. However, one might expect these new conceptions to generate reluctance to entrust infants to caregivers other than their natural mothers, which would in turn erode support for day-care. Yet acceptance of new views of motherhood among day-care staff members may have been shallower than it appears at first glance, because little if any opposition to day-care developed in Japan during the Taishō or early Shōwa periods. In this section I consider evidence for changing attitudes toward child-rearing and day-care during the early Taishō period, leaving late Taishō developments for discussion in the next chapter.

As we have seen, in the 1910s day-care centers were still mainly justified as a means of ameliorating the economic difficulties of lower-class families, as providers of moral training for children and parents, as protectors of children, or as a combination of these aims rather than as institutions to care for children while their mothers worked. Thus center statements of purpose frequently contained phrases such as "provides care for the children of persons who cannot work or whose work is hindered by preschool children" (Ōsaka Hoikuin), "to take in children of persons whose occupation is hindered by preschool children" (Izumio Aijien), or "gathers the children of the poor for the convenience of their guardians (*fukei*)" (Kōbe Kyōshūkai Hoikubu). However, day-care professionals' views of child-rearing showed a glimmer of change in one key respect during middle Taishō. Changes in the names of adult activities at child-care centers are an indication that attitudes toward child-rearing was beginning to shift.

During the late Meiji period, programs for adults were called parent meetings (*oya no kai*) or father-older brother meetings (*fukei kai*),[47] terms implying that responsibility for children lay not just with female family members, but with male members as well. The term "*fukei kai*," literally "father-older brother meetings," was derived from early modern Japanese household values that accorded authority over children to morally superior male members; in that sense, it can also be translated as "guardians." However, *fukei* implies its opposite, the unvirtuous, inferior woman, an older view that contrasted with the modern definition of the woman as "good wife, wise mother" (*ryōsai kenbo*) who was entrusted with the physical care and socialization of children. Yet the modern state retained a claim on the upbringing of its future citizens, because mothers shared responsibility for the mental and moral training of children with private and public schools under the compulsory education law.[48]

During early and middle Taishō, three new names for adult programs appeared. Another term for guardians' meetings, *hogosha kai*, was gender neutral, like the older terms. However, the other two terms, "mothers' meetings" (*haha no kai*) and "mother-older sister meetings" (*boshi kai*), implied that the activities at these gatherings were for females. As the evening adult programs generally consisted of lectures by teachers or visitors on child-rearing or other domestic matters, and occasionally entertainment, the emergence of these names indicates that day-care professionals increasingly associated girls and women rather than males or parents of both sexes with child-rearing, nutrition, cooking, sewing, household finances, and consumption.

The early Taishō trend toward feminization of the names of adult programs can be measured quantitatively. In 1912 the terms "parent meeting" and "father-older brother meeting" predominated in the eight existing child-care centers; there were no mothers' or mother-older sister meetings.[49] Six years later, among thirty-six centers for which information is available, the proportion having either parents' or guardians' meetings had dropped from 100 percent to 46 percent, while one-third held mothers' or mother-older sister meetings.[50] The change took place as centers founded during the 1910s tended to name their adult education programs for female members, while older centers did not rename their adult activities.

Western conceptions of the mother-child relationship continued to appear in the writings of leading Japanese child welfare specialists during early Taishō. Previously these views of child-rearing had occasionally surfaced in Japanese experts' descriptions of Western day-care facilities, especially in the writings of those who were Christians or who had studied social work overseas. Such views of parent-child relationships surfaced in the writings of day-care experts such as Ogawa, Takada Shingō, and Namae, all of whom had studied relief work in the United States or Europe.[51]

In "On Daytime Child-care Work," Ogawa referred to day-care as "substituting for mothers." This view again diverged from the existing consensus concerning day-care goals, which justified child-care facilities as replacements for laborers, families, parents, or guardians in caring for preschoolers.[52] Following Western child protection experts, Ogawa described the mother-child bond as "the closest natural relationship" and praised the practice of nursing as a means of preserving infant health.[53] Thus Ogawa's emphasis on the importance of the mother's role in child care is in part a consequence of his enthusiasm for breast feeding, a special concern of the European pronatalists and child relief work specialists who sought to reduce infant mortality by discouraging urban mothers from entrusting their infants to negligent rural wet nurses. But deaths from sending babies to the countryside and mothers' refusal to nurse their offspring did not constitute major social problems in prewar Japan. In fact, Ogawa could have mentioned the Japanese custom of shared nursing, in which children separated from their mothers by desertion or illness and infants of milkless mothers were suckled by female neighbors; surely he was must have known of this practice. The infants received the benefits of nursing through such sharing, but not from the milk of their own mothers.[54] Clearly Ogawa's enthusiasm for things German extended beyond support for German justification of day-care to idealizing Western conceptions of child-rearing and womanhood and to zealous encouragement of breast feeding, an unnecessary effort in early twentieth-century Japan.

Takada also emphasized the mother's central role in child-rearing in his 1914 lecture, "Child Protection Work in America," an address to the seventh annual Kanka Kyūsai Jigyō Kōshūkai (Symposium on relief and reform works), sponsored by the Home Ministry. In his lecture Takada stated that

> we must remember that day-care is a philanthropic work which is a necessary evil, and that even for persons in poverty, nothing surpasses care at the mother's bosom. Thus if care can take place at home, it brings happiness to the child, and the mother who cares for the child can receive assistance. This system is called the allowance system or the poor mother's pension system.[55]

In explaining American practices, Takada echoed early twentieth century American views that the mother was the best possible caregiver for children, especially infants. By the late 1910s belief in the irreplaceable role of mothers in child care led Americans to favor mothers' pensions over institutional child care as a means of helping impoverished families. Since "nothing surpasses care at the mother's bosom," subsidizing needy mothers to raise children at home was preferable to having them sent to day-care centers while mothers worked. Takada concluded that for American women motherhood took precedence over income earning. Takada's failure to criticize American child-rearing attitudes or mothers' pensions suggests that he was probably not opposed to their adoption in some form in his homeland, yet he continued to advocate the expansion of institutional child care in Japan.

While Ogawa listed many positive aspects of day-care and promoted its diffusion in Japan, he nonetheless referred to child-care centers in unflattering terms, labeling them "a necessary evil."[56] Takada also accepted growth of institutional child care as inevitable in Japan's emerging industrial society. In a lecture on relief work at a women's college, he stated that "[u]nder today's economic conditions, it is impossible to support a household through the efforts of a single working-class male. As day-care centers belong to the category of preventive work rather than relief work, I would like to have the Ōfūkai Takujisho become a model to stimulate the development of these facilities in our country."[57]

Thus early Taishō reports on day-care and child protection work in foreign countries began to reflect not only Western institutional practices, but Western views of motherhood and child-rearing as well. Western rationales for day-care and other children's institutions in this era assumed that mother-child bonds should be very intimate and that nurturing by mothers constituted the best possible care for children, especially infants. Breast feeding by the mother improved an infant's chances for survival and laid a foundation for sound development. The assumption in the West that a special bond existed between mother and child was the principal reason that institutional child care was justified as a substitute for the mother rather than the father, parents, or other caregivers.

In late Meiji Japan, when child-care centers were first introduced, early modern Japanese ideas of child-rearing that permitted a broad range of family members to tend to infants transformed Western justifications of the day-care center. In Europe, proponents had justified institutional child care as a replacement for mothers while in Japan supporters presented it as a substitute for working parents or guardians rather than mothers alone. Yet over time, child-care ideas and practices in Japan began to change. By the Taishō period urban Japanese mothers, especially among the salaried classes, were becoming isolated in the home and were gaining leisure time,[58] while "good wife, wise mother" had governed women's higher education for nearly two decades. These trends facilitated acceptance of Western-influenced notions of child-rearing, that is, the assignment of greater responsibility for child care to mothers as opposed to servants or other household members, beyond small circles of Christians and highly educated relief experts and day-care professionals.

The early Taishō descriptions of foreign day-care work in relief journals also promoted increasing awareness of new notions of mother-child relationships. The emergence of new terms for adult programs at some centers suggests that such views were becoming widespread among many day-care professionals. Yet the predominance of older arguments in official day-care documents belies this assertion. During the Taishō era, even among middle-class professionals, the new conceptions of motherhood and childhood had gained limited acceptance.

For example, in 1917 the Tokyo Metropolitan Relief Section (Tōkyō-fu Kyūsaika) issued a report describing contemporary Tokyo day-care facilities and discussing future city plans. The report stated that the purpose of day-care was to "protect and educate children" in place of their parents (ryōshin) when work prevented parents from discharging this responsibility themselves and referred to adult education programs as "parent meetings" (oya no kai). It also noted that historically day-care centers had been "philanthropic works" providing "assistance to family finances." This report, outlining the official views of the relief bureau of Japan's largest city, still adhered to the logic of the late Meiji day-care tracts.[59] Clearly, the old ideas still had the power to influence government officials and relief policies.

Furthermore, new centers founded in early Taishō still employed traditional arguments that did not assume the principal adult beneficiaries of day-care were female. Senjū Hoikuen, established in May 1916, described itself as an institution designed to guide children of busy parents and guardians:

> They cannot give adequate supervision and education to their beloved children due to the lives they lead. Therefore the bad children form gangs in the narrow lanes to make mischief and quarrel and inferior thought is fostered, an intolerable situation. Therefore to save these children from this harmful social environment and also to let their guardians (*fukei*) [literally, fathers and elder brothers] engage in work with ease of mind, this center was established.[60]

Several features of Senjū Hoikuen's aims and program are also worth noting. First, the range of eligible children was extended. The center served children of small businessmen as well as working-class youngsters for educational and economic reasons. Second, the provision of child-care services is still not predicated on an assumption that the work of mothers, in contrast to that of fathers, is damaging to children. Third, the founders intended day-care to instill proper values in preschoolers to keep them from misbehaving, while its objectives for older users were to assist parents' work and impart new knowledge to family members. Finally, in order to work more effectively with its preschoolers, Senjū Hoikuen held monthly father-older brother meetings to educate the children's families. The topics of the meetings, intended for fathers and siblings as well as mothers, included "talks . . . on child-rearing, hygiene, and spirit (*seishin*)," and the center staff estimated that the meetings "have a favorable effect."[61] All in all, the objectives of Senjū Hoikuen fell within the late Meiji–early Taishō consensus. By the mid-1910s turn-of-the-century views of day-care center purposes and parental roles had not yet been supplanted.

Conclusion: The Significance of Early Taishō Trends

By the middle of the Taishō era a very small but influential minority of day-care center and child welfare professionals began to circulate new ideas of child-rearing responsibility and mother-child relationships in their descriptions of foreign day-care work. These new views, originating in the West, emphasized the need for close contact between mothers and children, to the exclusion of other family members. Exposure to new conceptions of child-rearing in leading experts' writings and lectures did not persuade those at lower levels of day-care work to abandon earlier justifications of Japanese day-care, although partial acceptance of the new views brought about changes in the naming of evening adult programs. Thus the trend toward calling evening adult programs "mothers' meetings" instead of "parent" or "father-older brother" meetings signals subtle shifts in attitudes toward child-rearing taking place in the day-care world.[62]

During the first half of the Taishō era private day-care institutions predominated, yet strong endorsements from local and national officials played a key role in spurring the steady expansion of child-care facilities. The overlapping concerns of day-care professionals and government officials help account for the continuing support of bureaucrats and other prominent Japanese for the fledgling day-care movement. Since the Restoration, nationalism had dominated the political and intellectual climate in Japan. The promise of institutional child care to accelerate national progress continued to give day-care great appeal during the 1910s.

In the first two decades of the twentieth century day-care programs emphasized individual solutions to dilemmas of urban poverty and industrialization. The key was individual moral improvement; parents' hard work and savings would better the circumstances of lower-class families. If children acquired these values, the ranks of the poor would diminish. Of course, other solutions to the problems of of poverty, industrialization, and national integration emerged— labor and tenant unions, universal suffrage, minority organizations, and socialist and communist activism. However, as the twentieth-century progressed, social work experts, philanthropists, and Home Ministry officials maintained their enthusiasm for individual, moral solutions to the social problems of industrialization and urbanization.

In sum, during the 1910s child-care advocates believed that improved socialization of the urban lower classes would benefit all parties concerned: the children, parents, and households in metropolitan slum and back street districts, as well as society and the nation. Instilling values such as thrift, industry, and discipline would raise both household incomes and national productivity. In addition, steady expansion brought about a professionalization of day-care work. And, whether or not they so intended, leading day-care experts contributed to the diffusion of new conceptions of the mother-child relationship. Their emphasis on the special care for infants that only mothers could provide contrasted sharply with widespread willingness to employ caregivers such as siblings, grandparents, child baby-sitters, apprentices, and wet nurses to mind young children. These nineteenth-century practices, rooted in household labor needs, inhibited rapid diffusion of new conceptions of motherhood and child-rearing, yet by the 1920s the growing influence of new ideas on day-care professionals (but not on the center users) was clearly visible.

6

Late Taishō Day-Care
New Justifications and Old Goals

By the 1920s two of Japan's most renowned day-care experts, Namae Takayuki, the former KSKH director who became a Home Ministry official, and Tokunaga Yuki, director of Futaba Yōchien, began to discuss day-care as an institution to protect working mothers, a departure from previous rationales for child-care centers as aid to working parents and the household economy and as providers of education to poor urban children and their parents. In deemphasizing fathers' needs for institutional child care, Namae and Tokunaga may have reinforced the inclination of some lesser day-care professionals to stress the crucial role of mothers in child-rearing, a trend that was already visible during the 1910s. However, even during the 1920s insistence on the overarching importance of mothers to the exclusion of other caregivers in the rearing of young children was far from universal. While some nationally renowned child-care specialists and Home Ministry officials adopted this view of motherhood, municipal relief officials and many ordinary day-care teachers were less than enthusiastic in endorsing new conceptions of motherhood.

Despite the diffusion of new attitudes toward motherhood, Japanese enthusiasm for institutional day-care continued unabated during the late Taishō era, as demonstrated by solid numerical growth, a broadening geographic distribution of child-care facilities, and the development of new types of centers. As the 1920s progressed, permanent day-care facilities began to spread beyond the great metropolitan regions to smaller cities. Seasonal centers sprang up in rural villages. The first public day-care centers were established in the great cities, and the total number of day-care centers spiraled upward. During the 1920s the pace of establishment quickened to twenty to forty centers per year from 1922 to 1926, compared to five to ten per year between 1918 and 1921. By 1926, the final year of the Taishō era, 273 centers were operating in Japan, compared to the 15 that existed in 1912.[1] The expansion of child-care facilities prompted the Ministry of Education to recognize the viability of day-care centers as educational institutions for young children. In 1925 the ministry modified its regulations to allow kindergartens to become more like day-care centers. The new rules authorized greater flexibility in curriculum, a larger maximum enrollment, longer operating hours, and infant care.

Just as rising awareness of ideas about mothers' special role in child-rearing had not undermined Japanese receptivity to day-care in the first half of the Taishō era, neither did it do so in the second half of the period. The sternest criticisms leveled by prominent experts such as Ogawa Shigejirō and Takada Shingō went no further than calling day-care a "necessary evil," and both continued to recommend expansion of Japan's child-care facilities during the 1910s and beyond. Neither they nor Namae and Tokunaga harped on the faults of day-care. Also conspicuously absent are lengthy discussions of the harm to infants caused by daily separation from their mothers or the superiority of nurturing by the mother at home as compared to institutional care. In contrast, as the twentieth century progressed, U.S., French, German, and English child protection experts increasingly stressed the irreplaceable role of mothers in the nurturing of children. Western experts dismissed day-care centers as at best a necessary evil and instead recommended other types of child welfare institutions—mothers' pensions, milk depots, mother-child clinics, nursing rooms in factories, and motherhood education programs—that promoted maternal care of infants. Support for day-care strengthened only in the face of dire circumstances, for example, the need to mobilize women for wartime production. In the West, conventional wisdom held that the benefits of reduced infant mortality due to maternal care of young children outweighed the advantages of providing economic aid and moral education to the urban poor, the primary Japanese motivations for supporting day-care.[2]

In order to explain the seeming paradox of day-care in Japan—steady expansion of facilities and positive attitudes toward institutional child-care despite the diffusion of unfavorable viewpoints—this chapter scrutinizes late Taishō (1920s) changes in experts' views, adult programs, center regulations, and the behavior of urban lower-class mothers. These reveal shifts in arguments for day-care and views of motherhood as well as the strength of their appeal to leaders in the day-care field, rank and file workers at child-care facilities, and lower-class urban parents who entrusted their children to the centers.

Namae Takayuki and the New Views of Motherhood

New rationales for day-care appeared in the writings and speeches of Namae during mid-Taishō and remained in his writings throughout the pre-World War II era. After serving as the first director of KSKH, Namae rose to national prominence as a relief and child welfare expert after his appointment in 1909 to the Local Affairs Bureau of the Home Ministry. Although a commissioned employee (*shokutaku*) rather than a lifetime bureaucrat, Namae regularly spoke on relief and child protection at Home Ministry relief symposia held throughout Japan. In 1919 he served as Japan's official representative to the White House Conference on Children in the United States, an indication of his stature as a top child welfare expert. In 1921 he became a professor in Japan's first social work department at Japan Women's College (Nihon Joshi Daigakkō)[3] in Tokyo and continued to lecture widely and to publish numerous articles and books concerning child protection and social work.[4]

As the late Taishō era progressed, a new theme arose in Namae's justifications for day-care centers. During his tenure as director of the Kobe child-care centers (*hokanjo*) at the time of the Russo-Japanese War and of the exemplary KSKH facilities (*hoikujo*) established after that war, the institutional regulations and organizational records had not described these day-care projects as institutions to assist working mothers, despite the fact that female-headed families comprised the great majority of the *hokanjo* and *hoikujo* users.[5] Nor had Namae defended day-care as assistance to working mothers in "Taisei ni okeru kyūji jigyō" (Child relief work in the West), an article appearing in 1909 in the second issue of *Jizen* (Charity), organ of the newly-founded Chūō Jizen Jigyō Kyōkai (Central Charitable Work Association). Rather, Namae contended that in the West, "the concentration of the poor in cities, the imbalance of supply and demand for labor, and household economic difficulties calling for both husband and wife to work . . . are the reasons why *hoikujo* become necessary."[6]

Namae argued that industrial Japan needed day-care projects and specified many benefits that would result from their establishment. Urban working-class families, he wrote, gave little consideration to the education (or cultivation, *kyōyō*) of their children. Assuming that the child makes the man, Namae reasoned that undisciplined lower-class children would grow up to be intractable adults. In order to mitigate the harmful social conditions surrounding poor children, Namae recommended that the handful of existing Japanese child-care facilities be increased in number, and he also proposed that local authorities operate day-care centers, or at least provide financial assistance to such facilities. After his initial appeal for a substantial broadening of the nation's network of day-care facilities, Namae went on to list six advantages child care would bring to Japan: 1) education of the enrolled children; 2) home improvement (*katei kairyō*); 3) increased production (*seisan no zōka*); 4) a decrease in the infant mortality rate; 5) the prevention of poverty; and 6) aid to deceased veterans' children.[7] In closing, Namae argued that prevention of poverty and the rescue of children constituted pressing social issues in Japan and called for Japanese to cultivate a spirit of charity (*jikei*) and relief (*saisei*), which would stimulate the founding of day-care centers as well as other types of relief and benevolent institutions in Japan.

In his 1909 article Namae had considered the benefits of day-care for children, their homes, and the nation, but had not specified advantages for mothers alone. Four out of six of Namae's benefits—education, home improvement, reduced infant mortality, and special aid to veterans' offspring—would improve children's lives, and three of these four—education, home improvement, and aid to veterans' children—promised to better family life as well. Namae thus could assert that greater productivity would raise family income and contribute to the prevention of poverty, because the earnings of factory operatives and home-workers were wholly or partly based on piece rates.

According to Namae, the nation as a whole stood to gain much from establishment of day-care. By educating lower-class children, improving home life, decreasing infant mortality, increasing production, and preventing poverty Japan would nurture upright, healthy citizens, increase economic output, and diminish relief expenditures, thereby hastening her development into a first-class nation (*ittōkoku*). As presented by Namae, day-care offered something for everyone, from needy urban children and their parents to humanitarians, educators, social reformers, patriots, industrialists, and government officials. While a mere listing of advantages could not block the genesis of opposition to day-care, presenting a large number of potential benefits, particularly many for the nation as a whole, blunted criticism of institutional child care. Significantly, Namae offered not a single disadvantage, giving opponents of child-care centers no opening for attack.

Six years later, however, a new awareness of gender differences began to appear in Namae's arguments for institutional child care. In 1915, in "On Day-Care Work," published in the Osaka relief journal *Kyūsai kenkyū* (Research on relief), Namae again linked the need for child care to the prevention of poverty, one of the evils of modern civilization, but in contrast to his earlier assertions that day-care helped working parents, for the first time Namae argued that day-care assisted *mothers* with their occupations:

> As the struggle for existence becomes harsher, the number of losers and unfit suffering from livelihood difficulties increases. Both husband and wife in many impoverished families must work as serious livelihood difficulties are an evil frequently accompanying the civilization of today. . . . [Under

these conditions], children under school age become a nuisance and inter-fere with work. It becomes easier for mothers to work if they can entrust their children to day-care.[8]

Thus by 1915, rather than emphasizing that day-care enabled guardians or par-ents of both sexes to earn income, Namae contended that child-care centers freed mothers for paid employment, although he recognized that both parents in poor households needed to work. The assertion that day-care assisted mothers and their paid employment in households with two working parents illustrates Na-mae's shift toward a view that mothers had primary responsibility for rearing children. However, as before, Namae continued to acknowledge the benefits of hard work and increased productivity for both the household economy (and therefore for children) and society.

During late Taishō Namae continued his retreat from presenting institu-tional child care as an aid to parents regardless of gender or to the household as an economic unit and showed signs of emphasizing its advantages to mothers and children. In the chapter on child protection work (*jidō hogo jigyō*) in his clas-sic 1923 textbook, *Shakai jigyō kōyō* (Outline of social work),[9] Namae defined "the major purposes of day-care" as

> 1) protection of mothers (*hahaoya no hogo*) and 2) protection of children (*jidō no hogo*). In the first instance, child care frees mothers from involvement with their children when they engage in work at home or outside the home. It allows mothers to labor with peace of mind and furthermore it increases their labor efficiency, which raises their income. As for the second instance, day-care gathers infants and toddlers . . . during the day and provides them with appropriate care and education in place of their mothers.[10]

Here, as before, Namae discussed the advantages of day-care for mothers pri-marily in terms of their work performance—ease of mind on the job and higher earnings. Examination of the revised edition of his book, published in 1933, re-veals that in the early Shōwa period, Namae's views of the purpose of institu-tional child care had not changed.[11]

Tokunaga Yuki's Views on Motherhood, Feminism, and the Logic of Day-Care

The arguments for day-care of Tokunaga Yuki (1887–1973), director of Futaba Yōchien from 1910 until her death,[12] also underwent a transformation during the Taishō era—one more sweeping than that of Namae's. The establishment of a refuge for mothers and children at Futaba Yōchien in 1922 illustrates the extent to which Tokunaga had developed a special concern for their protection, a belief that led her to found new programs in addition to daytime child care and evening parent meetings during the 1920s. The new conceptions of motherhood that assumed mothers should be the primary providers of care to young children infused Tokunaga's justifications for day-care and other child welfare programs. Yet at the end of the Taishō era, she continued to defend day-care. By 1925 institutional child care served not simply as a means of improving the finances and character of the poor, but also as a means of freeing middle-class women to engage in educational and socially useful activities outside the home. Although Tokunaga did not publish prolifically, she presented her views concerning the operation, programs, and benefits of day-care facilities to a steady stream of ordinary and eminent visitors who toured Futaba Yōchien (Futaba Hoikuen after 1916) and to child protection workers, social work professionals, and members of the general public who attended her lectures in various parts of the country.[13]

When considered from a present-day perspective stressing the need for equal participation of father and mother in child-rearing, Tokunaga's simultaneous embracing of the special nature of the mother-child bond and a feminist impulse, a desire to promote women's social participation in affairs outside the home—self-cultivation and community service for middle-class women and wage labor for lower-class women—may seem contradictory. However, studies suggest that in nineteenth- and twentieth-century Japan and Western nations such as the United States and France, many individuals and movements seeking changes in women's situations have assumed women's difference from men, including women's primary responsibility for the home as wives and mothers.[14] Thus some individuals and movements that accepted women's domestic destiny enlarged the range of female activities, but they did so in order to strengthen their positions as members of or advocates for collectives to which they belonged—families, communities, or nations—rather than to seek participation in new activities or other changes for women in their own right. That is, it must be kept in mind that arguments grounded in women's difference are not necessarily incompatible with quests for change in the norms and roles of womanhood, including egalitarian assumptions and demands.[15]

While evidence concerning Tokunaga's early views on day-care and motherhood is scarce, from childhood her intellectual boldness was striking. Encouraged by her older brother, she converted to Christianity as a child and maintained her faith despite the continuing taunts of other youngsters in the neighborhood. Despite her family's poverty, she convinced her father to allow her to continue her education beyond the primary level. But her hunger for knowledge extended beyond Christian education at church; she coveted lessons at Tokyo Prefecture Second Higher Girls' School (*Tōkyō Furitsu Daini Kōto Joshi Gakkō*). As a high school student, she read forbidden novels such as Christian socialist Kinoshita Naoe's *Hi no hashira* (Pillar of fire) and *Ryōnin no jiyū* (Freedom of a good person),[16] which encouraged involvement with social problems, and circulated them to classmates, including Yamakawa Kikue (1890–1980), who later became one of Japan's leading Marxist feminists.[17]

While still in high school, Tokunaga decided to devote her life to Christian good works among the poor. From growing up near Samegahashi, she mingled with "people who, no matter how hard they worked, were poor . . . [and] from living in such poverty, their hearts also became impoverished." Moved by their plight, Tokunaga chose to dedicate her life to "work that enriches the hearts of such wretches, which above all, reflects the glory of God." Overall, Tokunaga was more academically oriented, more serious, and less feminine in a conventional sense than other girls at the school who read only the assigned textbooks and skipped cooking lessons to huddle around entertaining magazines. Tokunaga's distinctive qualities earned her the unflattering nickname of "Father."[18]

Tokunaga's intellectual interests extended to feminism as well. After graduation Tokunaga held the famous late Meiji feminist, Hiratsuka Raichō (1886–1971), in great esteem. In 1915 she sent a gorgeous, expensive baby kimono to the impoverished, unmarried Hiratsuka, who was then pregnant by the man with whom she was living and was being hounded by the press. Tokunaga also collected all issues of Hiratsuka's feminist magazine, *Seitō* (Bluestocking), published from September 1911 to February 1916, except those banned by government censors, and kept a scrapbook of newspaper clippings on Hiratsuka's activities.[19]

After graduating from girls' higher school in 1908, Tokunaga became a full-time teacher at Futaba Yōchien, but she had previously worked as a volunteer there during the summer of 1907. Just two years after her initial appointment at Futaba Yōchien, the two founders, Noguchi Yuka and Morishima Mine, elevated her to the position of director (*shunin*). Mention of Tokunaga is scant, and the annual reports are virtually the sole source of information concerning Tokunaga's ideas during her early career. Yet continuity in the discussions of motherhood and day-care goals in the 1908–1910 yearbooks suggests either that her early views in these matters were similar to those of Noguchi[20] or that, if Tokunaga's views differed from those of the two founders, they were not printed in the annual reports.

Although Tokunaga's great admiration for the unconventional, outspoken Hiratsuka demonstrates a capacity for thinking that must have differed from Noguchi's, there are compelling reasons to believe that her ideas about day-care and motherhood at this time had much in common with those of her mentor. First, as Protestant converts, both Noguchi and Tokunaga had doubtless been influenced by turn-of-the century Western ideals of Christian womanhood that stressed the uniqueness of the bonds between mother and child. And the feminist ideas of Hiratsuka that Tokunaga admired were not incompatible with Christian views of womanhood. Influenced by Ellen Key's writings, Hiratsuka asserted that motherhood should be the center of women's existence and that the state should protect mothers, who performed work indispensable to society as the bearers and rearers of the next generation. Second, it is likely that the ideals of Noguchi, a highly intelligent, well-educated Christian woman and head of one of the most prestigious kindergartens in Japan, must have had considerable influence on Tokunaga, fresh out of school with little experience in education or child protection work when she became a full-time teacher at Futaba Yōchien.[21] Finally, while Noguchi would not have appointed Tokunaga, who had only two years of full-time teaching experience, over senior teachers to the position of director had she not trusted Tokunaga's judgment and abilities, it seems unlikely that Noguchi would have selected such a young, inexperienced director if Tokunaga's views had differed radically from her own.

By 1914, four years after her appointment as director, there are indications that Tokunaga was becoming firmly established as a leader in her own right at Futaba Yōchien. Her name appeared for the first time alongside Noguchi's and Saitō's (Morishima's married name) at the end of "Shiritsu Futaba Yōchien Kakuchō Shuisho" (Expanded statement of purpose of Futaba Private Kindergarten), the final section of the annual report that year.[22] Yet when compared with the reports of 1909 and 1910, the 1914 annual report reveals no major shift in objectives, programs, or justifications for child care. Furthermore, there is virtually no difference between the 1914 and 1900 statements of purpose. The 1900 statement presented day-care at Futaba Yōchien as a boon to children and both parents rather than to mothers alone. The 1914 expanded statement of purpose reiterated those aims: "to save children from their environment and to educate them" and to "remove children from underfoot and let parents ply their trades with ease."[23]

However, in subsequent years Tokunaga transformed Futaba Yōchien from a pauper's kindergarten emphasizing the moral education of poor parents and preschool children into Futaba Hoikuen, a pair of day-care centers offering a panoply of social services to a broad range of slum residents. Changing the name to Futaba Hoikuen in July 1916 removed the center from the nominal jurisdiction of the Ministry of Education and placed it under the authority of the Home Ministry as a social project (*shakai jigyō*).[24] Under Tokunaga, Futaba also entered an era of expansion. In June 1916 a second center, the Shinjuku branch, opened. By the following year total enrollment stood at 393 children—265 at the Samegahashi center and 128 at the new facility. In addition, new programs serving older children and adults—a paupers' elementary school (1918), afterschool day-care (1919), a children's library, evening sewing classes, a refuge for mothers and children, an evening medical clinic, a wholesale market (all in 1922), and a meal distribution program (1927)—proliferated at the Shinjuku branch after the middle of the Taishō period.[25] The founding of these programs confirmed Futaba Hoikuen's shift from primarily focusing on the education of poor preschool children and their parents to emphasizing social and relief work with a broader spectrum of the local community, including infants under three, school-aged children, and adults without children who needed food or medical care. After 1922, then, Futaba Hoikuen functioned much like a settlement.[26]

Examination of the events and ideas surrounding the establishment of the women's and children's shelter provides valuable insights into Tokunaga's views of motherhood in the 1920s. As director of Futaba Hoikuen, Tokunaga must have supported the decision to found the refuge (*Haha no Ie,* literally, Mothers' House), because its creation involved a major shift in the utilization of existing resources.[27] The space for day-care shrank by almost 50 percent when one of the two classroom buildings was converted into eight large and two small family apartments for the refuge. The Mothers' House provided housing and employment for mothers impoverished by widowhood, divorce, or separation from their husbands. Its establishment was grounded in assumptions about women's differences from men—mothers' special relationships with their children and the need to preserve that precious bond. While the Mothers' House was established for the "protection of families," a phrase that would seem to permit the sheltering of both fatherless and motherless families, a later passage in the report clearly stated that the Mothers' House aimed to assist female-headed households only:

> The purpose of the *Haha no Ie* is to encourage women's independence and self-sufficiency. Despite experiencing poverty and loneliness, mothers depend on their children and children on their mothers in order to live under adverse circumstances safely, happily, and with hope.[28]

The goal of the Futaba Hoikuen women's shelter was to help single mothers stand on their own two feet—psychologically and economically—after voluntary or involuntary separation from their husbands. In this difficult endeavor, the bond between mother and child glimmered like a ray of sunshine, a precious resource for the desperate female-headed families who sought refuge in the Mothers' House. However, this logic acknowledged neither a similar tie between father and child nor similar needs on the part of single fathers. Thus the Mothers' House excluded single fathers, although jobless, homeless men living with children might have been as overwhelmed as destitute women by the twin responsibilities of income earning and child-rearing. Thus the founding of the Mothers' House contrasted with Futaba Yōchien's original purposes. In 1900 Noguchi and Morishima, women of a previous generation, aimed to assist fathers *and* mothers in educating and nurturing their offspring, but under Tokunaga, Futaba Hoikuen commenced a project assisting only mothers and children.

It is likely that the work of the Christian Women's Reform Society (Kyōfūkai) in rescuing women from licensed and unlicensed brothels inspired the establishment of the Mothers' House. Before founding the refuge Tokunaga reluctantly referred homeless, destitute women with children to the Jiaikan, a project that aimed to rescue women from prostitution, but she thought it unsuitable for young single women or former housewives with children. The conviction that families headed by ordinary women needed a separate shelter seems to have spurred Tokunaga to start the Mothers' House.[29]

Given Tokunaga's admiration for Hiratsuka and her acquaintance with Yamakawa, the intense debates involving Hiratsuka, Yamakawa, Yosano Akiko (1878–1957), and Yamada Waka (1879–1957) may also have influenced Tokunaga's decision to found the Mothers' House. The motherhood protection debates (*bosei hogo ronsō*), which took place from January 1916 to January 1919, exposed Tokunaga and many other educated women to a wide variety of perspectives on the social importance of motherhood, women's and children's needs, and the means to satisfy those needs.[30]

Within three years after the close of the motherhood protection debates, Tokunaga had drawn up plans and secured financial resources to take concrete action to protect mothers and children. However, Tokunaga's conceptions of motherhood protection did not closely resemble those of any of the four major figures in the debate. She was less optimistic about the strengths of individual women than Yosano. In Tokunaga's view, not all women could achieve independent livelihoods through individual efforts alone; some women, especially those suddenly faced with the need to support themselves and their children, required assistance from others to achieve this end. Nor did she envision women retreating to the home to rear children as their major contribution to society, as Hiratsuka advocated in the debates; rather, Tokunaga welcomed women's wider social participation in employment, relief work, and cultural activities. Unlike Yamakawa, Tokunaga did not insist that motherhood protection could be brought about only by revolution, yet in contrast to Yamada, she did not wholeheartedly support "good wife, wise mother" (*ryōsai kenbo*), the state's ideology of womanhood promoting female devotion to the domestic arts of household management and child-rearing.[31] Evidence for Tokunaga's stance derives from analysis of the circumstances under which women entered the Mothers' House. Over the years, the Mothers' House sheltered not only widows and women deserted by their husbands, but also admitted mothers (and even single childless women) who had abandoned their homes to live as they pleased rather than persuade or force them to return home to live as obedient wives or daughters. In these instances, the Mothers' House operated as a refuge for some women who chose to escape the confines of the male-dominated household (*ie*).[32]

In the early Shōwa period, Tokunaga explicitly linked the Mothers' House to motherhood protection in "Takujisho no shimei" (The purpose of day-care centers), a 1927 address to the Niigata Prefecture Social Work Association. She explained that the Mothers' House sprang "from a heart concerned with the happiness of children and from considering the protection of motherhood."[33] Tokunaga continued to present the Mothers' House as an institution for women and children rather than a facility benefiting men or bolstering family life in general and to assume that a special bond existed between mothers and their children—an assumption that accented women's differences from men.

However, the Niigata speech also revealed a striking shift in Tokunaga's ideas concerning the purposes of day-care, one that articulated a desire to equalize male and female social participation in the public world—that is, an egalitarian impulse. Tokunaga's novel views of the utility of institutional child care for urban middle-class and farm women appeared alongside standard arguments aimed at the urban poor that had been employed since the founding of Futaba Yōchien in 1900. Tokunaga contended that

[i]n cities, day-care centers are essential in areas where the needy are concentrated. To assist family life, to save young children from a fearful environment, to uplift and improve the locality, even a little bit [is the purpose of day-care centers]. In industrial areas, they are needed to watch children [in place of] of mothers during daytime working hours. They are

necessitated by many other circumstances, such as the busy seasons in agricultural areas. And some sort of temporary, mobile day-care centers are becoming necessary for busy mothers of the intellectual classes (*chishiki kaikyū*) who seek to absorb new knowledge at lectures and seminars.[34]

Thus by the end of the Taishō era Tokunaga's vision of potential users for institutional child care had broadened. No longer did centers need to limit themselves to offering assistance to families of the urban poor; day-care could be of use to busy rural mothers as well as to middle-class wives who ventured out of their homes for education rather than employment. Tokunaga extended care to leisured, middle-class women in support of female intellectual and cultural endeavors. This vision and the rationale for the Mothers' House, then, confirm Tokunaga's feminist leanings. Of greater significance for the study of day-care, her broadened view of the refuge's mission transformed child care from a means of assimilating the urban lower classes into a tool to help middle-class women expand their horizons, because only mothers in prosperous families had the money and leisure to attend lessons and lectures. In offering support to middle-class women's efforts at self-cultivation, Tokunaga generated another new justification for day-care, one that verged on openly challenging the state's "good wife, wise mother" ideology of womanhood.

Late Taishō Changes in Adult Programs

Changes in the adult program at Ishii Kinen Aizenen (Ishii Memorial Aizenen, hereafter Aizenen),[35] the successor to Aizenbashi Hoikujo, also reflect the influence of new conceptions of motherhood.[36] Due to generous funding from Kurashiki City textile magnate Ōhara Magosaburō, Aizenen carried on the diverse activities of its predecessor—a day-care program, an evening elementary school, and a lecture series for adults—and added new programs as well—a children's library, a social problems research project, and an institute to train day-care teachers. However, after 1918 there were two separate programs for infants and toddlers—a day nursery for children under two and a "kindergarten" for children ages two to six. The program for older preschoolers was in reality a day-care center, because its emphasis was on care as well as education of the children of working parents for seven hours each day, operating hours that far exceeded those permitted to kindergartens under the 1899 Ministry of Education regulations.[37]

The establishment of a separate program for mothers at Aizenen suggests that staff awareness of gender differences, or at least teachers' willingness to reshape activities according to gender considerations, had heightened around

Children and teachers in the playground of the Ishii Kinen Aizenen Foundation facility, circa 1920. Courtesy of Ohara Institute for Social Research, Hosei University.

1920, because the new mothers' meetings (*haha no kai*) were premised on two distinctions—one between mothers and the general public and another between the knowledge required by mothers and that needed by the public at large. That is, assumptions that mothers bore special responsibilities for the care of young children and that mothers alone (rather than both mothers and fathers or all adult members of the community) should be informed of new ideas of child-rearing underlay both the name and content of the new adult program.

Originally, parents' or guardians' meetings had not been held at Aizenen or its predecessor. Instead, Aizenen had offered lectures to the general public on topics ranging from hygiene (*eisei*) and child-rearing (*ikuji*) to morality (*dōtoku*), public morals (*fūki*), arts and sciences (*gakujutsu*), and current affairs (*jiji mondai*). Of course, the parents and guardians of pupils were welcome to attend, but the lectures were open to anyone who wished to listen.[38] However, by 1920 the staff had created a separate mothers' association, and its purpose was "improvement and progress of the home life of proletarians (*musansha kaikyū*, literally, propertyless class) in the neighborhood," with lecture topics directly related to family life—child care, hygiene, and morals—rather than the diverse subjects discussed in the general lecture series.[39] This shift parallels the segregation of child care and home management topics from national and international political

news in magazines for intellectuals, Christians, and the aspiring middle-class between the 1880s and 1910s analyzed by Kazue Muta, although the Aizenen
changes began later and continued into the 1920s.[40]

In contrast to Aizenen's earlier lecture program, the new mothers' association
vested mothers (as opposed to fathers, mothers-in-law, fathers-in-law, the entire
family, or the community) with responsibility for uplifting home life. Furthermore, excluding discussions of broader political, economic, and cultural trends
and providing information only on domestic topics at the mothers' meetings suggests that the staff assumed a mother's world was limited to the home and that
mothers did not need to acquire knowledge about general, national, or global affairs. Conversely, although detailed information regarding changes in the content
of the general lecture series is not available, to the extent that child-rearing and
household management disappeared from the general lecture series, the specialization of mothers in domestic matters would have been further reinforced. In
1926 the format of the mothers' meeting expanded to include practical instruction in cooking and sewing as well.[41] The establishment of the mothers' association in addition to the existing public lectures suggests that by late Taishō
Aizenen director Tomita Zōkichi and his staff had come to regard child care and
the well-being of the home as the special and limited domain of mothers.

New attitudes toward motherhood also influenced programs at other day-
care centers founded after the middle of the Taishō period. Most of the new centers holding evening programs for parents called them "mothers' meetings."
Analysis of the adult programs at fifty-four child-care centers established between 1915 and 1924 reveals that 38.9 percent of them held mothers' meetings
or mother-older sister meetings, while 35 percent offered no regular parent programs at all. Parents' meetings, guardians' meetings, and father-older brother
meetings (*fukei kai*) were established by only 24.1 percent of the centers founded
during that decade.[42] A comparison of middle and late Taishō trends in the naming of adult programs shows that 46 percent of the child-care centers in the 1918
sample held regular guardians', father-older brother, or parents' meetings, which
suggests expectations of male participation. Less than a decade later, in 1925,
the proportion of institutions sponsoring such meetings had fallen to 24 percent,
while mothers' and mother-older sister meetings constituted nearly 40 percent
of adult programs, up from 30 percent in 1918. Private child-care centers—for
example, Aikoku Fujinkai Takujisho, Kōbokan, and Aomori Hoikuen, founded
in 1924, 1919, and 1920, respectively—held mothers' meetings, in contrast to
newly founded public day-care centers (see the following section), which tended
to offer evening programs for guardians rather than exclusively for mothers.

The Unchanging Logic of Regulations

Although new attitudes toward motherhood influenced experts' publications and speeches as well as adult programs at day-care centers during the 1920s, as in earlier years such attitudes had little impact on one crucial aspect of institutional child-care—the regulations and statements of purpose that established centers' goals, programs, personnel, and basic operating procedures. Despite renowned child protection experts' increasing emphasis on child-care centers as institutions designed to help working mothers, the regulations of new and previously established centers generally failed to distinguish by gender the adults who enrolled their children. The regulations continued to refer to parents in gender-neutral terms such as guardians and laborers, because in late Taishō the older orientation toward improving family livelihood and educating children predominated in the goals of the new networks of public day-care centers founded in the great cities of Tokyo, Kyoto, and Kobe,[43] and in the aims and thus the charters of private centers as well.

As we have seen, regulations defined key aspects of centers' operation—eligibility, enrollment and withdrawal procedures, fees, hours, holidays, personnel, staff responsibilities, and organizational structure—and they sometimes specified goals, finances, children's activities, adult programs, and other services as well. In a way, it is not surprising that little reference was made to mothers in the articles discussing eligibility, enrollment, and withdrawal, because besides mothers, the regulations needed to allow fathers, other relatives, and foster parents to register children for care. However, in composing the sections describing center purposes and parent programs, writers had greater discretion. Although they could have presented day-care centers as an aid to working mothers or their livelihoods, in nearly all instances they clung to the late Meiji day-care purposes of helping laborers, parents, or guardians; assisting family livelihood; and caring for young children—which were premised on old rather than new conceptions of mother-child relationships.

For example, the 1921 Kyoto municipal day-care center regulations were clearly informed by older justifications for child care. Article one stated that "[t]he purpose of the *takujisho* is to increase the labor efficiency of the children's guardians and families. Moreover, they plan for care of children under six and home improvement (*katei kaizen*)." Furthermore, if a parent or guardian behaved inappropriately, the youngster would be cut off from care. "Care will be refused under the following circumstances: . . . 2) When it is judged that the child's guardian or family is lazy at work or is habitually extravagant."[44] There

Teachers leading group play outside at a public child-care center, Tsuru-machi No. 2 Day-Care Center, an Osaka municipal facility, circa 1920. Regarding the Osaka municipal centers, see note 41. Courtesy of Ohara Institute for Social Research, Hosei University.

is no hint that the founders of the Kyoto municipal child-care facilities viewed day-care as assistance to working mothers in particular. Rather, the Kyoto city regulations hoist the old standards of improving productivity, increasing income, and helping guardians and families.

Nor did the Tokyo municipal day-care facilities emphasize assistance to working mothers. Tokyo's first public day-care centers, called *takujiba,* were founded in 1921. Their regulations (*kitei*) admitted needy "city residents' children between 6 months old and school age," while the Users' Creed (*Takujisha Kokoroe*) cited two reasons for denial of care: "when the guardian does not zealously work" and "when the director judges that care is not necessary." Care was also refused if the center had reached maximum enrollment, if the child was ill, or if the child was judged likely to be a bad influence on the other pupils. Finally, the article concerning the adult program stated that "[g]uardians' meetings will be held once a month."[45] The language of the regulations strongly suggests that Tokyo, like Kyoto, did not found its child-care facilities primarily to help mothers.

The late Meiji logic of raising productivity and household income also infused the regulations of the five public day-care centers founded between 1922 and 1928 in several cities in Fukuoka Prefecture, far to the west of Kyoto and Tokyo. The Omoda City Day-Care Center (*takujisho*) began taking in children in a poor area in 1928, just after the end of the Taishō era. Its purpose was "to make it convenient for residents to earn a living." Staff members were instructed to "give attention to the balanced development of minds and bodies of the young children enrolled, to cherish them, and to think constantly of improving the work efficiency of those who entrust their children, by setting their minds at ease." The regulations of Hachiman City's two day-care facilities, founded in factory districts in 1925, indicate that here, too, child care aimed to promote lower-class parents'—not just mothers'—work: "Our city gathers and protects young children for the convenience of those residing here who engage in labor." The rules of the day-care centers in the other two Fukuoka cities presented similar arguments, as did those of the Kobe Municipal Day-Care Centers, established in 1923 in order to "care for the infants and toddlers of laborers."[46]

Furthermore, many private centers also stressed helping children, improving work, and uplifting family life rather than assisting mothers during late Taishō. In establishing a child-care project in 1926, Jikyōkan[47] staff members

Ryūsenji Day-Care Center, a Tokyo municipal facility. It was rebuilt as a ferro-concrete structure after the great Kanto Earthquake of 1923. Courtesy of Ohara Institute for Social Research, Hosei University.

desired to "protect the children of our residents who get underfoot and to encourage the livelihood of the residents doing piecework."[48]

Five out of the ten Buddhist and nonsectarian private centers in Fukuoka
Prefecture pursued similar goals—as one set of regulations stated, "to care for
children who hinder their parents' livelihood."[49] The regulations of three of the
five remaining private centers also reiterated the late Meiji rhetoric concerning
day-care goals: "to gather and protect young children for the convenience of
those residing in the city who engage in labor (*rōmu*)," "to take in and care for
young children of families having youngsters who hinder their occupation in order to ease their livelihood," and "to take in and care for young children for the
convenience of the family livelihood."[50]

Of course, regulations expressed the official views of cities, organizations, and
individuals who founded public and private day-care centers during the late
Taishō era. At all centers, but particularly at the public day-care facilities, officials, philanthropists, and child relief specialists strove to make institutional child
care appeal to a broad range of the population—both the lower-class families who
would use the centers and the powerful, wealthy individuals whose influence,
good will, and money helped sustain the centers. During the 1920s wholehearted
acceptance of new views of mother-child relationships still tended to be limited

Free play outdoors at Ryūsenji Day-Care Center, circa 1920. Courtesy of Ohara Institute for Social Research, Hosei University.

to a small number of Japanese who had encountered Western conceptions of womanhood through higher education or Christianity. Therefore, in order to maintain broad community support, most municipal and private day-care centers continued to ground their rationales in older views of womanhood, presenting themselves as institutions assisting poor or working-class preschoolers and their households, rather than as institutions operating primarily to help mothers.

While popular conceptions of child-rearing were still strongly influenced by early modern ideas, a glimpse into the day-to-day world of late Taishō child-care centers reveals that staff members, who ranged from helpers without formal training to teachers with certificates from higher girls' schools, held diverse views of center purposes and implictly of motherhood. Some teachers regarded their work as assistance to guardians, laborers, or livelihoods, while others asserted that their work eased the plight of working mothers. Itō Yamashika, a teacher at Futaba Takujiba, a Tokyo municipal day-care center in Honjo Ward,[51] aimed to help guardians, not just mothers. She described her work in this way: "[W]e rescued the children from bad habits and danger. Guardians could leave their beloved children without worrying, and be thankful to be able to work fully without children in the way."[52]

In contrast, Miwa Kiku at Ryūsenji Takujiba, another Tokyo municipal facility, recalled in an interview about her work as a teacher: "It was necessary to work together with mothers to educate the children. The teachers and mothers

Children and teachers doing an indoor lesson at Ryūsenji Day-Care Center. Courtesy of Ohara Institute for Social Research, Hosei University.

planned to keep in contact with each other. The teachers needed to listen to mothers' expectations, and mothers, to teachers' admonitions so that contradictions between center and home life would not develop." In Miwa's view the primary task of day-care was to work with preschoolers and their mothers; she did not consider it essential to consult fathers or other family members regarding home improvement or the children's development.[53]

As we have seen, the contention that day-care helped mothers continued to appear in articles and lectures by well-known day-care professionals and continued to influence the form of evening adult education programs; nevertheless, it had relatively little impact on the written regulations governing child-care centers. How can we explain the persistence of the old arguments for day-care during late Taishō? It seems quite likely that in order to maximize support for day-care among the general public and the lower-class parents whose children attended the centers, the regulations omitted new, unfamiliar views of motherhood that might arouse controversy or opposition.

At a glance, the idea of helping mothers' work does not seem to differ greatly from the old justifications of moral improvement and raising productivity. However, the new view of motherhood implied that child care and housekeeping alone, not productive work, constituted a woman's proper task, a potentially disturbing idea to many urban lower-class women and men and to significant numbers of progress-minded Japanese in the higher ranks of society. Such a view also clashed with the older view, discussed in chapter 2, which assumed that not only the mother, but older children and other adults in a household, would engage in child care and productive work for the sake of the household (*ie*). In the 1920s poor urban women needed to earn income through participation in piecework, family enterprise, or wage labor to make ends meet. And since lower-class men and women in both the city and countryside were accustomed to thinking of women as active participants in productive or income-earning labor, acceptance of new notions of motherhood demanded changes in attitudes and the conduct of daily life that they could not easily implement.[54] Thus the urban and rural lower classes were inclined to ignore or perhaps even resent the novel view of womanhood and the new arguments for child-care centers premised on it.

In contrast, more prosperous Japanese, especially the salaried classes, had less need for mothers' income and greater commitment to ideals of social and national progress. While patterns of new middle-class women's lives might change, if ordinary women lessened their participation in productive work to devote more time to child-rearing, not only would the income of lower-class households fall, but national productivity would also decline and social unrest and relief expenditures might increase. Educated Japanese, including many officials, concluded that their late-developing country could not insist that ordinary mothers abandon productive work to concentrate exclusively on domestic chores such as child-rearing and housekeeping.[55] Thus for the most part, regardless of personal sentiments among day-care professionals regarding motherhood, the old justifications continued to predominate in day-care regulations.

Motherhood in the Lower Classes

Despite the enthusiasm of leading child-care authorities and some rank-and-file staff members for new views of motherhood and its appearance in some experts' writings, during the 1920s there is little evidence that novel conceptions of motherhood had won acceptance among the urban lower-class parents who brought their children to day-care centers. Embracement of new notions of womanhood that disapproved of mothers' income earning work would not only have undermined poor urban parents' willingness to bring their children to day-care centers, but might have jeopardized the very existence of their households. In the absence of other materials, in order to recover center users' attitudes it is necessary to extract or extrapolate their views from sources written by middle-class professionals.

Inoue Teizō, author of several tracts on urban living conditions, found in 1922 that parents in urban lower-class districts still failed to groom and supervise their children and that child baby-sitters still shared infant care with mothers. He reported of one neighborhood: "Dirty children played guilelessly outside; all were undernourished. When I looked at the scene from a distance, it seemed like an earthly hell." In the Asahi-chō slum in Tokyo's Yotsuya Ward, home to a branch of Futaba Hoikuen since 1916, Inoue glimpsed child baby-sitters among the unkempt children roaming its narrow backstreets. In the Minami Senjū district, busy mothers had little time to devote exclusively to child-rearing. Inoue noted the harried state of mothers inhabiting the district: "Babies cried beside housewives (*okamisan*) with untidy hair who were working frantically at piecework." Here, the lack of housing amenities rendered cooking, bathing, and laundering difficult as families occupied rooms in wooden longhouses (*nagaya*) without artificial lighting, plumbing, water supplies, or kitchen facilities.[56]

During the 1920s the accounts of day-care staff stressed neglect of the physical aspects of child-rearing among urban poor families. Teachers noted that overall their pupils looked bedraggled, had health problems, and exhibited rough behavior. Parents and other caregivers had little time for child-care fundamentals such as washing, grooming, dressing, and feeding their infants and toddlers. While Inoue mentioned that children did not always receive proper meals, center teachers reported that children still frequently arrived in the morning with matted hair and grimy faces. Thus staff members began the day by washing faces, picking lice from hair, combing tangled locks, and clipping fingernails. As many children did not take baths at home, centers with ample budgets continued to include bathing facilities as standard equipment. And since most families could not afford medical care, nurses and visiting doctors regularly treated day-care pupils for trachoma and skin diseases.[57]

Regarding other aspects of the rearing of young children, teachers' accounts confirm Inoue's observation that mothers shared responsibility for the care of preschoolers with other household members, but they also suggest that parents at times attempted to discipline children rather than simply allowing them to run loose in the streets, as Inoue had reported. At Tokyo's Furukawabashi Hoikujo, teachers noted that siblings rather than mothers brought infants and toddlers to the day-care center:

> [T]hey come happily hand in hand with older brothers and sisters. . . . [W]e dress the hair of those with wild locks. We tell them to wash their faces in the morning, but many still come dirty, so we wash their faces for them.[58]

Teachers at Tokyo municipal centers criticized parents for inconsistency in child training, but did not accuse them of neglecting discipline altogether. They stated that while on the one hand, parents still indulged their young children by giving them allowances on demand and letting them play freely outside, on the other hand parents would yell at their offspring or punish them severely by beating, moxa,[59] or confinement in closets when irritated. According to the teachers, the oscillation between harshness and permissiveness produced tough, aggressive children who were difficult to control.[60]

A Tokyo social bureau report argued that children's characters were the result of the general slum environment as well as their coarse, unharmonious home life. "The children's mental outlook reflects the influence of their family and environment. They use rough language, quarrel, lack obedience, and are undisciplined."[61] Kuwahara Yotsu, a teacher working in Tokyo's Tomigawa district, concurred that children were tough, but noted that the younger ones at least were both fond of their parents and amenable to center training:

> I'm not sure about other day-care centers, but there are many wild children here. While some are playing house, others burst in and cause a ruckus. Or they follow other children and strike them from behind. . . . Being quick to quarrel is the outstanding characteristic of children here.

The small children, the three and four year olds, need a lot of attention when they first come to the center because they cry all day. Yet the bad habits of the little ones improve readily, while the bad habits of the ones near school age don't seem to get much better.[62]

These reports strongly suggest lower-class failure to conform to the emerging private ideal of middle-class womanhood—a full-time child-rearer and home-maker and scientific home manager—or to the state's ideal of "good wife, wise mother" carefully training future citizens.

Parental attitudes are difficult to measure, yet the available evidence does not suggest that lower-class parents' behavior or their attitudes regarding the rearing of young children had undergone a significant transformation by the 1920s. Higher incomes, a decline in married women's workforce participation, and higher rates of school enrollment created the possibility for mothers in the upper reaches of the urban lower class to devote greater attention to housework and nurturing children, but one detects virtually no signs of such behavior among the lower strata during the late Taishō period. It seems that new conceptions of motherhood or childhood that could have generated new child-rearing practices and opposition to mothers' employment and day-care found little acceptance among Japan's urban lower classes by the 1920s.

Implications for Day-Care Acceptance

In earlier chapters, I argued that early modern acceptance of a wide range of household members as caregivers for infants and toddlers facilitated Japanese acceptance of institutional child-care in the opening decades of the twentieth century. Despite these native attitudes, one would expect that as new conceptions of child-rearing emphasizing the essential role of the natural mother in upbringing gained acceptance, support for day-care would decline. However, this did not happen in prewar Japan, and it is interesting to consider why this was the case.

First, as we have seen, there were limits to the diffusion of new conceptions of the mother-infant bond. By late Taishō, the idea that infant care was the primary responsibility of mothers had gained substantial numbers of adherents among the educated classes who formulated policies and founded institutions, but it had not taken root among the urban lower classes who brought their children to day-care facilities. Also, an important sector of the day-care world, the supervisors of the new public child-care centers, dared not display too much sympathy for the new conception of motherhood as it potentially undercut state

goals of raising productivity, keeping relief expenditures low, and promoting national development. Overall, assumptions regarding caregivers to infants had
not changed enough to undermine support for day-care among important segments of the Japanese public.

Second, strong official support for day-care continued unbroken into the late
Taishō era and beyond. Despite increased attention directed toward relief programs for adults after the 1918 Rice Riots, the Home Ministry continued to
promote and finance programs for children. Programs for children continued to
be regarded quite favorably as preventive rather than ameliorative works. In
1923 the top five categories of social projects receiving Home Ministry funds
(*shōreikin*) were orphanages (35.4 percent), clinics (15.2 percent), day-care centers (12.9 percent), paupers' schools (7.8 percent), and reformatories (4.6 percent); child-welfare projects accounted for 60.7 percent of the total projects receiving awards. The awards for 1929 displayed the same pattern.[63] Clearly in
1930 the Home Ministry's Social Bureau continued to regard child-care centers
as indispensable social projects, and it continued to offer late Meiji arguments
in support of day-care centers, focusing on increasing productivity and household income rather than assisting mothers in caring for children:

> Daytime child-care projects do not simply give infants and toddlers healthy
> care; they also have the purpose of increasing the labor efficiency and im-
> proving the household. Recently, due to the development of industry and
> the concentration of laborers in cities, the need for this type of project is
> felt more and more keenly.[64]

Thus nationalism continued to play a key role in shaping Japanese receptivity to day-care, as concern for national economic development and the quality of future citizens that surfaced in late Meiji did not diminish during late
Taishō.[65] Despite decades of national achievement, during late Taishō local and
national officials (both relief specialists and others) as well as progress-minded
Japanese outside the government still judged that the nation could derive substantial benefits from institutional child care.

The view that proper attitudes would spur national productivity still contributed greatly to the appeal of day-care, as it had in the past. The arguments
that day-care would increase the economic productivity of families, workers, parents, and mothers and that child-care centers would properly educate youngsters
fit perfectly with this set of economic and moral concerns. For this reason, de-

spite some increased recognition of mothers' roles in child-rearing, regulations of late Taishō centers still harped on themes of boosting labor efficiency and helping family livelihood.

Social and political concerns also enhanced the appeal of day-care. Many members of the respectable classes were unnerved by the clamor of tenants and workers for influence in economic and political affairs in the 1920s. Although the precise content of the education that lower-class children would receive at day-care centers was not spelled out in the regulations, exemplary curricula at leading institutions such as Futaba Hoikuen, the KSKH centers, and Aizenen remained united in the goal of instilling hard work, thrift, cleanliness, and discipline—not only in young children, but in older family members as well. The centers stressed the importance of education, but they emphasized moral training and school attendance as obligations to the state more than learning as a means of upward occupational or social mobility. The late Meiji argument that day-care built good character still boosted the appeal of day-care centers in the age of impending universal suffrage. In addition, by preventing pauperism, day-care centers would undercut the social basis for the labor, tenant, and socialist movements, thereby contributing to political stability.

Yet the novel emphasis on helping mothers rather than on simply boosting productivity for the sake of nation, family, or children, seen most clearly in Tokunaga's ideas, may also reflect emergence of ideas that women existed as individuals rather than solely as daughters and mothers laboring for the family and that it was worthwhile for women to take part in activities outside the home. By the early Taishō era even conservatives had come to accept women's participation in philanthropy, relief work, and some aspects of education, while feminists pressed for women's rights to engage in wage labor and professional work, creative endeavors, and politics. At the close of the Taishō era female activists, including Tokunaga, invoked feminist notions of increasing women's social and cultural participation as a reason for creating day-care centers, in contrast to the statist aims of raising industrial or national productivity and maintaining the household, the bedrock of the imperial state.

The themes of productivity and moral training pervading discussions of institutional child care indicate that support for day-care in Japan did not hinge solely on views of who should care for children. On the other hand, the fact that assumptions antithetical to day-care were not deeply embedded in nineteenth-century Japanese conceptions of child-rearing, childhood, and motherhood encouraged Japanese to embrace day-care positively, with few misgivings and little ambivalence.

The rise of new conceptions of child-rearing and motherhood during the Taishō era, which made mothers' care central to the healthy nurturing of infants, added a new complexity to the issues involved in the Japanese acceptance or rejection of day-care. The late-developer context of Japanese nation-building that fostered concern for productivity, stability, and national strength worked against a wholehearted embrace of new mother-centered views of child-rearing. Throughout the period under study, substantial numbers of leading Japanese remained unequivocal supporters of day-care for the good of the society, state, or nation as much as for the benefit of households and children.[66]

Viewed from the perspective of the times, institutional child care still seemed to offer a tidy solution to the problems of urban poverty and national development, benefiting all interested parties—poor children and their families as well as the nation and society. The question of how smoothly this solution in fact accommodated the interests of the various parties is an important one, and it will be considered in the concluding chapter.

7

Conclusion

In this study I have explored two factors contributing to acceptance of day-care centers, new institutions providing both education and care to young lower-class children, in early twentieth-century Japan. In brief, the main factors were nineteenth-century child-care attitudes and practices and deep-seated nationalism. Nineteenth-century ordinary and elite child-rearing customs and practices help explain why Japanese did not reject institutional care for infants, but they cannot explain why child-care centers flourished in prewar Japan. As we have seen, desire for national progress took diverse forms in the period under study. Besides the development of constitutional politics and policies of capitalist industrialization, war, and empire building by bureaucrats, politicians, and industrialists, other public-minded individuals, including volunteers and professionals in charitable and relief work, also sought the national good. The discourses created by day-care proponents to introduce and justify institutional child care as well as the regulations and programs of individual day-care facilities linked their aims to pressing national issues such as the molding of a citizenry suited to the challenges of economic and imperial expansion and the amelioration of new social problems resulting from industrial and urban development. While day-care programs also attempted to accommodate the needs of lower-class children and parents, as perceived from a middle-class perspective, their justifications contained explicit and implicit benefits for society or the nation as a whole. In concluding, I will summarize the main arguments of this study and discuss some of the implications for Japanese studies and comparative women's history and gender studies.

Reprise

In the preceding chapters I have argued that two aspects of nineteenth-century child-rearing attitudes and practices fostered positive responses to day-care facilities when they initially appeared in Japan at the beginning of the twentieth century. The first was the willingness of all classes to assign the daily care of young children to kin and nonkin household members as well as to the birth mother. While an heir was necessary to maintain continuity, family values as practiced in daily life stressed hard work for the sake of the household and obedience to coresident in-laws rather than child-rearing or child-bearing as the essence of a young wife's role. The widespread practices of adopting children and placing them out for apprenticeship or training further illustrate Japanese tolerance for the rearing of children by persons other than their own mother and father. That is, children, even young ones, could be raised outside their natal households.[1] The widespread acceptance of nonmaternal caregivers assumed a second important aspect of child-rearing—a conception of child care in day-to-day life consisting of the relatively simple tasks of keeping a young child safe and well fed. The person who provided daily care for an infant or toddler was not necessarily responsible for socialization, that is, for the instilling of proper speech and manners and the transmission of social, vocational, and other knowledge. Thus nineteenth-century norms had not required that mothers be the primary providers of either care or education to children.

The goals and justifications of Japan's first day-care centers set the pattern for institutions founded later, in part because segments of the national bureaucracy, such as the Relief Section (later the Social Affairs Section) of the Home Ministry's Local Affairs Bureau and its successor, the Social Affairs Bureau, soon began to endorse day-care centers' aims, programs, and organization. Futaba Yōchien established moral education as a primary objective for Japanese day-care, while the KSKH centers placed greater emphasis on family economic assistance. For both the private centers established before World War I and the networks of municipal child-care centers founded after the 1918 Rice Riots, economic justifications had greater appeal than educational objectives; however, the fact that day-care professionals tended to regard moral improvement as a prerequisite to financial betterment minimized the tensions between these two objectives. Whether centers gave priority to educational or economic aims, they emphasized the transmission of a common core of values such as industry, savings, frugality, cleanliness, order, obedience to authority, and respect for formal education to lower-class pupils and their parents.

Many basic elements of the programs of later private and public centers, such as the children's curriculum, operating hours, low cost health care, snacks, and parent education meetings, followed the examples set by Futaba Yōchien and KSKH. Like KSKH, large, well-funded centers could offer a broad range of services, including dawn to dusk operating hours, meals, and baths. Futaba

Yōchien and the KSKH centers not only established models for subsequent centers, their aims and practices won approval for day-care among government officials, industrialists, and others from the upper ranks of society who could readily support values such as social stability and heightened economic productivity. For local elites and national leaders, arguments that child-care centers would promote social and national progress greatly enhanced the appeal of institutional child care.

Nationalism in Japan remained a substantial wellspring of support throughout the prewar era because day-care professionals continued to stress the social utility of day-care. However, the social and cultural context in which their proprosals were received shifted as changing conceptions of womanhood asserting the need for constant, close contact between the biological mother and her child began to displace older notions of motherhood and child-rearing, especially in the educated middle-classes. By the mid-1910s leading day-care experts seemed at the vanguard of those accepting the new views of motherhood. Yet contrary to what one might expect, the diffusion of novel conceptions of mothering did not undermine elite approval of institutional child care. Perhaps family need for the income earned by wives as pieceworkers, petty entrepreneurs, unpaid household labor, and wage workers in the households of millions of ordinary Japanese aligned with a national need for cheap labor, or the desire for economic growth fostered acceptance of the paid and unpaid productive labor of lower-class Japanese women. In other words, it is likely that strong household and national imperatives underlay the resilience of older views of motherhood among lower-class parents, day-care staff members, relief and social workers, public-spirited individuals, industrialists, and national and local officials. Thus from the mid-1910s the aims and programs of day-care centers reflected contradictory views of womanhood that coexisted in the larger society—older views of women as mainstays who contributed to household survival through hard work at both productive and reproductive tasks, and newer views of women as specialists in the nonremunerative domestic activities of child-rearing, cooking, cleaning, washing, sewing, and budgeting. The former notion tended to quell complaints about working mothers by middle-class specialists in early childhood education and relief work and accounted for the scarcity of language specifying the gender of the adult beneficiaries of day-care, but the latter undergirded the post-World War I trend of calling the adult programs "mothers," rather than "parents" meetings.

Thus despite the diffusion of new views emphasizing mothers' responsibility for infant care, support for institutional day-care did not decline in Japan during the 1920s and beyond. Government officials overseeing child-care facilities displayed little public receptivity to the new views of motherhood, and neither state nor private day-care professionals seem to have made major changes in the statements of purpose and bylaws during the 1920s. Nor did the parents of day-care pupils appear strongly to support the new views of motherhood. A style of child-rearing involving long hours of concentrated attention to only the nurturing of infants and toddlers was impractical for women in the lower ranks of society; lack of leisure time prevented them from providing more intensive care and instruction to their children. The families who actually used day-care, therefore, had reasons to remain sympathetic to its fundamental goals and programs.

Social Control

Day-care was largely a private, middle-class endeavor supported by government officials at the national, prefectural, and local levels. The involvement of social elites and the state raises the issue of social control. One might ask: to what extent did institutional child care operate as an agent of social control? How successful was institutional child care in persuading lower-class parents and children to adopt values and behavior useful to the middle-class professionals and bureaucrats who favored day-care? Conversely, one might also ask about the benefits of child-care centers from the lower-class point of view. What is certain is that the values taught at the day-care centers tended to coincide with those of bureaucrats, because the staff members were generally educated, middle-class professionals who shared many fundamental values with government officials. Both groups tended to favor industrialization, order, hygiene, education, and advancement of national progress and prestige.

Day-care teachers' efforts to impart values compatible with state goals have already been extensively discussed, but it is important to add that the middle-class teachers may have underestimated the diligence and discipline of the urban lower classes. The problems of the urban poor and working-class families may have stemmed as much from structural constraints such as low income, insecure employment, and poor housing as from lack of positive moral qualities. Moreover, although child-care proponents occasionally noted the low wages and long working hours endured by the day-care children and their families, the teachers' inclinations to focus on the moral failings of the poor overlooked the social origins of some of the problems. More to the point, one might ask whether the lower classes resented the harangues of middle-class intruders. There is not much evidence suggesting that the children and parents resented day-care teachings, although the deferential manner and financial constraints of the parents may have masked resentment, opposition, or resistance to the advice of the staff members.[2]

The available evidence[3] suggests that affection motivated parents to want to do well by their children, but that financial and time constraints prevented them from adopting teachers' advice concerning children's clothing, family nutrition, and child-rearing practices. For example, when given inexpensive alternatives, parents made changes in family diets. On the balance, then, it is likely that parents and children received some benefits, principally in the area of health, from contact with day-care centers. But there are few signs of long-term economic gains or thorough moral transformations of parents or children, because day-care centers do not appear successfully to have counteracted the social, economic, and cultural influences that shaped the daily existence and values of the urban lower classes. The limited focus of the day-care activity meant that whatever the intentions of the staff members and policymakers, the success of day-care centers as agents of social control was incomplete.

Class Differences in Changes in Motherhood, Childhood, and Child-Rearing

This study suggests the importance of considering class differences in analyzing social change in prewar Japan. In closing, I would like to venture a few generalizations about the relationship between child care, childhood, and motherhood in urban lower and upper classes, although at present these are still largely uncharted zones of Japanese social history. In proceeding, it is useful to consider the following two points. First, norms and attitudes may differ from actual behavior. In other words, the conduct of child care—treatment of children and the amount of time devoted to child care in the household division of labor—may change while attitudes do not. Conversely, attitudes may change in advance of behavior, or they may change while behavior does not. Second, ideas and behavior may vary by social class. For at least two reasons, then, it may be more useful to think that child care, childhood, and motherhood coexist in a loose set of relationships rather than in a rigid, tightly linked configuration.

I suggest that this set of flexible links between notions of childhood, motherhood, and childcare existed in the early modern period, and that although new notions of childhood and motherhood emerged in the modern era, they coexisted for decades with older views. In early modern Japan, a rather fluid internal division of labor allowed many different types of household members—fathers, grandparents, siblings, apprentices, and servants—to care for children, and standards of care were adequate but relatively undemanding. Although class differences in child care and childhood experiences existed in Japan before the Restoration, there was no strongly held conviction that children were weak, helpless, and in need of constant care and protection. Rather, early competence in children was valued; outside the upper classes, six- and seven-year-olds were called on to help with domestic and productive chores as well as to make financial contributions to the household. Infants received affection and protection from harm, but there was no concept that proper mental and psychological development depended on close ties with the mother. Furthermore, a separation between biological motherhood and caregiving existed in nineteenth-century Japan. Mothers did not necessarily provide daily care for the children they bore. Obviously, the absence of beliefs that only the mother could adequately rear children facilitated acceptance of nonmaternal child care inside and outside the home.

After the Restoration Japanese conceptions of childhood and motherhood slowly began to change; however, such ideas did not change at the same rate, and the pace of change also varied by class. The state played a leading role in the rise of new conceptions of childhood. When the government established compulsory education policies, it in effect defined children as students, which made them dependents rather than workers or earners valued for their economic contributions to the family. The need of ordinary families for children's labor at home and the income children could earn outside the home moved families to resist compulsory education, forcing the government to experiment with various policies to make education more palatable to the masses.

The diffusion of childhood as a dependent stage of life (in practice if not in conception) roughly paralleled families' acquiescence to the state's demands for school attendance. However, the government's major aim was not to remake families' conceptions of childhood; it sought compliance with the law in order to build a better citizenry. Therefore, to officials it did not matter that ordinary parents only grudgingly acknowledged the de facto lengthening of childhood. During the late Taishō period persistence of the old logic of childhood is clearly illustrated by the attitudes of small artisan families in Shitaya Ward, Tokyo. These lower-class (but not poor) families did not hesitate to make youngsters quit school to work in the family occupation in the middle of the final (sixth) year of primary school. If graduation had a symbolic meaning for them, it clearly did not override household labor or economic needs. And lower-class Shitaya parents still willingly apprenticed children to other small artisans and shopkeepers, rather than sending them on to higher schooling.[4]

As for motherhood, although some officials and enlightenment intellectuals introduced new ideas in the 1870s, bureaucratization and industrialization separating workplace and home did much to create a new division of labor among families of salaried workers—officials, teachers, journalists, clerks, managers, and technicians—in the cities. As in the case of childhood, it appears that practices of motherhood, and wifehood changed in advance of attitudes. And here, too, the role of the state is evident, although its role was at first indirect. Only at the turn of the century, when Ministry of Education officials made "good wife, wise mother" (*ryōsai kenbo*) the core of women's education, did the state make deliberate, large-scale attempts to reconfigure motherhood. As with changes in childhood, the diffusion of new ideas of womanhood proceeded unevenly among the lower and middle classes, for two main reasons. First, during the initial decade of the twentieth century, the introduction of "good wife, wise mother" began in the higher girls' schools, which poor girls rarely attended, and second, books, pamphlets, and magazine articles spreading new notions of womanhood had little circulation among lower-class women. Over time, however, as the literacy rate of nonelite women rose, they also began to read women's magazines.[5]

Womanhood, wifehood, and motherhood are neither static nor synonymous. As mentioned previously, "good wife, wise mother," the state's new ideology of womanhood, had new implications for women's roles as mothers. It lessened the stigma of inferiority that had justified limiting women's responsibility for child care during the Tokugawa era. Many officials in the modern state became willing to mobilize women for the strenuous efforts required to build a powerful industrial nation, although women were granted quite limited participation in the public spheres of government and economy.[6] If the unprecedented mobilization of women, which Ueno Chizuko calls the "nationalization of women,"[7] sprang in part from government officials' perceptions of the difficulties Japan faced in its quest for development, one might also say it was facilitated by a lessening of day-to-day male authority in growing numbers of households due to the separation of home and workplace in the modern economy.

Yet a certain degree of tension existed between the duties of a "good wife" and a "wise mother." A woman's task as "wise mother" was to train children to become industrious, patriotic citizens who would be useful to the nation-state. However, as a "good wife," a Japanese woman participated in productive and reproductive activities for the sake of the eternal household (*ie*). In nuclear families young wives were the sole managers, but in multigenerational households they obeyed their mothers-in-law until the senior generation retired. In the still-numerous merchant and farm families woman's labor involved participation in the family trade as well as housework and child-rearing. It is possible that the government's simultaneous injunctions to women to devote greater efforts to socializing their children and to increasing productivity operated as a speed-up of ordinary women's work.

Passages to Modernity: Home, Childhood, and Gender

Day-care centers can be seen as part of a diffuse movement to reform various aspects of Japanese life to suit the urban industrial age. The changes in family diet, clothing, and home budgets recommended by journalists, home economists, hygienists, doctors, and educators for middle-class families sprang from this spirit of innovation. The lectures on nutrition, hygiene, and child-rearing at the parent meetings of day-care centers also offered lower-class mothers and fathers the means to reshape home life in accordance with modern principles of domestic science, child study, medicine, and psychology. In the transition to the urban, industrial order, not only the economy and polity, but culture, including home life, had to be reconstructed in the name of civilization and national progress.

But Japan's transition to modernity after 1868 also involved changes in age and gender stratification. Although the state's objective was the formation of a new citizenry ready to engage in the affairs of an industrial, imperial nation, its compulsory education policies of the early 1870s also marked a giant step in the modern reconstruction of the child as student, future citizen, and consumer, in contrast to the early modern child as productive and reproductive laborer for a household and lifelong resident of a local community.

The reworking of gender proceeded more slowly and less clearly. By 1890 the state had denied women direct public roles as soldiers, voters, bureaucrats, and elected officeholders; however, it had not yet formulated for them a positive role for participation in the new nation-state. At the end of the nineteenth century one segment of the state, the Ministry of Education, resolved the issue by supporting "good wife, wise mother," an imprecise formulation asserting that private domestic labor in the home would be women's indirect contribution to the common good. However, some early twentieth century official discourses on womanhood endorsed restricted public roles for women. The conspicuous role of the empress in philanthropic work indicates state support for a voluntary role for women in the fields of charity, patriotic, and relief or social work. And two Home Ministry policies—its unwavering support for day-care and its commendations to women who supported their households when others could not—suggest that, more than the Ministry of Education, the Home Ministry favored retention of women's productive labor.[8] Ironically, it can be said that in remaking childhood, the prewar Japanese state succeeded at a task it had not intended to undertake. The greater irony is that while the prewar state consciously attempted to reconstruct womanhood (and thus gender as well), it did not achieve notable consistency in its own ideologies or practices, much less compel the majority of women to weave its discourses into the center of their daily lives.

Like the other institutions of socialization and care, day-care centers were involved in the complexities of reconstructing age and gender in the modern age, and they were implicated in the state's endeavors. As private institutions, the goals and programs of most child-care facilities in the first three decades of the twentieth century fostered values and behavior that tended to advance state aims and policies. Clearly, they supported state policies regarding children. As municipal institutions, child-care centers acted as an arm of local government in attempting to mold not only children but also their parents into diligent, thrifty, productive citizens, and most private centers did likewise. Furthermore, private and public child-care centers assisted the diffusion of modern conceptions of the child as student and dependent by unambiguously aligning themselves with the state's compulsory education policies. While it could be argued that obligatory education undermined the work ethic, the state chose to defer children's participation in wage labor until after graduation in order to build the character and skills of its future citizens during the four to six years of compulsory schooling.

Regarding changes in notions of womanhood and gender, the role of child-care centers is less clear. On the one hand, women found full-time employment and occupied leadership positions in institutional child care during an age of limited opportunities for female influence in public affairs; most day-care employees were young, single, middle-class women. Since the government endorsed female participation in philanthropy and social work, women's activism as staff members, head teachers, and child welfare experts did not present a strong challenge to "good wife, wise mother." On the other hand, as wage earners outside household enterprises, especially in the case of married women who became veteran career employees and supervisors, female day-care professionals could be regarded as transgressors of the "good wife, wise mother" ideal.

Most day-care personnel were educated middle-class women; their influence on lower-class views of womanhood took place through informal parent-teacher contact when children were dropped off and picked up and during the parent meetings. After all, one of the main purposes of institutional child care was to safeguard preschool children while their parents worked. Offering long hours of care to assist women who worked in income-earning activities at home would not have offended supporters of either "good wife, wise mother" or female productivity, but day-care centers took in the children of women who worked outside the home as well. Centers did not, for example, distinguish between "good" women who labored at home and "bad" women who entered the wage-labor force. In fact, some facilities refused child care to women who were not employed, an endorsement of female productivity. In this respect, whether intentionally or not, child-care centers seemed closer to the Home Ministry's views of womanhood than those of the Ministry of Education. However, the shift from parents' or guardians' meetings to mothers' meetings and in some instances changes in the content of the adult programs suggest a rising emphasis on female domesticity, a stance that surely would have won the Ministry of Education's approval. In short, whether or not child-care professionals consciously tried to tailor their goals, programs, and operations to conform to official conceptions of womanhood, conceptions of gender in the day-care world reflected the inconsistencies of gender in early twentieth-century Japanese society.

The passage to modernity, then, involved more than simply the creation of new economic and political institutions; Japan's post-1868 transformation also generated changes in home life, childhood, and womanhood that have become invisible today. As Linda Nicholson has observed in the United States and Western Europe, in the evolution of modernity, the household, which once had been all—the fundamental social, political, and economic unit of society under control of a patriarchal head—gave way to a polity based on individual participation (and the gradual expansion of the electorate) and an economy dominated by production of goods in large, nonfamilial workplaces. Thus public and private "spheres" and the place of children, women, and men in them emerged during the modern era, as much by accident as by design.[9]

If we compare the evolution of gendered "public-private," "domestic-public," or "reproductive-productive" spheres[10] in Japan with that of other countries, it is evident that the rise of "good wife, wise mother" roughly parallels the emergence of female domesticity in England and republican motherhood in the United States and France.[11] Since monarchs, oligarchs, and political parties have comprised the major elements in the twentieth-century political system (except during World War II), an appropriate term for Japanese female domesticity might be "imperial motherhood," which calls attention to the nationalist motivations for its genesis and the infusion of nationalist aims into normative values and behavior for the female gender. In any case, a limited elevation of woman's status and a limited broadening of conceptions of her public influence took place under many self-consciously nationalist (and imperialistic) regimes embarking on a new course. The lessening conceptions of female inferiority, the emphasis on the education of women, and the homage paid to women as mothers of citizens or country stemmed from recognition of women's labor as mothers who influenced the fate of a nation by shaping the character of its future citizens. The endorsement of women's efforts in voluntary and professional charity and social work was also similar to that of Western nations, in part because Japanese writers and lecturers consciously drew on Western ideals and models in advocating these forms of public activity for women.

However, the differences are as striking as the similarities.[12] First, modern Japanese conceptions of womanhood more strongly affirmed women's productivity than did those of the United States, France, and Great Britain. While middle-class womanhood tended to be the normative standard in Japan as elsewhere, the industrious, frugal housewife rather than the elegant lady of leisure won the highest accolades, perhaps because of Japanese consciousness of the difficulties of trying to catch up to the industrialized, imperialist powers of the West. Second, the timing of changes in Japanese womanhood followed those of childhood, precisely the opposite of trends in the three Western nations. The changes in Japanese childhood stemmed from the state's compulsory education policies; thus social realities began to shift before conceptions of childhood altered. The reverse may have been true in the advanced Western powers. In Japan there was a predominance of state initiatives in the creation of new visions of womanhood, certainly in comparison with Great Britain and the United States, countries that preferred a weaker central political authority. Despite the strength of the centralizing French state, there were relatively few direct initiatives in gender policy. In Japan a highly centralized administration and the relative weakness of private religious, professional, and women's organizations regarding the reconstruction of gender left the state as the major arbiter of change.

In the end, the failure to achieve unified or consistent views stands out in day-care, as in state initiatives regarding gender in modern Japan. These difficulties may seem surprising in light of the success of the Japanese state in building an industrial economy, a strong military establishment, and an overseas empire. In the day-care world, the difficulties may have stemmed from ambivalence as well as the complexity of the task. In the case of the state, we might entertain the possibility that bureaucratic rivalries between the Home and Education Ministries contributed to the ambiguities of the state's definitions of womanhood. Or perhaps the inconsistencies loom larger in retrospect than they did at the time. Because only four decades had passed since abolition of the decaying early modern hereditary status hierarchy, early twentieth-century Japanese

leaders were not reticent in according differential treatment to respectable middle-class women and their less respectable lower-class sisters. Domesticity served
as an ideal for prosperous new middle-class women who were less likely to reside
with their in-laws and more likely to have had time and money to lavish on new
techniques of home management and child-rearing, while productivity (with
perhaps some degree of rising expectations regarding domestic accomplish-
ments) was still expected of women in poor, working-class, and small enterprise
households.[13]

In considering changes in womanhood during modern development, scholars in various fields have proposed that womanhood can function as a repository
of tradition in the face of anxiety regarding social change or colonial domina-
tion.[14] Admittedly, the day-care world was a limited universe, but it encom-
passed state officials, private volunteers and professionals, and diverse segments
of the urban lower classes. Although by and large it supported the aim of making good citizens of both children and parents, the evidence regarding changes
in womanhood among inhabitants of the day-care world suggests that the reformulation of gender in early twentieth century Japan imagined more alternatives
than simply freezing womanhood in the mold of the unchanging past or removing women from the turmoil of the outside world. While the strength of legacies from the past varied according to class and those lingering ideas and practices to some extent limited the possibilities for reconstructing womanhood and
gender, in passively allowing them to persist or even in positively invoking them,
the overriding concern seems not to allay fears of change but rather to create conceptions of gender fostering nationalist visions of progress—the development of
the economy, the military establishment, and the empire, and the integration of
the modern nation-state. This, in turn, allowed women limited agency in economy and society despite articulation of the norm of "good wife, wise mother."
The establishment and growth of day-care centers and the transformation of
motherhood and childhood that took place in early twentieth century child-care
centers were part of a larger process—the reconstruction of reproduction, which
required the creation of new male and female and young and old citizens to meet
the severe challenges of a harshly competitive, racist world order.

Epilogue
Since 1945

Examination of the early twentieth century beginnings of Japanese day-care offers insights into the construction of Japanese motherhood, childhood, and household life in the modern era—its link to changes in economy and state resulting from development driven by nationalism in an imperialist era. It may be equally illuminating to consider briefly some aspects of the evolution of motherhood, child-rearing, and day-care institutions in the contemporary or post-World War II era. In 1945 Japan lost its overseas colonies and endured foreign occupation. This national crisis was overcome not through armed aggression but through rebuilding the shattered economy and mounting an export drive in overseas markets. Since 1945 economic growth, legal and family changes, improved health care, better access to fertility limitation, rising educational levels, rapid urbanization, and government policies are among the many factors underlying ongoing changes in postwar Japanese womanhood, childhood, and day care.[1]

Close-up views of individual Japanese women reveal that diverse ideas and practices of motherhood coexist in postwar Japan, although they have often been obscured by the image of the "education mother" (*kyōiku mama*). Recent studies by Dorinne Kondo, Joseph Tobin, Harumi Befu, Glenda Roberts, Joy Hendry, Margaret Lock, Takie S. Lebra, Anne E. Imamura, Ann Allison, and Gail Lee Bernstein suggest that the education mother may be primarily an urban, new-middle class ideal attained by only a handful of women; that mothers are less likely to be the sole child-care provider in small enterprise and working-class households; and that acceptance of nonmaternal male and female caregivers is still widespread. However, households rely to a lesser extent on individual non-familial caregivers, although it is unclear whether this is so because it is less acceptable or because child care by servants is less widely available.

Although a 1972 survey cited by Takie Lebra indicates that 70 percent of female respondents felt children were a woman's purpose in life (*ikigai*) (versus 35 percent of male respondents), she found that her female interviewees shied away from labeling themselves education mothers. By the mid-1970s the term

"*kyōiku mama*" had acquired negative connotations. Newspapers as well as scholars criticized overly zealous mothers who drove their children too hard or who
controlled their sons by tying them to "mommy's apron strings." The alleged
results: unhappy children who turned to misconduct or suicide and maladjusted
young men who could not adapt to the rigors of the workplace, or even mother-
son incest.[2]

In the 1980s Joseph Tobin found no "education mothers" among the mothers at the kindergarten he observed, while one of Dorinne Kondo's respondents,
a female worker at a small factory, stated flatly, "Yeah, pushing the kid to study
doesn't do any good. . . . My kids were just born stupid!" Kondo observed that
many women of the small enterprise districts (downtown or *shitamachi*) of Tokyo
seemed "resigned in many ways to their place in life as people who work with
their hands, not with 'paper and pencil,'" and tended not to imagine their children gaining upward mobility through scholastic excellence. With barely
enough time to complete basic household chores after working seven hours a day,
these mothers lacked the time and energy to monitor their children's educational
programs in minute detail.[3]

For husbands in salaried positions, distant commutes and long hours greatly
reduce opportunities for involvement in domestic affairs, but this is not necessarily true for working-class and self-employed men. In 1986 Befu noted the participation of small enterprise men in child care:

> When there is . . . a family business, the father tends to be with his chil-
> dren much more of the day than a father who is a wage earner. . . . The fa-
> ther's continual presence in the immediate vicinity tends to offset the emo-
> tional bond between mother and child. Moreover, if the wife assists in the
> family business, as often happens, she is less accessible to the child than a
> full-time mother. If a full-time mother neglects her child, she has reason to
> feel guilty, but a mother who has to help her husband cannot be expected
> to attend to her child's every whim.[4]

In Roberts' study, some husbands of urban female factory workers shared not
only child-rearing but household chores as well. In the words of two women:

> I do cooking and the laundry. That's all. . . . Dad, my husband, that is, puts
> the kids in the bath, spreads out the bedding, does miscellaneous things for
> the kids, dresses them, and that sort of thing.

> I did all of it [housework and child care] when they were little. . . .
> [D]uring the holidays he'd look after them if they were crying . . . also af-
> ter he came home in the evening if they were crying and I was busy. But I
> always fed them and changed them. Now that he's a grandpa, he's a softy,
> and he makes them their bottles and changes diapers. . . . [F]or me, . . .
> [h]e'd only hold them [but I didn't expect more].

Some respondents shared child care and other domestic labor with coresident
mothers or mothers-in-law. Although most of them accepted women's greater
responsibility for domestic tasks and experienced stress or guilt due to the difficulties of balancing paid and unpaid labor in their daily routines, one woman
asserted that children are the responsibility of both parents, not just of the
mother alone.[5]

In rural areas and in small-enterprise households, acceptance of female productivity and nonmaternal care of infants lingered long into the postwar era, sustained by family need for a married woman's income rather than rural or urban
residence. During the late 1950s farm wife Haruko took her children to a nursery or the home of an older woman who baby-sat during the busy rice planting
season. She recalled that

> I envied the wives of the salaried men. . . . Their chores consisted of merely
> cooking and washing. For farmers' wives, cooking, washing, and caring for
> children did not count as work. In the morning, my husband and I always
> worked in the paddies together.[6]

Nearly two decades later in a Kyushu village, Hendry observed that that "it was
often a grandfather who was entrusted with the care of a small child."[7] In the
early 1980s in a mountainous region of central Japan, one small-enterprise
woman voiced acceptance of mothers' paid employment if child care is provided
by a family member:

> I think the system is at fault at present. At the moment a woman can only
> take two months for maternity leave and that's much too short. We need
> to have a system in which a mother stays with her child until it's three years
> old, and then she can go back to her old job. I don't think that leaving a
> newborn baby in a nursery is right at all, not for nine or ten hours a day. If
> *obāsan* [grandmother] is at home and provides the child care then that's
> fine, but so often that's not the way things are these days.[8]

In contrast, one urban working mother strongly supported the expansion of infant day-care; however, unlike their prewar counterparts, the officials in her district placed responsibility for infant care solely on the mother.

> I had a child in 1983. After my maternity leave was over, I decided to en-
> roll my baby in a day nursery, but none of the public facilities in Suginami
> Ward, Tokyo, would take an eight-week-old child. The only places I could
> find were private nurseries, where the conditions were poor, so . . . I had to
> choose whether or not to resign from my job. . . . The social conditions that
> would allow women with children to work simply did not exist. . . . I and
> some other women went to negotiate with the ward mayor, but an official
> there said . . . "It is natural for mothers to take care of their children until
> they have reached the age of three. We pity babies who are sent to day nurs-
> eries right after the end of maternity leave. There is no need to build day
> nurseries for eight-week-old babies."[9]

Although neither woman opposed women's paid employment, they held opposite views on the desirable form of child care for working mothers.

The ideas of motherhood, wifehood, work, and women's responsibilities of
the young women in the first generation to come of age in the postwar era were
influenced by the experiences and instructions of their mothers, although in the
end they made their own choices. One middle-class woman who did not follow
her mother's advice reflected:

> My father was wounded in the war. . . . [H]e died in 1946. . . . [M]y
> mother raised us by herself. . . . [S]he was a midwife—she couldn't really
> earn enough money because people were too poor to pay her, but we got by
> somehow. . . . We all respected my mother for her hard work and for the
> way she helped people in the middle of the night. We children took . . .
> turns to fix dinner and clean the house. . . . When I went to work I really
> set out to find a good husband and always planned to stop work once I got
> married, although my mother didn't really agree with this. She thought
> that it was being frivolous. She had thought a lot about the position of
> women, and she always said that in the future Japanese women would all
> take jobs as a matter of course. . . . I was twenty-six when I got married and
> had my first child at twenty-seven. . . . I won't go back to work even when
> the children are older. . . . My husband's company doesn't like wives to
> work; they think it gives a bad image to the company, as though they're
> not paying their employees enough.[10]

In sum, the voices of postwar Japanese women from rural and urban areas and from diverse occupations indicate that beyond the image of the education mother, it is not hard to discover behavior and attitudes that differ from normative expectations. Given that salaried male employees under lifetime employment—those who can support a full-time homemaker—probably have constituted no more than 30 percent of the labor force, this range of conduct and ideas is hardly surprising. Furthermore, recent evidence suggests an undercurrent of resistance to domesticity moving against the main current of female acceptance of marriage and motherhood, as well as reconfigurations of wifehood that expand women's horizons beyond the role of caretaker for children, husband, and the elderly in the home.[11] The birth rate, which in 1990 dropped to 1.53 children born to a woman during her lifetime, can be interpreted as a rejection of motherhood.[12] Lamented by some conservative male politicians as a danger to the Japanese race, fertility limitation has been justified by some women in terms of maternal responsibility. Prudence dictates not giving birth if the family is unwilling or unable to afford the costs of child-rearing; in particular, the costs of higher education loom as a crushing future burden.

Despite a conventional wisdom that extols female domesticity, especially motherhood, and expresses misgivings about women's permanent, full-time wage work, day-care continues to thrive in postwar Japan. In fact, by 1989 the proportion of married female employees had risen to 58 percent, in contrast to 33 percent in 1962, and in 1990, 36 percent of married women with children under age six participated in the labor force.[13] Nationwide the 1991 preschool attendance rate for five-year-olds was 96 percent; of these, 24 percent had attended day-care centers, while 64 percent had attended kindergartens. For all age groups in 1992, 1,622,323 youngsters were enrolled in 22,675 day-care centers, while 1,977,611 children attended 15,041 kindergartens.[14] For five-year-olds, then, some sort of preschool experience has become nearly universal, but the younger the age, the lower the rate of attendance at an institution.

In law and administration, differences between day-care centers and kindergartens remain in the postwar era. The Child-Welfare Law of 1947 brought day-care centers under national regulation for the first time under the Ministry of Health and Welfare, while kindergartens today remain under the juristiction of the Ministry of Education. Another continuity is the relationship between day-care centers and the state, but the links have become far more direct in the postwar era. Both public and private child-care centers receive local and national funds, and local governments determine admission to both public and private day-care facilities. The main criterion for admission is care for "babies and children who do not have sufficient care in their homes," which generally requires verification of the mother's employment and unavailability of other caretakers in the home.[15] One might say that the KSKH legacy of exclusionary enrollment—rejection of the unemployed—lingers. The fact that inadequacy of home care justifies admission to day-care is sometimes regarded as a stigma on children and families using institutional child care.

Institutions in underserved areas have been given greater flexibility since 1987, but as a rule kindergartens continue to operate in the morning for four hours a day, while child-care centers operate for about eleven hours a day. As before, both include a program of education for children, generally in keeping with the Ministry of Education's regulations for kindergartens.[16] Although holes in the day-care network include hours of operation that are too short for working professionals, a scarcity of infant care, inadequate provisions for sick pupils, and shortages of after-school programs for elementary school children, in 1991 Japan had the largest number of day-care facilities of any industrialized nation. Other issues include the reduction of relatively high student-pupil ratios, cutbacks in government subsidies (and therefore rising user fees), unifying the administration of early childhood institutions under either the Ministry of Welfare or the Ministry of Education, and center closures due to declining enrollment—a consequence of the plummeting birth rate.[17]

Because quality of upbringing is now a major aim, there has been a shift toward focusing on the welfare of the child; household economic improvement and education of parents have receded in the regulations. In practice, however, many scholars have emphasized the role of kindergartens and day-care centers in the shaping of mothers' attitudes and behavior through interaction between mothers and teachers on informal occasions and at meetings. And the attitude of officials, even if it is not explicitly stated in the regulations, is now unambiguous—responsibility for child-rearing belongs to mothers.[18] Under Ministry of Education guidelines, the postwar children's curriculum has required first six, then five, subjects: health, society, nature, language, music-rhythm, and drawing-handicrafts, with the last two combined since 1989 under the category "expression," but day-care centers also include practical instruction aimed at "fostering basic habits necessary for everyday life."[19]

In contrast to the teacher-centeredness of the mainstream prewar day-care classroom, which featured songs, crafts, lessons, and games led by the teacher, the curriculum today relies far more on peer participation. The need to resocialize parents to habits of thrift, cleanliness, and diligence has diminished during the prolonged prosperity from the mid-1950s to the end of the 1980s. Nonetheless, teachers continue to hold meetings to diffuse new information on child-rearing, nutrition, and other aspects of child-rearing and home life, but these are mainly intended for mothers. This is difficult to trace, as the lion's share of Western research on Japanese preschool education has focused on pedagogical methods and the child's transition from home and parental care to the school environment more than on the content of curriculum, in order to reveal broader patterns of participation in social and economic institutions beyond home and school and to explain Japanese values.[20]

Observations of postwar child-training methods in the home have highlighted cooperation attained through indulgence and fostering of children's dependence on mothers, rather than coercion through reliance on rigid rules, forceful speech, or physical punishment. Major practices such as carrying babies by binding them to the caregivers' back, cosleeping, cobathing, patience, and cajoling continue, although today these are performed by family members rather than hired individual caregivers.[21] On the whole, postwar methods resesmble those described by Smith and Wiswell for Suye Village in the 1930s, although roughly 90 percent of Japanese now reside in cities, and the workforce is employed in the manufacturing and service sectors rather than agriculture.

In closing, I return once more to images of women as indicators of social change. In the 1870s reform-minded nationalist intellectuals criticized upper-class Japanese women for hiring wet nurses to rear their children. In recent times the reigning empress has won praise from media for rearing her children herself. During the late nineteenth century the process of family change has often been described as "samuraization," largely due to the codification of household law in the 1898 Civil Code. Yet when considered from the point of view of child-rearing, the rising insistence on mothers as socializers of children and the declining employment of hired caregivers for infants and toddlers permits description of this crucial aspect of domestic modernity as a "commonerization" of the elite. The same can be said of the contemporary longing of the Heisei emperor for a home, children and parents residing together, unlike his own childhood—a wish fulfilled by his commoner queen.[22]

Although the empress and other upper-class women are only a tiny minority of Japanese women, social expectations of conformity to established values may be greater for elites, who often serve as models for the masses. If so, there are grounds for regarding this continuity of late nineteenth century and postwar expectations for upper-class Japanese mothers as a barometer of modernity, an indication of changes in how adult women should behave and how children should be treated—changes that originated in the far-reaching transformations as the nation was forged in the modern era. Other fascinating and significant transmutations and reconstructions of womanhood, childhood, family life, and child care, including new views and dissent from the conventional wisdom, will surely emerge in future investigations of postwar child-rearing, child-care institutions, motherhood, childhood, and family life.

Notes

Introduction

1. The early twentieth century falls in Japan's modern era (1868–1945), which is also called the pre–World War II or prewar era. It was preceded by the early modern (Edo or Tokugawa) period (1600–1867) and followed by the postwar or contemporary period (1945–present). Imperial reigns of this century have been: Meiji (1868–1912), Taisho or Taishō (1912–1926), Showa or Shōwa (1926–1989), and Heisei (1989–).

2. Carol Simon, "A Long-Distance Ticket to Life," 46. See also Ezra Vogel, *Japan's New Middle Class,* 47–60, 251–252, and 183–185, 232; Suzanne Vogel, "Professional Housewife: The Career of Urban Middle-Class Women," esp. 24–28; Takie Sugiyama Lebra, *Japanese Women: Constraint and Fulfillment,* 192–206; Anne Imamura, *Urban Japanese Housewives,* 76; Merry White, "The Virtue of Japanese Mothers," 150, 153–156; Deborah Fallows, "Change Comes Slowly for Japanese Women," 70, 74; Anne Allison, *Nightwork: Sexuality, Pleasure, and Corporate Masculinity in a Tokyo Hostess Club,* ch. 6.

3. Mikiso Hane, *Rebels, Peasants, and Outcastes: The Underside of Modern Japan,* 90.

4. Ibid., esp. 78–137; Robert J. Smith and Ella Lury Wiswell, *The Women of Suye Mura* and Mikio Kanda, ed., *Widows of Hiroshima,* trans. Taeko Midorikawa. Gail Lee Bernstein, *Haruko's World: A Japanese Farm Woman and Her Community,* suggests that postwar motherhood displayed significant continuities with that of the modern period; see also the epilogue.

5. Pioneering social history works in English include Hiroshi Hazama, "Historical Changes in the Life Style of Industrial Workers"; Ann Waswo, *Japanese Landlords: Decline of a Rural Elite;* Donald Roden, *Schooldays in Imperial Japan: A Study in the Culture of a Student Elite;* Earl Kinmonth, *The Self-Made Man in Meiji Japanese Thought: From Samurai to Salaryman;* Mikiso Hane, *Rebels, Peasants, and Outcastes.* These were followed by additional specialized studies such as Sharon Sievers, *Flowers in Salt, Japan: The Beginnings of Feminist Consciousness in Modern Japan;* Andrew Gordon, *The Evolution of Labor Relations in Japan: Heavy Industry, 1853–1955,* esp. ch. 2. For more recent works in modern women's history, see E. Patricia Tsurumi, *Factory Girls: Women in the Thread Mills of Meiji Japan;* Gail

Lee Bernstein, ed., *Recreating Japanese Women, 1600–1945;* Yoshiko Furuki, *The White Plum: A Biography of Tsuda Ume;* Barbara Rose, *Tsuda Umeko and Women's Education in Japan;* Janet Hunter, ed., *Japanese Women Working;* Helen M. Hopper, *A New Woman of Japan: A Political Biography of Kato Shidzue;* and Vera C. Mackie, *Creating Socialist Women in Japan: Gender, Labour, and Activism, 1900–1937.* Also important are other relevant works such as Joyce Lebra, Joy Paulson, and Elizabeth Powers, ed., *Women in Changing Japan,* and Mariko Tamanoi, *Under the Shadow of Nationalism: Politics and Poetics of Rural Japanese Women,* and major translations such as Tomoko Yamazaki, *The Story of Yamada Waka: From Prostitute to Feminist Pioneer;* Yukichi Fukuzawa, *Fukuzawa Yukichi on Japanese Women: Selected Works;* Mikiso Hane, ed. and trans., *Reflections on the Way to the Gallows;* Fumiko Kaneko, *Prison Memoirs of a Japanese Woman;* and Makiko Nakano, *Makiko's Diary: A Merchant Wife in 1910.* Regarding the history of modern manhood, see Gordon, *Evolution of Labor Relations;* Kinmonth, *The Self-Made Man;* Roden, *Schooldays in Imperial Japan;* Sakae Ōsugi, *The Autobiography of Ōsugi Sakae,* trans. Byron Marshall; Shibusawa Eiichi, *The Autobiography of Shibusawa Eiichi,* trans. Teruko Craig; Gregory M. Pflugfelder, *Cartographies of Desire: Male-Male Sexuality in Japanese Discourse, 1600–1950.* New topics such as the history of minorities, gender, and early modern and modern sexuality have also emerged. See, for example, Ian Neary, *Political Protest and Social Control in Pre-war Japan: The Origins of Buraku Liberation;* Michael Weiner, *Race and Migration in Imperial Japan;* Barbara Molony and Kathleen Uno, eds., *Gendering Modern Japanese History;* Tsuneo Watanabe and Jun'ichi Iwata, *The Love of the Samurai: A Thousand Years of Japanese Homosexuality;* Gary Leupp, *Male Colors: The Construction of Homosexuality in Tokugawa Japan;* Sumie Jones, ed., *Imaging Reading Eros;* and Pflugfelder, *Cartographies of Desire.*

Many specialized studies have treated peasants and rural residents in the modern era, with much attention to their participation in protests: Waswo, *Japanese Landlords;* Hane, *Rebels, Peasants, and Outcastes,* 23–103, 127–218; Daikichi Irokawa, *The Culture of the Meiji Period* (translation of *Meiji no bunka*); William W. Kelly, *Deference and Defiance in Nineteenth-Century Japan;* Herbert Bix, *Peasant Protest in Japan, 1590–1884;* Richard Smethurst, *Agricultural Development and Tenancy Disputes in Japan, 1870–1940;* George O. Wilson, *Patriots and Redeemers in Japan: Motives in the Meiji Restoration;* Takashi Nagatsuka, *The Soil: A Portrait of Rural Life in Meiji Japan,* trans. Ann Waswo.

Despite the flowering of social history in general, new monographs on the modern social history of urban lower-class life and culture are conspicuously few, a void this study helps to fill for the urban poor and for urban lower-class women. For the early modern period, see Gary Leupp, *Servants, Shophands, and Laborers in the Cities of Tokugawa Japan.* Many aspects of the work lives of male and female laborers and their associations are revealed in Stephen Large, *The Yuaikai 1912–1919: The Rise of Labor in Japan;* Stephen Large, *Organized Labor and Socialist Politics in Interwar Japan;* Hane, *Rebels, Peasants, and Outcastes,* 237–259, 284–290, 327–345; Gordon, *The Evolution of Labor Relations;* Tsurumi, *Factory Girls;* Stephen E. Marsland, *The Birth of the Japanese Labor Movement: Takano Fusatarō and the Rōdō Kumiai Kiseikai;* Andrew Gordon, *Labor and Imperial Democracy in Japan;* Masanori Nakamura, ed., *Technology Change and Female Labour in Japan;* Kazuo Niimura, *The Ashio Riot of 1907: A Social History of Mining in Japan.* A broader perspective of urban social movements can be found in Michael Lewis, *Rioters and Citizens: Mass Protest in Imperial Japan;* Sally Ann Hastings, *Neighborhood and Nation in Tokyo, 1905–1937;* and Sheldon Garon, *Molding Japanese Minds: The State in Everyday Life.*

6. Ichibangase Yasuko, Izumi Jun, Ogawa Nobuko, and Shishido Takeo, *Nihon no hoiku;* Urabe Hiroshi, Shishido Takeo, and Murayama Yūichi, *Hoiku no rekishi.* Although there are no English language histories of Japanese early childhood education or of the development of child welfare institutions, limited information is available in Early Childhood Education Association of Japan, ed., *Early Childhood Education and Care in Japan,* ch. 4, 5, 8, 11. General works on the history of modern education include Herbert Passin, *Society and Education in Japan;* Kaigo Tokiomi, *Japanese Education: Its Past and Present;* E. Patricia Tsurumi, *Japanese Colonial Education in Taiwan;* Edward Beauchamp, *Learning to Be Japanese: Selected Writings on Japanese Society and Education;* and Byron K. Marshall, *Learning to Be Modern: Japanese Political Discourse on Education.* For limited treatments of child welfare policies and institutions, see Takayuki Namae, "Standards of Child Welfare Work in Japan"; Toshio Tatara, "1400 Years of Japanese Social Work from Its Origins through the Japanese Occupation, 552–1952"; Hastings, *Neighborhood and Nation;* and Mutsuko Takahashi, *The Emergence of Welfare Society in Japan.*

Among the English language studies of the broader history of social welfare in Japan, the most comprehensive study remains Tatara, "1400 Years of Japanese Social Work." Tatara states that while the term "social work" is generally used in reference to a profession in which professionally trained social workers engage in a vairety of activities," [i]n Japan the distinction between *shakai jigyō* (social work) and *shakai fukushi* (social welfare) has not always been clear. The first use of the term 'social work' . . . was used to signify various methods other than the methods of *jizen* (charity) and *hinmin kyūsai* (poor relief) of dealing with needy persons," 5–7. In this book, in certain contexts *shakai ji-gyō* is also translated as "social project(s)"; because *"shakai fukushi"* is a later term, it did not appear in documents examined for this study. Although welfare specialists in contemporary Japan sometimes draw inspiration for voluntarism from overseas, as the evolution of the terminology suggests, modern social welfare in Japan developed from a strong early emphasis on private philanthropy and relief rather than state policies. Regarding the evolution of social welfare in modern Japan, a trajectory from private philanthropic and relief work toward greater direct government involvement, see also in Japanese, Yoshida Kyūichi, *Shakai jigyō riron no rekishi;* Yoshida Kyūichi, *Gendai shakai ji-gyō riron no rekishi;* and in English, Koji Taira, "Public Assistance in Japan: Development and Trends"; Masayoshi Chubachi and Koji Taira, "Poverty in Modern Japan: Perceptions and Realities"; W. Dean Kinzley, "Japan's Discovery of Poverty: Changing Views of Poverty and Social Welfare in the Nineteenth Century"; Stephen J. Anderson, *Welfare Policy and Politics in Japan: Beyond the Developmental State,* ch. 3; Hastings, *Neighborhood and Nation,* ch. 1–2; Garon, *Molding Japanese Minds,* ch. 1; and Takahashi, *The Emergence of Welfare Society in Japan,* ch. 2.

7. For example, see Carroll Smith-Rosenberg, "The Female World of Love and Ritual: Relations between Women in Nineteenth-Century America"; Nancy F. Cott, *The Bonds of Womanhood: Woman's Sphere in New England, 1780–1835;* Katherine Kish Sklar, *Catherine Beecher: A Study in American Domesticity;* Barbara J. Berg, *The Remembered Gate: Origins of American Feminism* Joan Kelly, "Family and Society."

8. See, for example, Linda Gordon, ed., *Women, the State, and Welfare;* Seth Koven and Sonya Michel, "Womanly Duties: Maternalist Politics and the Origins of Welfare States in France, Germany, Great Britain, and the United States, 1880–1920"; and Linda Gordon, "Social Insurance and Public Assistance: The Influence of Gender in Welfare Thought in the United States," and many of the works cited therein.

9. Examples of works emphasizing the state as an agent of women's oppression are Elizabeth Wilson, *Women and the Welfare State;* Carol Brown, "Mothers, Fathers, and Children: From Private to Public Patriarchy," 239–268; Elizabeth Fox-Genovese, "Placing Women's History in History"; and Mimi Abramowitz, *Regulating the Lives of Women: Social Welfare Policy from Colonial Times to the Present.* Many of these works also stress the control exerted by states over the working class as well. Works on modern Japan treating similar themes include Sharon Nolte, "Women, the State, and Repression in Imperial Japan"; Sharon Nolte and Sally Hastings, "The Meiji State's Policy toward Women, 1890–1910"; and

Yoshiko Miyake, "Doubling Expectations: Motherhood and Women's Factory Work under State Management in Japan in the 1930s and 1940s."

Some revisionist works that focus on women's influence on the state, particularly in the areas of relief, welfare, social policy formation, and entry into state bureaucracies, include Koven and Michel, "Womanly Duties"; Gordon, ed., *Women, the State, and Welfare;* and Gordon, "Social Insurance and Public Assistance." More general studies considering women's roles in modern public life include Bonnie G. Smith, *Ladies of the Leisure Class: The Bourgeoises of Northern France in the Nineteenth Century;* Christine Stansell, *City of Women;* Mary P. Ryan, *Women in Public: Between Banners and Ballots;* Kathleen D. McCarthy, *Women's Culture: American Philanthropy and Art, 1830–1930;* and Dorothy O. Helly and Susan B. Reverby, eds., *Gendered Domains: Rethinking Public and Private in Women's History,* to name but a few.

Western works treating women and state in modern Japan have tended to emphasize state control and women's resistance or the incompleteness of state initiatives. See Sievers, *Flowers in Salt;* Sharon Nolte, "Women's Rights and Society's Needs: Japan's 1931 Suffrage Bill"; Robert J. Smith, "Making Village Women into 'Good Wives and Wise Mothers'"; Hane, *Reflections on the Way to the Gallows;* Kathleen Uno, "Women and Changes in the Household Division of Labor"; Mariko Tamanoi, "Songs as Weapons: The Culture and History of *Komori* (Nursemaids) in Modern Japan"; Jennifer Robertson," Doing and Undoing 'Female' and 'Male' in Japan: The Takarazuka Review"; Kathleen Uno, "Origins of 'Good Wife, Wise Mother' "; Hopper, *A New Woman;* and Barbara Molony and Kathleen Molony, *Ichikawa Fusae: A Political Biography.* Gregory Pflugfelder, "Politics and the Kitchen: The Women's Suffrage Movement in Provincial Japan"; Sheldon Garon, "The Women's Movement and the Japanese State: Contending Approaches to Political Integration, 1890–1945"; and Nishikawa Yūko, "Japan's Entry into War and the Support of Women" argue that cooperation of women's organizations with the state also merits scholarly attention.

10. See Eugen Weber, *Peasants into Frenchmen: The Modernization of Rural France, 1870–1914,* esp. 303–338; Jacques Donzelot, *The Policing of Families,* trans. Robert Hurley; and Philippe Meyer, *The Child and the State,* trans. Judith Ennew and Janet Lloyd.

11. See Rachel Fuchs, *Abandoned Children: Foundlings and Child Welfare in Nineteenth-Century France;* George K. Behlmer, *Child Abuse and Moral Reform in England, 1870–1908;* Clark Nardinelli, *Child Labor and the Industrial Revolution;* Katherine Lynch, *Family, Class, and Ideology in Early Industrial France: Social Policy and the Working-Class Family.*

12. For the United States, see David Nasaw, *Children of the City: At Work and at Play.* For England, see Stephen Humphries, *Hooligans or Rebels? An Oral History of Working-Class Childhood and Youth 1889–1939;* see also Nardinelli's interesting assertion that child labor reform pitted child operatives and industrialists against adult male factory workers, *Child Labor and the Industrial Revolution,* 151. Regarding the history of children in China, see Ann Waltner, *Getting an Heir: Adoption and the Construction of Kinship in Late Imperial China;* Jon L. Saari, *Legacies of Childhood: Growing up Chinese in a Time of Crisis, 1890–1920;* and Anne Behnke Kinney, ed., *Chinese Views of Childhood.*

13. Three such analyses are: Linda Nicholson, *Gender and History;* Joan Scott, *Gender and the Politics of History,* esp. 1–50; and Anita Levy, *Other Women: The Writing of Class, Race, and Gender, 1832–1898.* Applications of such methodology to the study of gender in Japan include Dorinne Kondo, *Crafting Selves: Power, Gender, and Discourses of Identity in a Japanese Workplace;* Uno, "Women and Changes"; Kathleen Uno, "One Day at a Time: Work and Domestic Activities of Urban Lower-Class Women in Early Twentieth-Century Japan"; Kathleen Uno, "The Death of 'Good Wife, Wise Mother'?"

14. Works on women and political theory tracing the rise of separate male and female spheres include Jean Bethke Elshtain, *Public Man, Private Woman: Women in Social and Political Thought;* and Joan Landes, *Women and the Public Sphere in the Age of the French Revolution.* One work that questions such dualistic thinking is Judith Butler and Joan Scott, ed., *Feminists Theorize the Political.* Another work treating women and citizenship is Carol Pateman, *The Disorder of Women.*

15. Regarding gender role mutability as reflected in Japanese opinion polls, see Imamura, *Urban Japanese Housewives,* 14, and Uno, "Death of 'Good Wife, Wise Mother'?" 321–322. See also the epilogue of this book, esp. note 11.

16. See Nolte, "Women, the State, and Repression," 5; Nolte and Hastings, "The Meiji State's Policy"; and Uno, "One Day at a Time."

17. Uno, "One Day at a Time."

1. Beginnings

1. In this study, day- or child-care centers are defined as institutions that care for young children of working parents, devoting attention to youngsters' educational and physical needs. However, it is important to note that prewar Japanese day-care centers generally attempted to provide education and other services for parents as well.

2. See Yoshida Kyūichi, *Gendai shakai;* Ichibangase, et al., *Nihon no hoiku,* 2–58; Urabe, et al., *Hoiku no rekishi,* 2–32.

3. Local government and police administration were among the important powers delegated to the Home Ministry. Day-care first came to the attention of officials in the Relief Section (Kyūsaika) of the Local Affairs Bureau (Chihōkyoku), and they retained their interest after jurisdiction over relief matters was transferred to the Social Bureau (Shakaikyoku) in 1920.

4. The first yearbook of social projects also recommended establishment of relief institutions such as charity hospitals, orphanages, and paupers' schools. Naimushō, *Waga kuni ni okeru jikei kyūsai jigyō.*

5. Figures for the years 1919 to 1926, as well as other years, appear in Ichibangase, et al., *Nihon no hoiku,* 278. Total day-care and kindergarten enrollments can be estimated at about 3,000 and 30,600 in 1919 and 1926, respectively, assuming that center size averaged around 50 children.

6. In Japanese, his position was Naimushō shakaikyoku buchō. *Dai ikkai zenkoku jidō hogo jigyō kaigi hōkoku* (1925), 3, cited in Yoshida, *Gendai shakai,* 104.

7. See Okada Masatoshi, *Nihon no hoiku seido,* 33–55.

8. Regarding uses of the term "reproduction" (also referred to in its broadest sense as "social reproduction") in works analyzing gender or women's history, see Kelly, "Family and Society"; Nicholson, *Gender and History;* Levy, *Other Women;* and Rayna Rapp, Ellen Ross, and Renate Bridental, "Examining Family History," esp. 252.

   However, some writers propose to eliminate the productive/reproductive dichotomy, e.g., Levy, *Other Women;* Mary Poovey, *Uneven Developments: The Ideological Work of Gender in Mid-Victorian England;* Allison M. Jaggar, "'Reproduction' as Male Ideology," and others assert that reproduction should be considered part of the process of production, while Mary O'Brien, in *The Politics of Reproduction,* argues for an all-inclusive definition of reproduction encompassing not only birth, socialization, and care of children and adults, but the production of material goods as well.

9. Regarding the history of housework, see, for example, Glenna Matthews, *Just a Housewife;* Susan Strasser, *Never Done: A History of American Housework;* and Ruth Schwartz Cowan, *More Work for Mother: The Ironies of Household Technology from the Open Hearth to the Microwave.*

   Aspects of the history of child-rearing are treated in the chapters on individual countries in Joseph M. Hawes and N. Ray Hiner, eds., *Children in Historical and Comparative Perspective: An International Handbook and Research Guide,* as well as in monographs, including Philippe Aries, *Centuries of Childhood: A*

Social History of Family Life, trans. Robert Baldick; Linda Pollock, *Forgotten Children: Parent-Child Relations from 1500 to 1900;* Elisabeth Badinter, *Mother Love: Myth and Reality;* Warren Sussman, *Selling Mothers' Milk: The Wet-Nursing Business in France, 1715–1914;* and David Ransel, *Mothers of Misery: Child Abandonment in Russia.* Regarding child-rearing in modern Japan, see chapter 2 of this study. Kathleen Uno, "Japan," 389–419, surveys early modern, modern, and postwar developments.

10. Regarding Japan see Uno, "Women and Changes." See also Nicholson, *Gender and History.*

11. See Eli Zaretsky's suggestive essay regarding this process in the United States, "The Place of the Family in the Origins of the Welfare State," 188–224.

12. In Japan as elsewhere, the survival of children under five or six was more problematic than that of older children. Although Japan had fairly high infant mortality rates, which rose until 1919 and then declined, the population was growing rather than declining. Takayuki Namae, "Standards of Child Welfare Work in Japan."

13. This similarity of functions can call forth opposition to day-care centers.

14. See George Sansom, *The Western World and Japan;* Irwin Scheiner, *Christian Converts and Social Protest in Meiji Japan;* and Donald Shively, "The Japanization of the Middle Meiji," 77–119.

15. See, for example, Kenneth Pyle, *The New Generation in Meiji Japan.* There was a greater willingness to import arts and fashion as well as knowledge and techniques for industrial development and social control until foreign culture was suppressed during the war mobilization of 1930s.

16. It appears that the first day-care centers served both poor households and lower-class families who were not destitute. Yet in physical terms and in terms of income stability, the boundary between the poor and the lower class, or even between the poor and the middle class, was hazy in early twentieth century Japan, although the distinction between the poor and higher classes became more clear-cut as the century progressed. Around the turn of the century Japan had no huge slums; rather, there existed small settlements of the very poor in low-lying, damp areas and on the fringes of the great cities. Thus in some districts paupers lived next to the rich and powerful. The chronic prewar housing shortage in older cities meant that salaried workers occupied cramped quarters, and sometimes they had to reside in poorer districts. This, too, makes it difficult to categorize certain urban districts as the exclusive domain of the poor. Furthermore, the modern economy destroyed a number of traditional occupations; ruined households that turned to wage labor or marginal work such as day labor

and rag-picking might reside near families of artisans and petty merchants. Finally, during late Meiji the border between subsistence and poverty was thin. Illness or injury of the principal wage earner could plunge prosperous middle-class, as well as lower-class, families into want. However, by the late Taishō era differences in wages and consumption patterns more clearly distinguished the poor and working classes. Operatives for large enterprises had higher and more stable incomes than small enterprise and casual workers. In some respects the distinction between the upper and lower strata of the urban lower class still lacked clarity, as housing and social insurance were not well developed. See Masayoshi Chubachi and Koji Taira, "Poverty in Modern Japan"; Nakagawa Kiyoshi, *Nihon no toshi kasō;* Uno, "One Day at a Time"; and Akimasa Miyake, "Female Workers of the Urban Lower Class."

17. In fact, in his plans for reviving impoverished villages, late Tokugawa thinker Satō Nobuhiro (Shinen) proposed facilities resembling day-care centers to tend farmers' children while their parents worked in the fields, but these facilities were never built, and they apparently did not influence the post-Meiji development of institutions for young children. Urabe, et al., *Hoiku no rekishi,* 2; Murayama Sadao, "Meiji zenki no yōji hoiku no gaikan," 31–36.

18. Descriptions of prewar rural children appear in Smith and Wiswell, *The Women of Suye Mura,* xxxiv–xxxvi, 202–253; and Hane, *Rebels, Peasants, and Outcastes,* 29–101.

19. Sievers, *Flowers in Salt,* 93–94; Sally Hastings, "From Heroine to Patriotic Volunteer: Women and Social Work in Japan, 1900–1945." Poovey, in *Uneven Developments*, 9, suggests this was the case in nineteenth-century England as well.

20. Government surveys published in *Shokkō jijō* (1903) revealed that married women comprised from 3.2 to 34.1 percent of 2,400 female textile workers in seven factories, and from 11 to 60.6 percent of the 2,350 female operatives in eight other industries. A 1924 survey of over a dozen industries indicated that, on average, 17 percent of female operatives were married—ranging from 12 percent in the textile trade and 71 and 62.4 percent in the construction and metal industries, respectively. Fuse Akiko, *Atarashii kazoku no sōzō* 138, 147.

21. Regarding the concept of social control, see Jesse R. Pitts, "Social Control," 382; and Helen Everett, "Control, Social," 344. Regarding welfare and educational institutions, see, for example, Frances Piven and Richard A. Cloward, *Regulating the Poor: The Functions of Public Welfare;* Michael Katz, *In the Shadow of the Poorhouse;* and Samuel Bowles and Herbert Gintis, *Schooling in Capitalist America: Educational Reform and the Contradictions of Economic Life.* Regarding the state as an agent of patriarchy or gender control, see the works cited in note 8

of the preface. For Japan, see, for example, Fuse, *Atarashii kazoku no sōzō*; Suwa Yoshihide, *Hoiku no shisō: Katei kyōiku to yō, ho kyōiku no kōzō*; Gavan McCormack and Yoshio Sugimoto, *Democracy in Contemporary Japan*, 244.

24. Sievers, *Flowers in Salt*, 11–25, 109–113; Yukichi Fukuzawa, "On Japanese Women," "On Japanese Women, Part Two," (1885), in *Fukuzawa Yukichi on Japanese Women*, 6–32, 33–69.

25. Regarding the origins of social policy in Japan, see Byron Marshall, *Capitalism and Nationalism in Prewar Japan: The Ideology of the Business Elite, 1868–1941*, 51–76, 94–97; Sheldon Garon, *The State and Labor in Modern Japan*, 10–38; W. Dean Kinzley, *Industrial Harmony in Modern Japan: The Invention of a Tradition*, 1–25; and Hastings, *Neighborhood and Nation*. Stefan Tanaka, like Carol Gluck, suggests the importance of socialization to nationalist values in policies and thought during the Meiji and Taishō periods, "The concern for morals, proper behavior, good citizenship, loyalty to the emperor, and so on were emphasized for fear of discord and disintegration," *Japan's Orient: Rendering Pasts into History*, 14–15.

26. See Wilbur M. Fridell, "Government Ethics Textbooks in Late Meiji Japan," 823–833; and Richard J. Smethurst, *A Social Basis for Prewar Japanese Militarism: The Army and the Rural Community*.

27. Kenneth Pyle, "The Technology of Nationalism: The Local Improvement Movement, 1900–1918," 51–60; Harry Harootunian, "Introduction: A Sense of Ending and the Problem of Taisho," esp. 10–12, and chapter 4 note 24.

2. Child-Rearing in the Nineteenth Century

1. Regarding continuity and change in farming and village life, see Thomas C. Smith, *Agrarian Origins of Modern Japan*, 208–210; and Daikichi Irokawa, *The Culture of the Meiji Period*. As late as 1930 a majority of the labor force was employed in household enterprises. Uno, "Women and Changes," 18. Even in the early postwar years the percentage of the labor force in the "self-employed" and "family worker" categories totaled 59 percent in 1950 and 35 percent in 1960. Robert E. Cole and Kenichi Tominaga, "Japan's Changing Occupational Structure and Its Significance," 59, 64–65.

2. Fukutake Tadashi, *The Japanese Social Structure: Its Evolution in the Modern Century*, 18, 21.

3. Irokawa, *The Culture of the Meiji Period*, provides a sensitive, detailed account of many aspects of early Meiji rural change, but Western-language accounts of the social and cultural life of ordinary urbanites in the prewar era have yet to be written.

4. See Ronald P. Dore, *Education in Tokugawa Japan;* Herbert Passin, *Society and Education in Japan;* and Richard Rubinger, *Private Academies of Tokugawa Japan.* Sons of high-ranking or wealthy families—both warrior and commoner youth—attended the domain schools and Confucian academies; children of less prosperous households attended the village and city schools. Regarding women's education, see Kikue Yamakawa, *Women of the Mito Domain: Recollections of Samurai Family Life,* trans. Kate Wildman Nakai.

5. See also Uno, "Women and Changes," 22–30.

6. It was clearly established as the legal norm by the Civil Code of 1898. However, conflicting views in Japanese scholarship suggest that the nineteenth-century urban and rural lower classes may not have accepted the stem family with inheritance and succession by primogeniture as a normative household form. Uno, "Women and Changes," 23; Uno, "Japan," 390, 404.

7. Lutz Berkner, "The Stem Family and the Developmental Cycle: An Eighteenth Century Example," 399.

8. Or alternatively, before retirement of the head's father, the household might consist of a head, wife, and successor, plus successor's wife, children, and siblings. However, a household might be comprised of a single generation—the head and his wife—or two generations, i.e., head, wife, and children, due to poverty, divorce, or death.

9. Length and quality of service might improve their status as household members. For example, trusted elderly servants as well as parents might instruct children in proper behavior and household customs. See Kathleen Uno, "Questioning Patrilineality: On Western Studies of the Japanese *Ie,*" 569–594. On the dynamics of the early modern household in its social context, see Herman Ooms, *Tokugawa Village Practice: Class, Status, Power, Law.*

10. Richard K. Beardsley, John W. Hall, and Robert E. Ward, eds., *Village Japan,* 217. In contrast to *ie,* the term *"katei,"* rendered as "home" or "family," or occasionally "household," refers to the family as a social unit or set of domestic relationships developing from coresidence. *Setai,* or "household," refers to a domicile or residential unit. See also Ronald Dore, *City Life in Japan,* ch. 8–10, ch. 20; Susan Orpett Long, *Family Change and the Life Course in Japan,* 7–31; Uno, "Questioning Patrilineality," including the bibliography. Regarding the genesis of the middle-class *katei* in the modern period, see in English Yūko Nishikawa, "The Changing Form of Dwellings and the Establishment of the (Home) in Modern Japan," and Jordan Sand, "At Home in the Meiji Period: Inventing Japanese Domesticity"; lower-class developments are presented in Miyake, "Female Workers of the Urban Lower Class," and Uno, "One Day at a Time."

11. Harumi Befu, *Japan: An Anthropological Introduction,* 41. The law permitted the disowning only of retarded, mentally ill, or incurably profligate eldest sons.

12. Nobushige Hozumi, *Ancestor-Worship and Japanese Law,* 130. Hozumi stated that if the estate could support only one heir, the other children were not allowed to marry unless they obtained the means to support a household. During the late Tokugawa period girls generally married into other households; boys who remained at home or left the household as apprentices or servants frequently did not marry. Ibid., 138.

13. For this reason, anthropologist Chie Nakane has argued that the *ie* should be considered a corporate group, not a kinship group. *Kinship and Economic Organization in Japan.*

14. Ibid.

15. See Uno, "Questioning Patrilineality," 576–577; 589, notes 25–26.

16. The junior wife, the wife of the heir and successor, was also called the "young wife" or *yome.* Until retirement of the senior couple, her mother-in-law (*shūtome*), was called the "housewife," or in Japanese, *shufu* or *kaka.*

17. The authority of the adopted son who became household head was, however, weaker than that of a natural son who succeeded his father; as an insider, the wife of an adopted heir might possess considerable authority in business affairs as well as household matters. One would also expect such women to have had a strong voice in the rearing of their children, although I have not been able to find concrete evidence of this.

18. In her 1935 observations of social life in Suye, a rural hamlet in Kyushu, Wisell notes that when a new baby was born, the next-youngest child stopped nursing and began to sleep beside another household member besides the mother. During the day infants and the next-youngest children were carried around most frequently by sisters, grandmothers, and girl baby-sitters, but also by brothers. Fathers played a fairly active role in raising children. Smith and Wiswell, *The Women of Suye Mura,* 202–253.

19. The father of an infant might or might not be the household head, just as his wife, the child's mother, might or might not be the mistress of the household (the housewife or senior wife).

20. Isabella Bird, *Unbeaten Tracks in Japan,* 74. Bird traveled through villages in northeast Honshu in 1878 before foreigners were permitted to travel freely in Japan. Hideo Kojima, "Childrearing Concepts as a Belief-value System of Society and Individual."

21. Takai Toshio, *Watashi no jokō aishi,* 8–9. Takai's account as well as Bird's observations suggest that even in households without livelihood or property, fathers

could develop a strong emotional attachment to their successors, and that such paternal sentiments could lead to direct involvement in the care of young children.

22. Limited demographic data are available for the modern era, especially between 1870 and 1920. Mean household size (MHS) averaged 4.65 in 1870, 4.89 in 1920, 4.98 in 1930, and 5.00 in 1940. Rural-urban differentials are 4.99 rural MHS and 4.47 urban MHS for 1930 and 5.25 rural MHS and 4.62 urban MHS for 1940. Chie Nakane, "An Interpretation of the Size and Structure of the Household in Japan over Three Centuries," 523, 531. Regarding household composition in 1920, 53.2 percent of the nation's households consisted of two generations, while 27 percent consisted of three generations and 17.7 percent of one generation. In 1920 in rural counties respective figures were 52.2, 29.8, and 15.7 percent, and in the six great cities, 59.5, 12.8, and 27.4 percent. Irene Taeuber, *The Population of Japan,* 106.

23. Hane, *Rebels, Peasants, and Outcastes,* 83.

24. Dr. Matsuda also observed that "[n]owadays it is the young mother herself who carries the baby into the clinic. She is usually followed by her husband." Matsuda Michio, *Oyaji tai kodomo* (Tokyo 1966), cited in Hiroshi Wagatsuma, "Some Aspects of the Contemporary Japanese Family: Once Confucian, Now Fatherless?" 189; 206, note 27.

25. Hane, *Rebels, Peasants, and Outcastes,* 83. See also the discussion on grandmothers and child-rearing later in this chapter.

26. Despite its samurai status, I have treated the Kawakami household as an ordinary household, because it lacked sufficient income to hire servants to care for the children.

27. Gail Bernstein, *Japanese Marxist: A Portrait of Kawakami Hajime 1879–1946,* 6. Regarding grandmother's child in contemporary Japan, see Joy Hendry, *Becoming Japanese: The World of the Preschool Child,* 24, 48, 52–53, 55; and Ezra Vogel, *Japan's New Middle Class,* 224–226.

28. Tanaka Katsubumi, "Ie de hataraku kodomo," 245.

29. Kobayashi Hatsue, *Onna sandai,* 97–98.

30. Hyman Kublin, *Asian Revolutionary: The Life of Sen Katayama,* 11–17.

31. Tanaka, "Ie de hataraku kodomo," 246–248.

32. Chiba Hisao, *Meiji no shōgakkō,* 273–274.

33. Sugō Hiroshi, *Komori gakkō.*

34. Ishikawa Matsutarō, *Onna daigakushū.* In English, see Basil Chamberlain, *Things Japanese: Being Notes on Things Connected with Japan,* 67–76 or Atsuharu Sakai, "Kaibara Ekiken and 'Onna Daigaku,' " 43–56.

35. Yamazumi Masami and Nakae Kazue, *Kosodate no sho,* vols. 1–2.

36. Uno, "Women and Changes," 27–30; Yamakawa, *Women of the Mito Domain,* 19–23, 39–61, 85–100.

37. Sugō, *Komori gakkō,* 6–25; Ichiyō Higuchi, "Child's Play," in Robert Danly, ed. and trans., *In the Shade of Spring Leaves: The Life and Work of Higuchi Ichiyo, A Meiji Woman of Letters,* 276, 261–262; originally published in 1895–1896 as "Takekurabe."

38. Kobayashi, *Onna sandai,* 10, 12.

39. Smith and Wiswell, *The Women of Suye Mura,* esp. 146–147, 234–236.

40. Tanaka, "Ie de hataraku kodomo," 257.

41. Ibid. The girl left home in 1905.

42. Tamanoi, "Songs as Weapons," 808–809.

43. Nishimura Kōichi, "Shokunin no ko—totei kara oyakata made," 80, 91, 104.

44. Ibid., 91, 104.

45. For example, see Richard Bowring, ed. and trans., *Murasaki Shikibu: Her Diary and Poetic Memoirs: A Translation and Study;* and Helen Craig McCullough and William H. McCullough, trans., *A Tale of Flowering Fortunes.*

46. Ihara Saikaku, *Some Final Words of Advice,* trans. Peter Nosco, 226. However, early modern wet nurses or nannies might also serve until the betrothal of their charges, or after. Chikamatsu Monzaemon, "Yosaku of Tamba," 91–98; Etsu Inagaki Sugimoto, *A Daughter of the Samurai,* 84–85, 96–97.

47. See Yamazumi and Nakae, *Kosodate no sho,* 73–79, 95–99.

48. See Sugimoto, *A Daughter of the Samurai,* 3, also 7–16, 21–22, 84–85; and Shidzue Ishimoto, *Facing Two Ways,* 23.

49. Ihara, *Some Final Words of Advice,* 225–226.

50. Ibid., 228–229; Robert Danly, "A Brief Life," in Danly, ed. and trans., *In the Shade of Spring Leaves,* 7; Ihara Saikaku, *This Scheming World,* trans. Takatsuka Masanori and David C. Stubbs, 80–81.

51. Chikamatsu, "Yosaku of Tamba," 91–98.

52. Sugimoto, *A Daughter of the Samurai,* esp. 1–35; Chiyoko Higuchi, "Lady Kasuga, Mother of Shoguns," 38–42.

53. Danly, "A Brief Life," 7.

54. Ibid., 28, 43.

55. Kuwata Shingo, *Osanago no sono* (1876), cited in Ichibangase, et al., *Nihon no hoiku,* 15.

56. Fukuzawa Yukichi, *The Autobiography of Yukichi Fukuzawa,* 297–298.

57. Osamu Dazai, *Return to Tsugaru: Travels of a Purple Tramp,* xv–xvi, 152–154.

58. Hachihama Tokusaburō, "Keian no kenkyū," 230.

59. Smith and Wiswell, *The Women of Suye Mura,* 202–253.

60. For example, Cole and Tominaga estimate that male and female professional, managerial, and clerical employees comprised 12 percent of the labor force in 1920 and 13.6 percent in 1930. Cole and Tominaga, "Japan's Changing Occupational Structure," 60. However, the new middle class exerted social and cultural influence beyond its numbers because its ranks included journalists, writers, schoolteachers, professors, and government officials.

    Demographic as well as economic factors account for the scarcity of parents-in-law in urban households. Parents of rural migrants who established families in the cities tended to remain in the village with the *ie* successor. National figures on earlier household composition are unavailable, but Toda Teizō's *Kazoku kōsei,* the classic analysis of the 1920 census results, revealed that while 67.9 percent of rural (*gun*) households consisted of one- or two-generation households and 29.8 percent consisted of three-generation households, the corresponding figures for the six great cities were 86.9 and 12.8 percent. Cited in Taeuber, *The Population of Japan,* 106. (Female labor was negligible in 1920, but it comprised roughly 6 percent of the clerical category in 1930.) See also Kinmonth, *The Self-Made Man,* 279–280. Regarding household size, see Nakane, "An Interpretation," 531.

61. Naka, 86, 93.

62. Masaaki Kosaka, *Japanese Thought in the Meiji Era,* trans. David Abosch, 84.

63. In 1900 the overall enrollment rate was still only 82 percent, but in 1909 it leveled off and remained at about 97 percent. Kami Shōichirō, "Honryū no naka no gakkō kyōiku," 100.

64. Tanaka, "Ie de hataraku kodomo," 245.

65. "Nippori-chō jidō shūgaku jōkyō chōsa ni tsuite," 57–58; "Jidō kyōyō chōsa," 51, 56–58.

66. The first *komori gakkō* was founded in 1883. In 1891 many schools of this type were founded in Aichi and Nagano Prefectures. In 1899 a national educators' association recommended that *komori gakkō* be established at all public elementary schools. Thereafter, curriculum plans to implement this recommendation were drawn up in various prefectures ranging from the south of Kyushu to the northern central areas of Japan's main island, Honshu. The *komori gakkō* disappeared after World War II. Tanaka, "Ie de hataraku kodomo," 265–266. See also Tamanoi, "Songs as Weapons." Similarly, special factory and evening schools for children employed in other occupations were established around the turn of the century. Tanaka, "Ie de hataraku kodomo," 267–272.

67. See Ichibangase, et al., *Nihon no hoiku,* 2, 20; Urabe, et al., *Hoiku no rekishi,* 4–5; and Kōzu Zenzaburō, *Kyōiku aishi.*

68. The *gakusei,* the 1874 edict establishing Japan's centralized educational system, provided for the founding of "*yōchi shōgaku,*" best translated as nursery schools. Urabe, et al., *Hoiku no rekishi,* 3.

69. Monbushō rei dai sanjūnigō, "Yōchien hoiku oyobi setsubi kitei," issued June 28, 1899, cited in Urabe, et al., *Hoiku no rekishi,* 34–35.

70. This was true for both rural and urban lower-class families; however, urban families could not obtain supplementary food or fuel from the land. Also, weaker ties to their landlords made it more difficult for lower-class city dwellers to obtain paternalistic aid.

71. For example, E. Patricia Tsurumi documents 1901 wage differentials by gender at cotton spinning mills in Kansai, Japan's great industrial area, in *Factory Girls,* 149, table 8.2.

72. Evidence concerning the *kōjō takujisho* is sparse, but records indicate that many of the earliest operated at mines. See, for example, Fukuoka-ken shakai jigyō kyōkai, *Fukuoka kenka shakai jigyō.*

73. Kami Shōichirō and Yamazaki Tomoko, *Nihon no yōchien: Nihon no yōji kyōiku no rekishi,* 129–144.

74. The virtual absence of references to factory day nurseries in welfare and educational journals indicates that they did not capture the attention of turn-of-the-century social reformers as day-care centers did, most likely because day nurseries did not attempt to reform children's or parents' character or to improve home life.

75. The two groups did different types of work. Lower-middle class women performed skilled or semiskilled work such as embroidering handkerchiefs and finishing garments. Lower-class women did unskilled work such as gluing paper bags and attaching sandal thongs. See Uno, "One Day at a Time."

76. Fukaya Masashi, *Ryōsai kenbo no kyōikushugi;* Uno, "Origins of 'Good Wife, Wise Mother.' "

77. One can compare Japan's *ryōsai kenbo* and with the U.S. "republican motherhood" of the federal era; however, as prewar Japan was a constitutional monarchy, one might call *ryōsai kenbo* "imperial motherhood." See Mary Beth Norton, *Liberty's Daughters: The Revolutionary Experience of American Women, 1750–1800;* Linda Kerber, *Women of the Republic: Intellect and Ideology in Revolutionary America;* and Cott, *The Bonds of Womanhood.* See also Sievers, *Flowers in Salt,* esp. 112–113.

78. As industrialization proceeded, wage work in the new economic organizations outside the home was defined as men's work.

79. As filial piety to coresident parents or parents-in-law was of greatest importance, wives whose husbands had been adopted into the bride's household

(housedaughters) were not obliged to serve their husbands' parents. Rather, their husbands were obliged to obey their adoptive parents, who were at the same time their parents-in-law. Additional study of the dynamics of these relationships in concrete cases is needed. The 1898 Civil Code disregarded regional variations, mandating primogeniture, male succession, and thus the patrilineal stem family as the basic household unit throughout Japan.

3. Day-Care and Moral Improvement: The Case of Futaba Yōchien

1. The word *yōchien* signifies "kindergarten." In late nineteenth century Japan foreign kindergartens, mainly established by missionaries and Japanese Christian converts, kept young children a few hours a day for intellectual, moral, and spiritual education, but kindergartens did not offer all-day care to the children of working parents. In addition to employing the term "day-care center," I sometimes refer to Futaba Yōchien as a paupers' kindergarten (*hinmin yōchien*) because its founders described it as such until its name was changed to Futaba Hoikuen (Futaba Care Center) in 1916.

   Prewar Japanese day-care centers were referred to as *jidō hokanjo, hokanjo, hoikujo, takujisho, takujiba, yōjien, jidōen, hoikuba, hoikuen,* and *aijien,* but *hoikujo, takujisho,* and *takujiba* were the most frequently used terms. Factory day nurseries, or *crèches* (my translation of *kōjō takujisho*), provided long hours of custodial care for operatives' children, with little or no attention to their educational needs.

2. The next chapter discusses a second set of influential early child-care facilities, the Kobe Wartime Service Memorial Day-Care Association (Kōbe Seneki Kinen Hoikukai, or KSKH) centers.

3. See for example, Tsurumi, *Factory Girls;* Elizabeth Mouer, "Women in Teaching," 157–170; Margit Nagy, "Middle-Class Working Women during the Interwar Years," 199–216; Barbara Hamill Sato, "Japanese Women and *Modanizumu:* The Emergence of a New Women's Culture in the 1920s."

4. Hastings, "From Heroine to Patriotic Volunteer," 2–18; Nolte and Hastings, "The Meiji State's Policy," 151–172; Saji Emiko, "Gunji engo to katei fujin—shoki Aikoku Fujinkai ron," 116–143, esp. 142.

5. Yoshida Kyūichi, *Shakai jigyō riron,* 128, cf. 80. Despite the livelihood guarantees written into the postwar constitution, *fuyō gimu* precedes legal entitlement. Tsukamoto Tetsu, Ōtsuka Tatsuo, Urabe Hiroshi, and Kōkō Seiichi, eds., *Shakai fukushi jigyō jiten,* 50.

6. Hastings, "From Heroine to Patriotic Volunteer," 9.

7. Kaide Sumiko, *Noguchi Yuka no shōgai,* 116–125; Matsukawa Yukiko, "Jūkyū seikimatsu Kariforunia no mushō yōchien undō to waga kuni e no eikyō, Morishima Mine to Kariforunia yōchien renshū gakkō o chūshin ni," 28–29; Kami Shōichirō and Yamazaki Tomoko, *Hikari hono kanaredomo: Futaba Hoikuen to Tokunaga Yuki* 45–63.

8. Difficulties of women writers and artists during the Meiji era can be found in Sievers, *Flowers in Salt,* 162–188; Danly, "A Brief Life," 11–164; Brian Powell, "Matsui Sumako: Actress and Woman," 135–147.

9. Kaide, *Noguchi Yuka no shōgai;* Muraoka Suehiro, ed., *Futaba Hoikuen hachijūgonen shi;* Nakatani, 129–134; Monbushō, *Yōchien kyōiku kyūjūnen shi.*

10. Kami and Yamazaki, *Hikari hono kanaredomo,* 45–63; Agnes Snyder, *Dauntless Women in Early Childhood Education, 1856–1931,* ch. 5, esp. 106–109; Barbara Beatty, *Preschool Education in America: The Culture of Young Children from the Colonial Era to the Present.*

11. Kublin, *Asian Revolutionary,* 96–102, esp. 100–101; Muraoka, ed., *Futaba Hoikuen,* 22; "Katayama's Thanks," 5.

12. Kanzaki Kiyoshi, "Noguchi Yuka," 59.

13. The German educator Froebel (1872–1952) is credited with inventing the kindergarten. Frederick Mayer, *A History of Educational Thought,* 2d ed., 308.

14. In 1891, the Christian Uchimura Kanzō was dismissed from his teaching position at the elite First High School for refusing to bow to the Imperial Rescript on Education (issued in 1890). Conservative nationalists viewed this as proof that Christians' belief in God hindered development of loyalty to the emperor.

15. Kanzaki, "Noguchi Yuka," 60.

16. Urabe, et al., *Hoiku no rekishi,* 32–33. Also in Kaide, *Noguchi Yuka no shōgai,* 36.

17. Although there is no evidence that the two knew of Japanese factory day nurseries, Morishima was doubtless aware of American day nurseries from her overseas sojourn.

18. The regulations are reprinted in Urabe, et al., *Hoiku no rekishi,* 33–34.

19. The respective sites were Shimorokubanchō 27 banchi, Dote sanbanchō 7 banchi, and Shimorokubanchō 48 banchi, all in Kōjimachi Ward, and Samegahashi, Yotsuya Ward.

20. Kanzaki, "Noguchi Yuka," 62–63.

21. *Shiritsu Futaba Yōchien hōkoku* (hereafter *SFYH*) 1 (January–June 1900), 3–4. After the 1915 name change, from 17 (July 1915–June 1916) the title of the annual report became *Shiritsu Futaba Hoikuen hōkoku* (*SFHH*).

22. *SFYH* 7 (July 1905–June 1906), 2–3.

23. *SFYH* 9 (July 1907–June 1908), 10.

24. Ibid.

25. *SFYH* 4 (July 1902–June 1903), 4.

26. Ibid., 11; *SFYH* 5 (July 1903–June 1904), 5, 10. Descriptions of Shitadera-machi, one of Osaka's great slums, in the yearbooks of Aizenbashi Hoikujo (1905–1915; reopened as Aizenen Takujisho and Yōchien, 1915–) and articles in *Katei shūhō* (the weekly newspaper published at Japan Women's College [Nihon Joshi Daigakkō]) reveal similar conditions—overcrowded and dilapidated housing, marginal occupations, income shortfalls, and working wives and children—in early twentieth century cities.

27. The father's salary could not support the family, so the mother might take in sewing, give sewing lessons, or do skilled piecework at home.

28. Urabe, et al., *Hoiku no rekishi,* 33–34; Kanzaki, "Noguchi Yuka," 63–65; *SFYH* 1 (January–June 1900), 26–27; *SFYH* 16 (July 1914–June 1915), 9.

29. *SFYH* 1 (January–June 1900), 7–8.

30. *SFYH* 4 (July 1902–June 1903), 12.

31. *SFYH* 1 (January–June 1900), 24–25.

32. By the middle of the Taishō period the staff also had created programs for older siblings of their pupils as well. See chapter 6.

33. The names of the evening meeting might also be translated as "parent association" and "fathers' and mothers' association," respectively, but my usage follows late nineteenth century U.S. kindergarten terminology known to Morishima. See note 34, following.

34. In the United States, programs for parents at late nineteenth century free, or charity, kindergartens were almost invariably called "mothers' meetings" and were held in the afternoon, reflecting an assumption that care of preschool children was of greatest interest to mothers rather than fathers. The time of the meetings in the United States reflects cultural assumptions that mothers should not work; therefore meetings were held during standard working hours rather than at night.

35. *SFYH* 5 (July 1903–June 1904), 9.

36. *SFYH* 4 (January 1903), 11. Although parents shared responsibility for children, the division of labor was asymmetrical. The Futaba Yōchien staff may have felt that women had fewer recreational outlets than men despite greater burdens of housework and child care.

37. *SFYH* 2 (July 1900–June 1901), 6.

38. Regarding early modern views of family togetherness, see the discussion below in this section.

39. *SFYH* 2 (July 1900–June 1901), 8.

40. *SFYH* 5 (July 1903–June 1904), 10.

41. *SFYH* 2 (July 1900–June 1901), 9.

42. *SFYH* 4 (July 1902–June 1903), 14.

43. By the third decade of the twentieth century, however, the rise in literacy and the diffusion of newspapers, magazines, photographs, and motion pictures may have lessened the cultural gap between urban social classes.

44. The yearbooks did not restrict themselves merely to rosy reports of Futaba Yōchien's success. Noguchi mentioned the failure of her savings talk; the first yearbook mentioned that one disgruntled parent withdrew a child.

45. *SFYH* 1 (January–June 1900), 11–13.

46. Ibid., 24–25.

47. *SFYH* 6 (July 1904–June 1905), 6.

48. The third institution was located in northern, rural Yamagata Prefecture. Naimushō, "Yōji hoiku jigyō," *Waga kuni ni okeru jikei kyūsai jigyō*, 9–14.

49. *SFYH* 10 (July 1909–June 1910), 9.

50. Naimushō, *Naimushō senji jigyō nenkan.* The yearbook does not discuss these facilities in detail. One network of wartime day-care centers, the *jidō hokanjo* of the Kobe Women's Service Association, is briefly discussed in the next chapter.

4. Day-Care and Economic Improvement: The Kobe Wartime Service Memorial Day-Care Association

1. Kobe, one of Japan's six great prewar cities, is located over 400 km to the west of Tokyo.

2. When the war ended, the board of directors of the Kōbe Fujin Hōkōkai voted to close the facilities. The centers were saved by a personal appeal from the Kobe mayor and reopened under sponsorship of a new organization, KSKH.

3. *Hokanjo* literally means "places to keep children."

4. Hyōgo-ken shakai fukushi kyōgikai, ed., "Namae Takayuki to hobo-san tachi," *Fukushi no tomoshibi: Hyōgo-ken shakai jigyō senkakusha*, 256.

5. For example, when Namae represented Japan at the 1919 White House Conference on Children, he lauded these centers as exemplary early facilities. Namae, "Standards of Child Welfare Work."

6. Ōsaka-shi minseikyoku, ed., *Hoikujo no ayumi, 1909–1945,* 44.

7. The *hokanjo* regulations can be found in Kōbe Seneki Kinen Hoikukai, *Sanjūnen o kaerimite,* 16. Hereafter called *Sanjūnen.*

8. Ibid., 188, 189–190.

9. Ibid., 56.

10. Ibid., 55.

11. Ibid.

12. Ibid.

13. Ibid.

14. Ibid., 51.

15. The existing sources lack detailed information concerning the curriculum.

16. *Sanjūnen,* 48.

17. Despite the fact that the Kansai region was an economic, political, and cultural rival of Tokyo during the prewar era, the relative decline of Kansai since the loss of the colonies following Japan's defeat in World War II has fostered a certain degree of scholarly amnesia regarding the many innovations in relief institutions that developed there during the prewar era.

18. Only one day-care center existed in 1900. According to the table in Ichibangase, et al., *Nihon no hoiku,* 278, the number of centers had increased to 25 at the early Taishō era (1913). By the end of the Taishō period in 1926 there were 273 centers, which had tripled to 879 during the first decade of Shōwa (by 1935). In 1944, during World War II, 2,184 centers were in operation. Regarding the nationalistic content of kindergarten curricula that influenced day-care programs, see Murayama Seiichi, "Fukyūki no yōchien no hoiku katei (Meiji 30nen–Meiji 31nen)," 52, and his "Taishō ki no hoiku yonkō no naiyō," 89–93.

19. It is unlikely that "good wife, wise mother," (*ryōsai kenbo*), which the state had endorsed in 1899, or even the Western conceptions of motherhood, which intellectuals debated in the 1870s, could have displaced the old ideas of womanhood and motherhood by the first decade of the twentieth century. See Uno, "Origins of 'Good Wife, Wise Mother'"; Nolte and Hastings, "The Meiji State's Policy," 158–172.

20. The contrast with the adult activities at U.S. kindergartens is striking. Examination of the American periodical, *Kindergarten Magazine,* reveals that from 1893 to 1915 in the United States, gatherings for adults were called "mother's meetings." They were held during the day, when employed fathers and mothers would be unable to attend, implying that working and caring for children were mutually exclusive activities.

21. The latter is Carol Gluck's term. Carol Gluck, *Japan's Modern Myths,* 34.

22. Ibid., esp. ch. 5, 6, and 8.

23. Kinzley, *Industrial Harmony;* Hastings, "From Heroine to Patriotic Volunteer."

24. Harootunian, "Introduction," esp. 10–11; "Imperial Rescript on Thrift and Diligence (Boshin shōsho)," the official translation from *The Japan Yearbook,* 1911, 456, is cited in Wilbur M. Fridell, *Japanese Shrine Mergers, 1906–1912,* 111.

25. Smethurst, *A Social Basis,* xii–33.

26. See Gluck, *Japan's Modern Myths,* esp. 178–204; Pyle, "The Technology of Nationalism"; and Kenneth Pyle, "The Advantages of Followership: German Economics and Japanese Bureaucrats, 1890–1925," 421–430.

27. Gluck's term. See Gluck, *Japan's Modern Myths,* 12. Some urban initiatives are suggested in Gluck, 178–204. Pyle, "The Technology of Nationalism"; and R. P. Dore, "Factory Legislation in Nineteenth-Century Japan," 323–390, discuss the turn-of-the-century debate over factory legislation.

28. Gluck, *Japan's Modern Myths,* 201–202.

29. Ichibangase, et al., *Nihon no hoiku,* 39.

5. Nationalism, Motherhood, and the Early Taishō Expansion of Day-Care

1. This discussion of early Taishō centers includes institutions founded between the opening of the KSKH day-care centers in 1906 (Meiji 39) and the 1918 (Taishō 7) Rice Riots. Thus a handful of pre-1910 (late Meiji) facilities are treated in this chapter.

2. In addition, there still existed widespread acceptance of ordinary women's participation in income-earning activities. See chapter 2.

3. The other three were Yokohama, Nagoya, and Fukuoka. By 1926 day-care centers had been established in all six of Japan's great cities.

4. The major work in English on the 1918 Rice Riots (Taishō 7) is Michael Lawrence Lewis, *Rioters and Citizens.* Regarding social work in Japan in the late Taishō era, see Yoshida, *Gendai shakai,* ch. 6.

5. Early Taishō expansion rates were calculated from figures in Ichibangase, et al., *Nihon no hoiku,* 278. For later expansion rates, see chapter 6 of this book. I compiled the information on geographical distribution and center descriptions in Chūō jizen kyōkai, *Nihon shakai jigyō meikan* and Tōkyō-shi shakaikyoku, *Tōkyō-shi shakai jigyō meikan.*

6. The Kansai region surrounds the three great cities of Osaka, Kobe, and Kyoto. The former two were industrial and shipping centers; the latter was Japan's capital from 794 to 1868. The Kanto region includes Japan's largest city and capital, Tokyo, and the port city Yokohama.

7. The multiple centers of the KSKH and Kōsaikai networks had uniform curricula and programs, while these apparently varied at the four Kōenkai centers in Tokyo.

8. It opened as part of the Nihonbashi Dōjōkan (Nihonbashi Sympathy House) on July 21, 1909, in Shitaderamachi, an Osaka slum district, as a branch project

of Ishii Jūji's Okayama Orphanage, located in Okayama City, a prefectural capital one hundred miles west of Osaka. This orphanage was well-known in the Meiji period for introducing the family system of care for orphans to Japan.

9. Ishii first visited the KSKH centers on one of his trips from Okayama to Osaka.

10. Nor were mothers excluded from the category "laborer."

11. Ōsaka-shi minseikyoku, *Hoikujo no ayumi,* 85. The Kōsaikai directive creating the day-care division (*hoikubu*) passed the Kōsaikai board of directors in late 1913 by a nearly unanimous vote: eighteen for, one against, two absent; its sole opponent cited the need for further study. The directive mandated a program of physical care and education consisting of "1. Day-care of poor children, 2. Simple paupers' kindergartens, 3. Meals for the children." Ibid., 81–82.

12. Kōsaikai, *Zaidan hōjin Taishō gonenji dai ikkai nenpō,* 80.

13. Kōsaikai, *Zaidan hōjin Kōsaikai Taishō kunen dai yonkai nenpō,* 5.

14. The area it served was a *tokushu buraku,* an area occupied by former members of the Tokugawa outcast class. The old class system was abolished in early Meiji, but the former outcasts still suffered severe discrimination, as they do today.

15. Ōsaka-shi minseikyoku, *Hoikujo no ayumi,* 63.

16. It was founded in March 1914 as a philanthropic project by a local entrepreneur, Tanaka Shōzaburō, who later became an Osaka city council member.

17. Ōsaka-shi minseikyoku, *Hoikujo no ayumi,* 70.

18. Chūō jizen kyōkai, *Nihon shakai jigyō meikan,* 4–5.

19. Kōbe shiritsu hoikuen renmei, *Kōbe no hoikuenshi,* 47.

20. The special schools were called *tokushu shōgakkō,* while the club was named Tōkyō-shi Tokushu Shōgakkō Kōenkai. The association began in 1907 as the Tokushu Gakkō Jidō Kyūgokai, organized to provide shelter and medical treatment to children of the special elementary schools following the disastrous flood that year. Here one must recall that many of Tokyo's slums were built on low-lying land, making many of them very vulnerable to floods and high waves. Using the surplus from the flood assistance fund, the association was formed in 1910 to create and administer permanent relief programs, including the child-care centers, for families of the Tokushu Shōgakkō students. Katoda Keiko, "Waga kuni ni okeru hinji kyōiku," 95–96.

21. Chūō jizen kyōkai, *Nihon shakai jigyō meikan,* 103. The data in this yearbook are for the year 1918.

22. Literally, "Garden of Sympathy Day-Care Center for Young Children."

23. Sakamaki and an association of supporters supported Dōjōen, but it also received financial assistance from the Home Ministry and Tokyo Prefecture. Tōkyō-shi shakaikyoku, *Tōkyō-shi shakai jigyō meikan,* 20–21.

24. Ibid., 20.

25. Ibid.; Chūō jizen kyōkai, *Nihon shakai jigyō meikan,* 107.

26. Tōkyō-shi shakaikyoku, *Tōkyō-shi shakai jigyō,* 110.

27. Ibid., 111.

28. The establishment of municipal day-care centers and settlements is discussed in chapter 6.

29. Kōsaikai, *Zaidan hōjin Taishō,* 85.

30. After early Taishō, limited facilities for infant care were sometimes added to existing centers and included in plans for child day-care centers.

31. Ogawa held a doctorate in law. His initial specialization was reformatory work (*kanka jigyō*), but he later played a leading role in the creation of the district welfare commissioner system (*hōmenin seido*) in Osaka. In 1913 he moved from Tokyo to Kansai in order to assume a position in the Osaka City Kyūsai Kenkyūshitsu (Relief Works Research Office). He also became the guiding light of Osaka's Kyūsai Jigyō Kenkyūkai (Relief Work Research Association).

32. Ogawa Shigejirō, "Chūkan hoiku jigyō ni tsuite," 1–21. In addition, he briefly mentioned other German facilities for young children, including kindergartens, shelters for waifs (*kinderheim*), and preparatory schools (*fichurushure*).

33. Ibid., 3.

34. Ibid., 7.

35. Ibid., 1. Ogawa repeated these criticisms of Japanese day-care in a speech to a group of leading Tokyo industrialists in 1918. Ironically, the lecture ended with a tour of Futaba Yōchien, whose purposes and programs did not exemplify his views. Ogawa Shigejirō, *Yōji hoiku jigyō ni tsuite.*

36. Ogawa, "Chūkan hoiku," 2.

37. They are listed in the original order. Ibid., 18.

38. Ibid., 9.

39. Ibid., 10.

40. This facility closed in 1915, but reopened as Ishii Kinen Aizenen in 1917. As the latter, it is discussed in the following chapter.

41. He also once more blasted most Japanese day-care facilities as fakes, asserting that saving infant lives was the main purpose of day-care.

42. Kōsaikai, *Zaidan hōjin Taishō,* 82.

43. Izumio Aijien's goals were discussed earlier in this chapter.

44. Inada Jō, "Kōsaikai kakubu jigyō to sono shugi," 53.

45. Ibid., 54.

46. Namae Takayuki, "Hoiku jigyō ni tsuite," 81–88. The article is the text of a lecture he presented at the Home Ministry's annual Kanka Kyūsai Kōshūkai (Reform and Relief Symposium) on July 12, 1915.

47. This term was apparently first employed by KSKH; the word "*kai*" can also be translated "association" or "club." See also chapter 4.

48. See the discussion of child care and education in chapter 2.

49. Of eight centers, 50 percent were called *fukei kai;* 25 percent, *oya no kai;* together the two terms totaled 75 percent. One center had no adult program, and information was unavailable for one center. Information compiled primarily from Kōbe Seneki Kinen Hoikukai, "Zenkoku jidō hoiku jigyō ippan," *Jidō hoiku jigyō no gaiyō* 100–119; Tōkyō-fu kyūsaika, Yōji Chūkan hoiku.

50. More precisely, *oya no kai* constituted seven centers (19 percent); *fukei kai,* ten (27 percent); *haha no kai,* four (11 percent); *boshi kai,* seven (19 percent). Six centers, or 17 percent, had no adult educational program, while information was unavailable for two centers.

51. The views of the latter are discussed more extensively in the next chapter.

52. Ogawa, "Chūkan hoiku," 2. Cf. excerpts from this article cited earlier in this chapter.

53. Ibid., 11.

54. Cows were not raised in Japan before the Meiji era, so alternatives to nursing were few. Gruel from boiled rice was sometimes fed to babies, if the mother's milk failed.

55. Takada Shingō, "Beikoku ni okeru jidō hogo jigyō," 86.

56. Ogawa, "Chūkan hoiku," 11.

57. Gōchi Fumiko, "Maruyama Chiyo," 201.

58. Nakagawa estimates Tokyo lower-class women's employment rates, including piecework (*naishoku*), at roughly 70 percent during late Meiji–Taishō but states that by late Taishō–early Shōwa it had fallen to about 25 percent. Nakagawa Kiyoshi, *Senzen Tōkyō no toshi kasō,* 27.

59. Tōkyō-fu kyūsaika, *Yōji chūkan hoiku,* 1, 18–19.

60. Tōkyō-shi shakaikyoku, *Tōkyō-shi shakai jigyō meikan,* 376.

61. Ibid.

62. The discussion of these changes continues in the next chapter.

6. Late Taishō Day-Care: New Justifications and Old Goals

1. Ichibangase, et al., *Nihon no hoiku,* 278.

2. U.S. Department of Labor, Children's Bureau, *Standards of Child Welfare: A Report of the Children's Bureau Conferences May and June, 1919;* Nettie McGill, *Infant Welfare Work in Europe: An Account of Recent Experiences in Great Britain, Austria, Belgium, France, Germany, and Italy,* 81–107, 108–136.

3. In the prewar era regulations prohibited the establishment of colleges and universities (*daigaku*) for women, but in an English publication the founder called it a university. Jinzō Naruse, "The Education of Japanese Women," 219. After World War II this institution became Japan Women's University (Nihon Joshi Daigaku).

4. Until his retirement in 1923, in publications Namae's affiliation was listed as Home Ministry Commissionee. After retirement he lectured at well-known universities and continued to write sections of the yearbooks of the Chūō shakai jigyō kyōkai (Central Social Work Association) in the 1930s. Ichibangase Yasuko, ed., *Namae Takayuki shū*, 424–447; Hokkaidō jizen jigyō kyōkai, ed., *Kyūsai jigyō kōshūkai.*

5. See chapters 4 and 5. The *hokanjo* had served the families of soldiers stationed overseas during the war. Their successors, the *hoikujo,* gave first priority to the families of deceased and disabled war veterans, but they admitted children of employed nonveterans.

6. Namae Takayuki, "Taisei ni okeru kyūji jigyō," 44.

7. Ibid., 50.

8. Namae, "Hoiku jigyō ni tsuite," 81–88.

9. Iwamatsudō published the first edition in 1923. Namae revised and expanded the text for the fifth (1929) edition; the eighth edition was issued by Iwamatsudō in 1933. The discussion of this work is based on the 1923 edition reprinted in Ichibangase, ed., *Namae Takayuki shū*, unless another edition is specified.

10. Ichibangase, ed., *Namae Takayuki shū*, 266.

11. Namae Takayuki, *Shakai jigyō kōyō,* 363.

12. As explained later in this chapter, the institutional name was changed to Futaba Hoikuen in 1916 and has remained so to the present. When Futaba was reorganized as a foundation in 1935, Tokunaga became chair of the board of directors.

13. For example, in 1918, after a lecture on institutional child care by Ogawa Shigejirō, twenty-three representatives from fourteen large industrial firms, including Asahi Glass K. K. (Kabushiki Kaisha), Oji Silk Filiature K. K., Kanegafuchi Cotton Spinning K. K., and Japan Electrification Industries K. K., went to Futaba to observe day-care firsthand, an event sponsored by the Kōgyō Kyōikukai (Industrial Education Association), an Osaka organization headed by Uno Riemon. Ogawa, *Yōji hoiku jigyō ni tsuite,* 2.

14. Karen Offen, "Defining Feminism: A Comparative Historical Approach," 119–157; Naomi Black, *Social Feminism;* Uno, "Death of 'Good Wife, Wise Mother'?" esp. 318–320.

15. Yamakawa Kikue stated that Kinoshita Naoe's *Hi no hashira* (1904), translated as *Pillar of Fire,* was an inspiration to Tokunaga's Christian social activism. Yamakawa Kikue, *Onna nidai no ki* 118–119; Kami and Yamazaki, *Hikari hono kanaredomo,* 126.

16. Regarding broad changes in notions of womanhood and women's lives beginning around the Taishō period, see, for example Sievers, *Flowers in Salt,* esp. ch. 6–9; Noriyo Hayakawa, "Feminism and Nationalism in Japan"; Yasuko Imai, "The Emergence of the Japanese Shufu: Why a Shufu is More than a 'Housewife'"; Bernstein, *Recreating Japanese Women,* ch. 8–11; Hopper, *A New Woman of Japan;* Miyake, "Female Workers of the Urban Lower Classes"; Akiko Chimoto, "The Birth of the Full-Time Housewife in the Japanese Worker's Household as Seen through Family Budget Surveys"; Shizuko Koyama, "The 'Good Wife and Wise Mother' Ideology in Post–World War I Japan"; Hane, *Reflections on the Way to the Gallows;* Mackie, *Creating Socialist Women;* Barbara Hamill Sato, "The *Moga* Sensation: *Perceptions of the Modan Gāru in Japanese Intellectual Circles;*" Sato, "Japanese Women and *Modanizumu*"; and Molony and Molony, "Ichikawa Fusae."

17. Yamakawa Kikue, "Tokunaga Yuki no omoide," 6.

18. And, every year until Hiratsuka's child graduated from girls' higher school, Tokunaga sent her a birthday gift. Kami and Yamazaki, *Hikari hono kanaredomo,* 113–118, 273–278.

19. It is not possible to assess Tokunaga's relationship with Morishima. Morishima gradually became less involved with Futaba after her marriage to Saitō Seijirō in 1901. Kami and Yamazaki, *Hikari hono kanaredomo,* 47. And there are no sources that discuss her later ties to Futaba Yōchien or Futaba Hoikuen.

20. Noguchi's pupils at the Peers' Kindergarten included imperial princesses and the children of peers and great industrial houses such as Mitsui. See Ishimoto, *Facing Two Ways,* 41–52, also 55–74.

21. *SFYH* 15 (1914), 36.

22. *SFYH* 14 (1914), 1. For details concerning earlier Futaba justifications for daycare and views of motherhood, childhood, and family life, see chapter 3.

23. This was a fairly simple matter, because in offering infant care and extended hours and in caring for more than one hundred children, Futaba Yōchien violated the Ministry of Education regulations and had never been licensed as a kindergarten. In contrast, the Home Ministry did not establish uniform standards for child care or most other social projects during the pre–World War II era.

24. Muraoka, ed., *Futaba Hoikuen,* 40–52. In English see Kathleen Uno, "Day-Care and Family Life in Late Meiji–Taishō Japan," 30.

25. Cf. Aizenbashi Hoikujo and the Kōsaikai activities treated in the previous chapter, Ishii Kinen Aizenen and the municipal settlements discussed later in this chapter. While day-care centers that offered both education and long hours of care constituted the core of many prewar Japanese settlements, especially the public ones, in the United States settlements often included day nurseries, provided day-long custodial care, or charity (or free) kindergartens, which emphasized preschool education.

26. Neither the annual reports nor Muraoka, ed., *Futaba Hoikuen,* 43–48, clearly state whether Tokunaga, Noguchi, or both jointly made the decision to found the refuge. There is no evidence that Noguchi had developed interest in feminism or special aid to mothers, but Tokunaga had shown enthusiasm for Hiratsuka's ideas, which from 1913 onward explicitly emphasized the protection of motherhood. Thus it is likely that the Mothers' House was Tokunaga's idea, although such a drastic change in Futaba's program doubtless required Noguchi's consent.

27. *SFHH,* 20 (1922), 4–5.

28. Muraoka, ed., *Futaba Hoikuen,* 49.

29. In English see Laurel Rodd, "Yosano Akiko and the Taisho Debate over the 'New Woman,'" 175–198; and Diana Bethel, "Visions of a Humane Society: Feminist Thought in Taishō Japan," 92–95. In Japanese see Kōchi Nobuko, ed., *Shiryō bosei hogo ronsō;* and Arai Tomio, "Bosei ishiki no mezame," 130–157. Kōchi contains an extensive bibliography of the mid-Taishō debates on motherhood and motherhood protection.

30. In English important discussions of "good wife, wise mother" include Sievers, *Flowers in Salt,* 22–24, 109–113; Uno, "Women and Changes," 38–39; Nolte and Hastings, "The Meiji State's Policy," 153–171; Uno, "Origins of 'Good Wife, Wise Mother.'" Major Japanese works include Fukaya, *Ryōsai kenbo,* 1–270; Komano Yōko, "Ryōsai kenboshugi no seiritsu to sono naiyō," 142–143; Nakajima Kuni, "Boseiron no keitō," 62–66; Katano Misako, "Ryōsai kenboshugi no genryū," 32–57; Nagahara Kazuko, "Ryōsai kenboshugi kyōiku ni okeru 'ie' to shokugyō," 149–184; Tachi Kaoru, "Ryōsai kenbo"; Mitsuda Kyōko, "Kindaiteki boseikan no henyō to tenkei," 121–129; Koyama Shizuko, *Ryōsai kenbo to iu kihan;* and Haga Noboru, *Ryōsai kenbo ron.*

31. Kami and Yamazaki, *Hikari hono kanaredomo,* 222.

32. Niigata-ken shakai jigyō kyōkai, ed., *Takujisho no shimei,* 12.

33. Ibid., 2.

34. Ibid.

35. Aizenbashi Hoikujo was renamed Ishii Kinen Aizenen in honor of Ishii Jūji (1865–1914), its founder, a renowned Christian pioneer in orphanage work. Reorganized as a foundation (*zaidan hōjin*) free from organizational ties to Ishii's Okayama orphanage, it opened in a new building on the old Aizenbashi Hoikujo site in 1918.

36. Aizenbashi Hoikujo and its purposes were treated in chapter 5. Tomita Zōkichi continued to serve as executive director; after 1923 his wife Ei became director of the kindergarten. Uto Eiko, "Tomita Ei," 238.

37. Ōsaka-shi minseikyoku, *Hoikujo no ayumi,* 19. The inclusion of kindergarten may reflect Tomita Zōkichi's specialization in education rather than relief work.

38. *Ishii Kinen Aizenen jigyō hōkokusho,* 1917, 42; *Ishii Kinen Aizenen jigyō hōkokusho,* 1925, 3; *Ishii Kinen Aizenen jigyō hōkokusho,* 1926, 3–4.

39. Ōsaka-fu, *Ōsaka shakai jigyō yōran,* 120; *Ishii Kinen Aizenen jigyō hōkokusho,* 1925, 3.

40. Kazue Muta, "Images of the Family in Meiji Periodicals: The Paradox Underlying the Emergence of the 'Home,'" 62.

41. *Ishii Kinen Aizenen jigyō hōkokusho,* 1926, 4.

42. Of this 24.1 percent, guardians' meetings accounted for the smallest proportion, 5.6 percent, while father-older brother meetings represented only 7.4 percent. Parents' meetings comprised the largest proportion, 11.1 percent. Sources for these percentages and those immediately below are Tōkyō-fu, *Kannai jidō hogo jigyō,* and statements of purpose, regulations, and annual reports of individual centers.

43. In 1919 the Osaka City Day-Care Centers, Japan's first public child-care facilities, were established in public housing projects, but these centers admitted all children in the neighborhood to promote social interchange among its various classes for the benefit of rich and poor—much like American settlements—rather than focusing solely on improving the morals or household incomes of the poor. Ōsaka-shi minseikyoku, *Hoikujo no ayumi,* 67.

44. Kyōtō-shi, "Kyōtō-shi takujisho kitei," 109–110. The regulations are dated April 6, 1921.

45. Tōkyō-to kōritsu hoikuen kenkyūkai, "Tōykō-shi takuji hoiku kitei," 15.

46. Fukuoka-ken shakai jigyō kyōkai, *Fukuoka kenka jōsetsu takujisho ni kansuru chōsa* 3–33, esp. 5, 7, 23; Kōbe-shi, "Kōbe-shi hoikujo kitei," 20.

47. Jikyōkan was a private work project and lodging house in Osaka dating from the late Meiji era; its name may be translated as "house of strenuous effort."

48. Yoshimura Toshio, "Jidō hoiku," 45.

49. From the regulations of Aikoku Gohō Eishōji day-care centers, sponsored by the eastern and western women's associations of a Buddhist temple in the city of Kokura.

50. Fukuoka-ken shakai jigyō kyōkai, *Fukuoka kenka jōsetsu takujisho*, 29–64, esp. 33, 45, 48–53, 61.

51. Although the name is similar, this municipal center was not affiliated with Futaba Hoikuen, a private center located in Tokyo's Yotsuya Ward.

52. Tōkyō-shi shakaikyoku, *Takujiba no koto*, 2, 19, 20.

53. Uno, "Women and Changes," 35–39.

54. Ibid.; Nolte and Hastings, "The Meiji State's Policy," 152, 165–174, but cf. 157–163, 171–172; Uno, "Origins of 'Good Wife, Wise Mother.'"

55. Inoue Teizō, *Roku daitoshi no hinmin kutsu*, 3, 15. Despite the title, in it Inoue surveyed slum life in only four of Japan's six greatest cities: Tokyo, Nagoya, Kobe, and Osaka.

56. Ibid.

57. Tsukui Toshiko and Katsumata Sunako, "Furukawabashi Hoikujo ni tsuite," 343–344; Ōtsuka Yōko, "Shinsetsu Kōtōbashi Takujiba ni tsuite," 253; Tōkyō-shi shakaikyoku, *Takujiba no koto*, 19.

58. Ibid.

59. Moxa punishment consisted of burning a vegetable powder on a child's skin. The combustion supposedly cured a child's intractability, although it incidentally left a scar.

60. Tōkyō-shi shakaikyoku, *Takujiba no koto*, 10, 20; Tōkyō-to kōritsu hoikuen kenkyūkai, "Tōkyō-shi takuji hoikukitei," 83–84.

61. Tōkyō-shi shakaikyoku, *Takujiba no koto*, 19.

62. Kuwahara Yotsu, "Omoide," in Tōkyō-shi shakaikyoku, *Takujiba no koto*, 21.

63. There were twenty-two categories in all, including settlements, female rescue work, employment introductions, work projects, and public baths. "Shōreikin gokashi no onrei ni abiseru shakai jigyō dantai," 1143–1145. Naimushō shakaikyoku shakaibu, *Shōwa yonen shakai jigyō gaikan*, 124.

64. Naimushō shakaikyoku shakaibu, *Shōwa yonen shakai*, 123.

65. The argument that it was impractical to change the attitudes and behavior of ordinary Japanese women has some merit; however, the same argument can be raised concerning compulsory education. The government felt that compulsory education was crucial to national development; therefore, from the 1870s to the 1930s officials and private educators devised ways to promote school attendance.

66. Despite diligent searching for a number of years, I have not yet found documents written by Japanese articulating opposition to day-care.

7. Conclusion

1. Regarding socialization, early modern and modern schools educated children in social and occupational skills. There was little stress on the indispensability of the mother (young wife, or *yome*) in educating children; rather, other adults with more authority in the household played prominent roles in the socialization of children. In early modern times, formal schooling had begun to spread beyond the upper classes, especially in urban areas, and it became far more widespread three decades into the modern era.

2. Chubachi and Taira, "Poverty in Modern Japan"; Thomas C. Smith, "Right to Benevolence; Dignity and Japanese Workers, 1890–1920," 587–613; and Andrew Gordon, *The Evolution of Labor Relations in Japan,* 25–32, suggest that members of the urban lower class may have been grateful for the social recognition accorded them by relief works such as day-care centers.

3. The evidence in yearbooks and surveys of users is not lacking in candor, but it is still subject to bias, since middle-class teachers and supervisors wrote these works.

4. Kashima Kōji, *Taishō no Shitayakko,* 82–84.

5. See Sato, "Japanese Women and *Modanizumu.*"

6. For example, Sievers noted that women's participation in the Aikoku Fujinkai (Women's Patriotic Association) was a partial exception; however, men led the organization, and it unfailingly supported government policies. Sievers, *Flowers in Salt,* 114–115. Similarly, in 1932 a small group of women founded the Kokubō Fujinkai, but as army officers (and their wives) dominated the higher echelons, it became a national organization.

7. Ueno Chizuko, " 'Kokumin kokka' to 'jiendaa': 'Josei no kokuminka' o megutte," 8–45.

8. Saji, "Gunjiengo"; Hastings, "From Heroine to Patriotic Volunteer"; Nolte and Hastings, "The Meiji State's Policy." However, the Home Ministry policies probably endorsed wage work for lower-class and poor women. Day-care centers served lower-class children and parents, and the ministry did not praise wage-earning wives of able-bodied men.

9. Nicholson, *Gender and History,* 105–208, esp. 105–130. The evolution of gender from a male perspective falls outside the scope of this study, but it certainly deserves research in its own right.

10. The fact that these dichotomies are not synonymous and the fact that the meaning of each may shift according to context are issues that merit more attention, especially in theoretical projects. For example, "private" can mean "household"

and "private enterprise," or that which is not the state, but "private enterprise" acquires a "public" identity when considered in opposition to "household," the latter remaining in the "private" sphere.

11. Poovey, *Uneven Developments;* Levy, *Other Women;* Kerber, *Women of the Republic;* Norton, *Liberty's Daughters;* Smith, *Ladies of the Leisure Class;* Jane Rendall, *The Origins of Modern Feminism,* 33–140, 189–275.

12. While the comparisons here treat similarities and differences between Japan and three Western countries in processes of modern gender change, the intent is not to establish Japan's essential difference or uniqueness from the West, or to assert the essential unity of the West. Rather, my generalizations regarding Japanese difference in opposition to these three Western nations stem from the fact that they shared Judeo-Christian religious traditions and exchanges of knowledge regarding economic, political, and cultural ideas and institutions during early modern and modern times. In a lengthier discussion, I would better be able to distinguish between Japan and each of the three countries, and to add comparisons with non-Western regions.

13. Regarding lack of social respect accorded wage workers in the prewar era, see Smith, "Right to Benevolence"; Gail Lee Bernstein, "Women in the Silk-Reeling Industry in Nineteenth-Century Japan," 68; and Barbara Molony, "Activism among Women in the Taisho Cotton Industry," 228–229. Regarding changing attitudes toward women's work and standards of domestic management, see Uno, "One Day at a Time."

14. Berg, *The Remembered Gate;* Hannah Papanek, "Development Planning for Women," 15, cited in Sievers, *Flowers in Salt,* 15, 201, note 9; Partha Chatterjee, "The Nationalist Resolution of the Women's Question," 233–254.

Epilogue

1. Some very recent works on women in contemporary Japan include Joyce Gelb and Mariann Palley, *Women of Japan and Korea;* Kumiko Fujimura-Fanselow and Atsuko Kameda, eds., *Japanese Women: New Feminist Perspectives on the Past, Present, and Future;* AMPO Japan-Asian Quarterly, ed., *Voices from the Japanese Women's Movement;* Anne E. Imamura, ed., *Re-Imaging Japanese Women;* Sandra Buckley, *Broken Silences: Voices of Japanese Feminism.*

2. Lebra translates *ikigai* as "life's worth"; *Japanese Women,* ch. 5, esp. 162–165, 205–208. Despite the stereotype of Japanese men as workaholic businessmen, for male respondents children were second only to occupation, which was

chosen by 47 percent of the males surveyed. Gordon Matthews, *What Makes Life Worth Living? How Japanese and Americans Make Sense of Their Worlds,* found that the *ikigai* of most of Japanese women he interviewed lay in "being housewives and mothers . . . and in their committment to family," although there are a few signs of change, 47–152, esp. 101, 150–165. Regarding mothers or mother-hood as a source of social ills, see Lebra, *Japanese Women,* 205–208; Kyutoku Shigemori, *Bogenbyō;* Anne Allison, *Permitted and Prohibited Desires: Mothers, Comics, and Censorship in Japan,* esp. ch. 6. Regarding one child's perspective on the education mother, see Emiko Ochiai, *The Japanese Family System in Transition,* 37. Additional insights into contemporary motherhood can be gained from Hendry, *Becoming Japanese,* esp. ch. 4; Lois Peak, *Learning to Go to School: The Transition from Home to Preschool Life,* esp. ch. 1–3; Sumiko Iwao, *The Japanese Woman: Traditional Image and Changing Reality,* ch. 3, 5; Allison, *Permitted and Prohibited Desires,* ch. 4–5; see also the introduction to this book, notes 3 and 4.

3. Joseph Tobin, David Wu, and Dana Davidson, *Preschool in Three Cultures: Japan, China, and the United States,* 55–68, esp. 55; Kondo, *Crafting Selves,* 282–284.

4. Harumi Befu, "The Social and Cultural Background of Child Development in Japan and the United States," 17–18.

5. Glenda Roberts, *Staying on the Line: Blue-Collar Women in Contemporary Japan,* 140–167, esp. 156–158.

6. Bernstein, *Haruko's World,* 48–49.

7. Hendry, *Becoming Japanese,* 24, 48, 51.

8. Margaret Lock, *Encounters with Aging: Mythologies of Menopause in Japan and North America,* 94.

9. Yoshiko Tomizawa, "From Child Care to Local Politics," 196.

10. Lock, *Encounters with Aging,* 73–75.

11. Regarding single women and postponements of marriage, see Ochiai, *The Japanese Family System in Transition,* 118–120. Matthews Hamabata, *Crested Kimono: Power and Love in the Japanese Business Family,* 155–160, describes acquiescence to cultural norms following the shock of a failed rebellion. For insights into married women's changing expectations, see Elisabeth Bumiller, *The Secrets of Mariko: A Year in the Life of a Japanese Woman and Her Family,* esp. 27–28, 65–90, 304–307, 331–332, but cf. 308–310; Nancy Rosenberger, "Fragile Resistance, Signs of Status: Women between State and Media in Japan"; Susan Orpett Long, "Nurturing and Femininity: The Ideal of Caregiving in Postwar Japan"; and Ochiai, *The Japanese Family System in Transition,* ch. 6–8, 10.

12. Iwao, *The Japanese Woman,* 130–132.

13. Inoue Teruko and Ehara Yumiko, *Josei no deetabukku,* 89; Iwao, *The Japanese Woman,* 143. Regarding gender stratification in the labor force, see also Mary Brinton, *Gender and the Economic Miracle.*

14. Zenkoku hoiku dantai renrakukai and Hoiku kenkyūjo, eds. *Hoiku Hakusho,* 251–253; Japanese National Committee of OMEP, "Education and Care of Young Children in Japan,"12–13. The postwar terms *hoikuen* and *hoikujo* generally have been most often translated as "day nursery"; however, due to the emphasis on education rather than simple custodial care, I prefer the terms "day-care center" and "child-care center." Besides these works, other useful treatments of postwar early childhood education include Early Childhood Education Association of Japan, *Early Childhood Education and Care in Japan;* Hendry, *Becoming Japanese,* esp. 119–152; Tobin, et al., *Preschool in Three Cultures,* esp. 12–71, 188–221; and Peak, *Learning to Go to School,* but their in-depth observations of the latter three studies took place at kindergartens rather than day-care centers. Specialized studies of preschool pedagogy are listed in note 20. For general studies of education in postwar Japan, see Thomas Rohlen, *Japanese High Schools;* James Shields, *Japanese Schooling: Patterns of Socialization, Equality, and Political Control;* Merry White, *The Japanese Educational Challenge;* and Marshall, *Learning to be Modern.* Research on problems of Japanese children and education include Merry White, *The Japanese Overseas: Can They Go Home Again?;* Merry White, *The Material Child;* and Norma Field, "The Child as Laborer and Consumer: The Disappearance of Childhood in Contemporary Japan."

15. Japanese National Committee of OMEP, "Education and Care," 15–16; Sarane Spence Boocock, "Controlled Diversity: An Overview of the Japanese Preschool System," 46. For one mother's experience, see Mariko Fujita, "'It's All Mother's Fault': Childcare and the Socialization of Working Mothers in Japan," 80–90.

16. Nobuko Takahashi, "Child-Care Programs in Japan"; Boocock, "Controlled Diversity," esp. 44–55; Japanese National Committee of OMEP, "Education and Care," 27. Boocock discusses some of the differences between licensed and unlicensed child-care centers, and Takahashi includes a section on home day-care.

17. Iwao, *The Japanese Woman,* 143; Japanese National Committee of OMEP, "Education and Care."

18. Tomizawa, "From Child Care to Local Politics"; Fujita, "'It's All Mother's Fault'"; Peak, *Learning to Go to School,* 57–62; Tobin, et al., *Preschool in Three Cultures,* 55–71, 209–211; Allison, *Permitted and Prohibited Desires,* ch. 4–5.

19. Japanese National Committee of OMEP, "Education and Care," 15–16; an extended discussion of kindergarten educational goals is found in Peak, *Learning to Go to School,* ch. 6.

20. See, for example, Tobin, et al., *Preschool in Three Cultures,* 55–71; Peak, *Learning to Go to School,* ch. 6; Catherine C. Lewis," From Indulgence to Internalization: Social Control in the Early School Years"; and Toshiyuki Sano, "Methods of Social Control and Socialization in Japanese Day-Care Centers."

21. Among numerous works on this subject, see William Caudill and David W. Plath, "Who Sleeps by Whom? Parent-Child Involvement in Urban Japanese Families"; William Caudill and Helen Weinstein, "Maternal Care and Infant Behavior in Japan and America"; Katsumi Yokoe, "Historical Trends in Home Discipline"; Hendry, *Becoming Japanese,* ch. 3; Lebra, *Japanese Women,* 166–192; and Uno, "Japan." Regarding influences outside the home, see Millie R. Creighton, "'Edutaining' Children: Consumer and Gender Socialization in Japanese Marketing."

22. Kawahara Toshiaki, *Michiko Kōgō*; Kawahara Toshiaki, *Michiko sama to kōzoku tachi;* Toshiaki Kawahara, *Hirohito and His Times: A Japanese Perspective,* 178–196. Regarding the distinctive child-rearing practices of the former aristocracy, see Takie Lebra, *Above the Clouds: Status Culture of the Modern Japanese Nobility,* ch. 7.

Bibliography

Primary Sources

Chuō jizen kyōkai. *Nihon shakai jigyō meikan.* Tokyo: Chuō jizen kyōkai, 1920.

Fukuoka-ken shakai jigyō kyōkai. *Fukuoka kenka jōsetsu takujisho ni kansuru chōsa.* Fukuoka-shi: Fukuoka-ken shakai jigyō kyōkai, 1929.

———. *Fukuoka kenka shakai jigyō.* Fukuoka: Fukuoka-ken shakai jigyō kyōkai, 1929.

Futaba Hoikuen, 1928.

Futaba Hoikuen, 1934.

Hachihama Tokusaburō. "Keian no kenkyū." *Kyūsai kenkyū* 1, no. 9 (Sept. 1913), 230.

Hokkaidō jizen jigyō kyōkai, ed. *Kyūsai jigyō kōshūkai.* Sapporo: Hokkaidō jizen jigyō kyōkai, 1922.

Ichibangase Yasuko, ed. *Namae Takayuki shū,* Shakai fukushi koten sōsho 4. Tokyo: Ōsho shoten, 1982.

Inada Jō. "Kōsaikai kakubu jigyō to sono shugi." *Kyūsai kenkyū* 3, no. 11 (Nov. 1915), 43–54.

Inoue Hide. "Takujisho ni tsuite." *Ōfūkai hachijūnen shi.* Ed. Ōfūkai hachijūnen shi shuppan iinkai. Tokyo: Ōfūkai hachijūnen shi shuppan iinkai, 1984.

Inoue Teizō. *Roku daitoshi no hinmin kutsu.* 1922.

Ishii Kinen Aizenen jigyō hōkokusho, 1917.

Ishii Kinen Aizenen jigyō hōkokusho, 1925.

Ishii Kinen Aizenen jigyō hōkokusho, 1926.

Ishikawa Matsutarō. *Onna daigakushū.* Tokyo: Heibonsha, 1977.

"Jidō kyōyō chōsa." *Tōkyō-fu shakai jigyō kyōkai kaihō,* no. 17 (1922).

"Katayama's Thanks." *Commons* 3, no. 24 (April 1898), 5.

Kōbe Seneki Kinen Hoikukai. *Jidō hoiku jigyō no gaiyō.* Kobe: Kōbe Seneki Kinen Hoikukai, 1919.

———. *Sanjūnen o kaerimite.* Kobe: Kōbe Seneki Kinen Hoikukai, 1935.

Kōbe-shi. *Kōbe-shi shakai jigyō gaiyō.* Kobe: Kōbe-shi, 1924.

Kōchi Nobuko, ed. *Shiryō bosei hogo ronsō.* Tokyo: Domesu shuppan, 1984.

Kōsaikai. *Zaidan hōjin Kōsaikai Taishō kunen dai yonkai nenpō.* Osaka: Kōsaikai, 1920.

————. *Zaidan hōjin Taishō gonenji dai ikkai nenpō*. Osaka: Kōsaikai, 1916.

Kyōtō-shi. *Kyōto-shi shakai jigyō gaiyō*. Kyoto: Kyōtō-shi, 1925.

Miyoshi, Taizō. "Philanthropy in Japan." In *Fifty Years of New Japan,* vol. 2. Ed. Shigenobu Okuma. London: Smith, Elder, & Co., 1910; rpt. New York: Kraus Reprint Co., 1970, 101–112.

Naimushō. *Naimushō senji jigyō nenkan*. 1905.

Naimushō. *Waga kuni ni okeru jikei kyūsai jigyō*. 1908.

Naimushō shakaikyoku shakaibu. *Shōwa yonen shakai jigyō gaikan*. Tokyo: Naimushō shakaikyoku, 1930.

Namae Takayuki. "Taisei ni okeru kyūji jigyō." *Jizen* 1, no. 2 (Oct. 1909), 35–47.

————. "Hoiku jigyō ni tsuite." *Kyūsai kenkyū* 3, no. 7 (July 1915), 81–88.

————. *Shakai jigyō kōyō*. Tokyo: Iwamatsudō, 1933.

Naruse, Jinzō. "The Education of Japanese Women." In *Fifty Years of New Japan,* vol. 2. Ed. Shigenobu Okuma. London: Smith, Elder, & Co., 1910; rpt. New York: Kraus Reprint Co., 1970, 192–225.

Niigata-ken shakai jigyō kyōkai, ed. *Takujisho no shimei*. Shakai jigyō sankō shiryō daini gō. 1927.

"Nippori-chō jidō shūgaku jōkyō chōsa ni tsuite." *Tōkyō-fu shakai jigyō kyōkai kaihō*, no. 11 (1920), 57–58.

Ogawa Shigejirō. "Chūkan hoiku jigyō ni tsuite." *Kyūsai kenkyū* 1, no. 3 (Oct. 1913), 1–21.

————. *Yōji hoiku jigyō ni tsuite*. Shokkō mondai shiryō, Series A, no. 273. Osaka: Shokkō kyōikukai, 1918.

Ōsaka Jikyōkan. *Ōsaka Jikyōkan no jūnananen*. Osaka: Ōsaka Jikyōkan, 1928.

Ōsaka-fu. *Ōsaka shakai jigyō yōran*. Osaka: Ōsaka-fu, 1920.

Ōtsuka Yōko. "Shinsetsu Kōtōbashi Takujiba ni tsuite." *Yōji kyōiku* 21, no. 7 (July 1921), 251–257.

Shiritsu Futaba Yōchien Hōkoku, nos. 1–16 (1900–June 1916).

Shiritsu Futaba Hoikuen Hōkoku, nos. 17–21 (July 1916–1920).

Shiritsu Futaba Hoikuen Nenpō, nos. 22–25 (1921–1928).

"Shōreikin gokashi no onrei ni abiseru shakai jigyō dantai." *Shakai jigyō* 6 (1923), 1143–1145.

Takada Shingō. "Beikoku ni okeru jidō hogo jigyō." *Jizen* 5, no. 11 (Nov. 1914), 84–92.

Takeuchi Ayako. "Ōfūkai takujisho ni okeru keiken, yon." *Katei shūhō* (Jan. 15, 1915).

Toda Teizō. *Kazoku kōsei*. Tokyo: Shinsensha, 1920.

Tōkyō-fu. *Kannai jidō hogo jigyō*. Tokyo: Tōkyō-fu, 1925.

Tōkyō-fu kyūsaika. *Yōji chūkan hoiku*. Tokyo: Tōkyō-fu, 1917.

————. *Tōkyō-shi shakai jigyō meikan*. Tokyo: Tōkyō-shi shakaikyoku, 1920.

Tōkyō-shi shakaikyoku. *Takujiba no koto.* Tokyo: Tōkyō-shi shakaikyoku, 1925.

Tōkyō-to kōritsu hoikuen kenkyūkai. *Watakushitachi no hoikushi,* vol. 1. Tokyo: Tōkyō to kōritsu hoikuen kenkyūkai, 1980.

Tsukui Toshiko and Katsumata Sunako. "Furukawabashi Hoikujo ni tsuite." *Yōji kyōiku* 21, no. 10 (Oct. 1921), 343–344.

———. "Tokunaga Yuki no omoide." *Jidō bungei* 10, no. 3 (Jan. 1965), 6.

Yamakawa Kikue. *Onna nidai no ki.* Tokyo: Heibonsha, 1972.

Yamazumi Masami and Nakae Kazue, eds. *Kosodate no sho,* vols. 1–2. Tokyo: Heibonsha, 1976, 1977.

Yoshimura Toshio. "Jidō hoiku." In Ōsaka Jikyōkan, *Ōsaka Jikyōkan no jūnananen.* Osaka: Ōsaka Jikyōkan, 1928.

Secondary Works

(For works published in Japan, names are listed in Japanese order, surname first.)

Abramowitz, Mimi. *Regulating the Lives of Women: Social Welfare Policy from Colonial Times to the Present.* Boston: South End Press, 1988.

Allen, Ann Taylor. *Feminism and Motherhood in Germany, 1800–1914.* New Brunswick, N.J.: Rutgers University Press, 1991.

Allison, Anne. *Nightwork: Sexuality, Pleasure, and Corporate Masculinity in a Tokyo Hostess Club.* Chicago: University of Chicago Press, 1994.

———. *Permitted and Prohibited Desires: Mothers, Comics, and Censorship in Japan.* Boulder, Colo.: Westview Press, 1996.

AMPO, ed. *Voices from the Japanese Women's Movement.* Armonk, N.Y.: M. E. Sharpe, 1996.

Anderson, Stephen J. *Welfare Policy and Politics in Japan: Beyond the Developmental State.* New York: Paragon House, 1993.

Arai Tomio. "Bosei ishiki no mezame." In *Bosei o tou,* vol. 2. Ed. Wakita Haruko. Kyoto: Jinbun shoin, 1985, 130–157.

Arichi Tōru. *Kindai Nihon no kazokukan, Meiji hen.* Tokyo: Kōbundō, 1977.

Aries, Philippe. *Centuries of Childhood: A Social History of Family Life.* Trans. Robert Baldick. New York: Vintage, 1972.

Badinter, Elisabeth. *Mother Love: Myth and Reality.* New York: Macmillan, 1980.

Beardsley, Richard K., John W. Hall, and Robert E. Ward, eds. *Village Japan.* Chicago: University of Chicago Press, 1959.

Beatty, Barbara. *Preschool Education in America: The Culture of Young Children from the Colonial Era to the Present.* New Haven, Conn.: Yale University Press, 1995.

Beauchamp, Edward, ed. *Learning to Be Japanese: Selected Writings on Japanese Society and Education.* Hampden, Conn.: Linnett Books, 1978.

Befu, Harumi. *Japan: An Anthropological Introduction.* San Francisco: Chandler Publishing Co., 1971.

Befu, Harumi. "The Social and Cultural Background of Child Development in Japan and the United States." In *Child Development and Education in Japan.* Ed. Harold Stevenson, Hiroshi Azuma, and Kenji Hakuta. New York: W. H. Freeman, 1986, 55–62.

Behlmer, George K. *Child Abuse and Moral Reform in England, 1870–1908.* Stanford: Stanford University Press, 1982.

Berkner, Lutz. "The Stem Family and the Developmental Cycle: An Eighteenth-Century Example." *American Historical Review,* no. 77 (1972), 398–418.

Berg, Barbara. *The Remembered Gate: Origins of American Feminism.* New York: Oxford University Press, 1978.

Bernstein, Gail Lee. *Japanese Marxist: A Portrait of Kawakami Hajime 1879–1946.* Cambridge, Mass.: Harvard University Press, 1976.

———. *Haruko's World: A Japanese Farm Woman and Her Community.* Stanford: Stanford University Press, 1983.

———. "Women in the Silk-Reeling Industry in Nineteenth-Century Japan." In *Japan and the World: Essays in Honour of Ishida Takeshi.* Ed. Gail Lee Bernstein and Haruhiro Fukui. New York: St. Martin's Press, 1988, 54–77.

Bernstein, Gail Lee, ed. *Recreating Japanese Women, 1600–1945.* Berkeley: University of California Press, 1991.

Bethel, Diana. "Visions of a Humane Society: Feminist Thought in Taishō Japan." *Feminist,* international issue no. 2 (1980), 92–95.

Bird, Isabella. *Unbeaten Tracks in Japan.* New York, 1880; rpt. Tokyo: Charles E. Tuttle, 1984.

Bix, Herbert. *Peasant Protest in Japan, 1590–1884.* New Haven, Conn.: Yale University Press, 1986.

Black, Naomi. *Social Feminism.* Ithaca, N.Y.: Cornell University Press, 1988.

Boocock, Sarane Spence. "Controlled Diversity: An Overview of the Japanese Preschool System." *Journal of Japanese Studies* 15, no. 1 (1989), 41–66.

Bowles, Samuel, and Herbert Gintis. *Schooling in Capitalist America: Educational Reform and the Contradictions of Economic Life.* New York: Basic Books, 1976.

Bowring, Richard, ed. and trans. *Murasaki Shikibu: Her Diary and Poetic Memoirs: A Translation and Study.* Princeton, N.J.: Princeton University Press, 1982.

Brinton, Mary C. *Women and the Economic Miracle: Gender and Work in Postwar Japan.* Berkeley: University of California Press, 1993.

Brown, Carol. "Mothers, Fathers, and Children: From Private to Public Patriarchy." In *Women and Revolution: A Discussion of the Unhappy Marriage of Marxism and Feminism.* Ed. Lydia Sargent. Boston: South End Press, 1981, 239–268.

Buckley, Sandra. *Broken Silence: Voices of Japanese Feminism.* Berkeley: University of California Press, 1997.

Bumiller, Elisabeth. *The Secrets of Mariko: A Year in the Life of a Japanese Woman and Her Family.* New York: Times Books, 1995.

Butler, Judith, and Joan Scott, eds. *Feminists Theorize the Political.* New York: Routledge, 1992.

Caudill, William, and David W. Plath. "Who Sleeps by Whom? Parent-Child Involvement in Urban Japanese Families." In *Japanese Culture and Behavior: Selected Readings.* Ed. Takie S. Lebra and William P. Lebra. Honolulu: University of Hawai'i Press, 1974, 277–312.

Caudill, William, and Helen Weinstein. "Maternal Care and Infant Behavior in Japan and America." In *Japanese Culture and Behavior: Selected Readings.* Ed. Takie S. Lebra and William P. Lebra. Honolulu: University of Hawai'i Press, 1974, 225–276.

Chamberlain, Basil. *Things Japanese: Being Notes on Things Connected with Japan.* 1893; rpt. Tokyo: Charles E. Tuttle, 1965, 67–76.

Chatterjee, Partha. "The Nationalist Resolution of the Women's Question." In *Recasting Women in India: Essays in Colonial History.* Ed. Kukum Sangari and Sudesh Vaid. New Brunswick, N.J.: Rutgers University Press, 1990, 233–254.

Chiba Hisao. *Meiji no shōgakkō.* Hirosaki-shi, Aomori-ken: Tsugaru shobō, 1971.

Chikamatsu, Monzaemon. "Yosaku of Tamba." In *Major Plays of Chikamatsu.* Trans. Donald Keene. New York: Columbia University Press, 1961, 91–130.

Chimoto, Akiko. "The Birth of the Full-Time Housewife in the Japanese Worker's Household as Seen through Family Budget Surveys." *U.S.-Japan Women's Journal, English Supplement* no. 8 (June 1995), 37–64.

Chubachi, Masayoshi, and Koji Taira. "Poverty in Modern Japan: Perceptions and Realities." In *Japanese Industrialization and Its Social Consequences.* Ed. Hugh Patrick. Berkeley: University of California Press, 1976, 391–437.

Cole, Robert E., and Kenichi Tominaga, eds. "Japan's Changing Occupational Structure and Its Significance." In *Japanese Industrialization and Its Social Consequences.* Ed. Hugh Patrick. Berkeley: University of California Press, 1976, 53–95.

Cott, Nancy F. *The Bonds of Womanhood: Woman's Sphere in New England, 1780–1835.* New Haven, Conn.: Yale University Press, 1977.

Cowan, Ruth Schwartz. *More Work for Mother: The Ironies of Household Technology from the Open Hearth to the Microwave.* New York: Basic Books, 1983.

Creighton, Millie R. "'Edutaining' Children: Consumer and Gender Socialization in Japanese Marketing." *Ethnology* 33, no. 1 (1994), 35–52.

Danly, Robert, ed. and trans. *In the Shade of Spring Leaves: The Life and Work of Higuchi Ichiyo, A Meiji Woman of Letters.* New Haven, Conn.: Yale University Press, 1981.

Dazai, Osamu. *Return to Tsugaru: Travels of a Purple Tramp.* New York: Kodansha International, 1985.

Donzelot, Jacques. *The Policing of Families.* Trans. Robert Hurley. New York: Pantheon, 1979.

Dore, Ronald P. *City Life in Japan.* Berkeley: University of California Press, 1958.

Dore, Ronald P. *Education in Tokugawa Japan.* Berkeley: University of California Press, 1964.

———. "Factory Legislation in Nineteenth-Century Japan." *Comparative Studies in Society and History* 23 (1969), 323–390.

Early Childhood Education Association of Japan, ed. *Early Childhood Education and Care in Japan.* Tokyo: Child Honsha, 1979.

Elshtain, Jean Bethke. *Public Man, Private Woman: Women in Social and Political Thought.* Princeton, N.J.: Princeton University Press, 1981.

Everett, Helen. "Control, Social." In *Encyclopaedia of the Social Sciences,* vol. 4. New York: The Macmillan Co., 1931, 344.

Fallows, Debra. "Change Comes Slowly for Japanese Women." *National Geographic* 177, no. 4 (April 1990), 52–83.

Field, Norma. "The Child as Laborer and Consumer: The Disappearance of Childhood in Contemporary Japan." In *Children and the Politics of Culture.* Ed. Sharon Stephens. Princeton, N.J.: Princeton University Press, 1995, 51–78.

Fox-Genovese, Elizabeth. "Placing Women's History in History." *New Left Review,* no. 133 (May–June 1982).

———. "Government Ethics Textbooks in Late Meiji Japan." *Journal of Asian Studies* 29 (1970), 823–833.

Fridell, Wilbur M. *Japanese Shrine Mergers, 1906–1912.* Tokyo: Sophia University Press, 1973.

Fuchs, Rachel. *Abandoned Children: Foundlings and Child Welfare in Nineteenth-Century France.* Albany: State University of New York Press, 1984.

Fujimura-Fanselow, Kumiko, and Atsuko Kameda, eds. *Japanese Women: New Feminist Perspectives on the Past, Present, and Future.* New York: Feminist Press, 1995.

Fujin mondai shiryō shūsei. 10 vols. Tokyo: Domesu shuppan, 1976.

Fujita, Mariko. " 'It's All Mother's Fault': Childcare and Socialization in Japanese Day-Care Centers." *Journal of Japanese Studies* 15, no. 1 (1989), 67–92.

Fujitani, Takashi. *Splendid Monarchy: Power and Pagentry in Modern Japan.* Berkeley: University of California Press, 1996.

Fukaya Masashi. *Ryōsai kenbo no kyōikushugi.* Nagoya: Reimei shobō, 1976.

Fukutake, Tadashi. *The Japanese Social Structure: Its Evolution in the Modern Century.* Tokyo: University of Tokyo Press, 1982.

Fukuzawa, Yukichi. *The Autobiography of Yukichi Fukuzawa.* Trans. Eiichi Kiyooka. New York: Columbia University Press, 1960.

―――. *Fukuzawa Yukichi on Japanese Women: Selected Works.* Trans. Eiichi Kiyooka. Tokyo: University of Tokyo Press, 1988.

Furuki, Yoshiko. *The White Plum: A Biography of Ume Tsuda.* New York: Weatherhill, 1991.

Fuse Akiko. *Atarashii kazoku no sōzō.* Tokyo: Aoki shoten, 1984.

Garon, Sheldon. *The State and Labor in Modern Japan.* Berkeley: University of California Press, 1987.

Garon, Sheldon. "Women's Groups and the Japanese State: Contending Approaches to Political Integration, 1890–1945." *Journal of Japanese Studies* 19, no. 1 (1993), 5–41.

Garon, Sheldon. *Molding Japanese Minds: The State in Everyday Life.* Princeton, N.J.: Princeton University Press, 1997.

Gelb, Joyce, and Mariann Palley, eds. *Women of Japan and Korea: Continuity and Change.* Philadelphia: Temple University Press, 1994.

Gluck, Carol. *Japan's Modern Myths.* Princeton, N.J.: Princeton University Press, 1985.

Gōchi Fumiko. "Maruyama Chiyo." In *Shakai jigyō ni ikita joseitachi.* Ed. Gomi Yuriko. Tokyo: Domesu shuppan, 1973, 203–226.

Gordon, Andrew. *The Evolution of Labor Relations in Japan: Heavy Industry, 1853–1955.* Cambridge, Mass.: Harvard University Press, 1985.

―――. *Labor and Imperial Democracy in Japan.* Berkeley: University of California Press, 1992.

Gordon, Linda. "Social Insurance and Public Assistance: The Influence of Gender in Welfare Thought in the United States." *American Historical Review* 97 (1992), 19–54.

Gordon, Linda, ed. *Women, the State, and Welfare.* Madison: The University of Wisconsin Press, 1990.

Haga Noboru. *Ryōsai kenbo ron.* Tokyo: Yūzankaku, 1992.

Hamabata, Matthews. *Crested Kimono: Power and Love in the Japanese Business Family.* Ithaca, N.Y.: Cornell University Press, 1990.

Hane, Mikiso. *Rebels, Peasants, and Outcastes: The Underside of Modern Japan.* New York: Pantheon, 1982.

Hane, Mikiso, ed. and trans. *Reflections on the Way to the Gallows.* Berkeley: University of California Press, 1988.

Harootunian, Harry. "Introduction: A Sense of Ending and the Problem of Taisho." In *Japan in Crisis: Essays on Taisho Democracy.* Ed. Bernard S. Silberman and H. D. Harootunian. Princeton, N.J.: Princeton University Press, 1970, 3–28.

Hashimoto, Mitsuru. "The Social Background of Peasant Uprisings in Tokugawa Japan." In *Conflict in Modern Japanese History: The Neglected Tradition.* Ed. Tetsuo Najita and J. Victor Koschmann. Princeton, N.J.: Princeton University Press, 145–163.

Hastings, Sally. "From Heroine to Patriotic Volunteer: Women and Social Work in Japan, 1900–1945." Michigan State University Working Papers on Women in International Development, no. 106. November 1985.

Hastings, Sally Ann. *Neighborhood and Nation in Tokyo, 1905–1937.* Pittsburgh: University of Pittsburgh Press, 1995.

Hawes, Joseph M., and N. Ray Hiner, eds. *Children in Historical and Comparative Perspective: An International Handbook and Research Guide.* Westport, Conn.: Greenwood Press, 1991.

Hayakawa, Noriyo. "Feminism and Nationalism in Japan." *Journal of Women's History* 7, no. 4 (1995), 108–119.

Hazama, Hiroshi. "Historical Changes in the Life Style of Industrial Workers." In *Japanese Industrialization and Its Social Consequences.* Ed. Hugh Patrick. Berkeley: University of California Press, 1976, 21–52.

Helly, Dorothy O., and Susan B. Reverby, eds. *Gendered Domains: Rethinking Public and Private in Women's History.* Ithaca, N.Y.: Cornell University Press, 1992.

Hendry, Joy. *Becoming Japanese: The World of the Preschool Child.* Honolulu: University of Hawai'i Press, 1986.

Hendry, Joy. "The Role of the Professional Housewife." In *Japanese Women Working.* Ed. Janet E. Hunter. New York: Routledge, 1993, 224–241.

Higuchi, Chiyoko. "Lady Kasuga, Mother of Shoguns." *The East* 7, no. 6 (June 1971), 38–42.

Hopper, Helen M. *A New Woman of Japan: A Political Biography of Katō Shidzue.* Boulder, Colo.: Westview Press, 1996.

Hozumi, Nobushige. *Ancestor-Worship and Japanese Law.* 1912; rpt. Plainview, N.Y.: Books for Libraries Press, 1973.

Humphries, Stephen. *Hooligans or Rebels? An Oral History of Working-Class Childhood and Youth 1889–1939.* New York: Basil Blackwell, 1981.

Hunter, Janet, ed. *Japanese Women Working.* New York: Routledge, 1993.

Hyōgo-ken shakai fukushi kyōgikai, ed. *Fukushi no tomoshibi: Hyōgo-ken shakai jigyō senkakusha.* Kobe: Hyōgo-ken shakai fukushi kyōgikai, 1961.

Ichibangase Yasuko, Izumi Jun, Ogawa Nobuko, and Shishido Takeo. *Nihon no hoiku.* 3d ed. Tokyo: Domesu shuppan, 1980.

Ihara Saikaku. *This Scheming World.* Trans. Takatsuka Masanori and David C. Stubbs. Tokyo: Charles E. Tuttle, 1965.

———. *A Japanese Family Storehouse Or the Millionaires' Gospel Modernised.* Trans. G. W. Sargent. Cambridge: Cambridge University Press, 1969.

———. *Some Final Words of Advice.* Trans. Peter Nosco. Tokyo: Charles E. Tuttle Co., 1980.

Imai, Yasuko. "The Emergence of the Japanese Shufu: Why a Shufu is More Than a 'Housewife.'" *U.S.-Japan Women's Journal, English Supplement* no. 6 (January 1994), 44–65.

Imamura, Anne. *Urban Japanese Housewives.* Honolulu: University of Hawai'i Press, 1987.

Imamura, Anne E., ed. *Re-Imaging Japanese Women.* Berkeley: University of California Press, 1996.

Inoue, Teruko, and Yumiko Ehara, eds. *Josei no deetabukku.* Tokyo: Yūhikaku, 1991.

Irokawa, Daikichi. *The Culture of the Meiji Period.* Princeton, N.J.: Princeton University Press, 1985.

Ishida Takeshi. *Meiji seiji shisō shi kenkyū.* Tokyo: Miraisha, 1954.

Ishimoto, Shidzue. *Facing Two Ways.* New York: Farrar and Rhinehart, 1935.

Iwao, Sumiko. *The Japanese Woman: Traditional Image and Changing Reality.* Cambridge, Mass.: Harvard University Press, 1994.

Jaggar, Alison M., and William L. McBride. "'Reproduction' as Male Ideology." *Women's Studies International Forum* 8, no. 3 (1985), 185–196.

Japan National Committee of OMEP. "Education and Care of Young Children in Japan." 1992. (Pamphlet)

Jones, Sumie, ed. *Imaging Reading Eros.* Bloomington: East Asian Studies Center, Indiana University, 1996, 1–12.

Kaide Sumiko. *Noguchi Yuka no shōgai.* Tokyo: Kirisuto shimbunsha, 1974.

Kaigo, Tokiomi. *Japanese Education: Its Past and Present.* Tokyo: Kokusai Bunka Shinkokai, 1968.

Kami Shōichirō. "Honryū no naka no gakkō kyōiku." In *Gekidōki no kodomo,* vol. 6 of *Nihon kodomo no rekishi.* Ed. Kami Shōichirō. Tokyo: Daiichi hōki, 1977.

Kami Shōichirō and Yamazaki Tomoko. *Nihon no yōchien: Nihon no yōji kyōiku no rekishi.* Tokyo: Rironsha, 1974.

―――. *Hikari hono kanaredomo: Futaba Hoikuen to Tokunaga Yuki.* Tokyo: Asahi shimbunsha, 1980.

Kanda, Mikio, ed. *Widows of Hiroshima.* Trans. Taeko Midorikawa. New York: St. Martin's Press, 1989.

Kaneko, Fumiko. *Prison Memoirs of a Japanese Woman.* Trans. Jean Inglis. Armonk, N.Y.: M. E. Sharpe, 1992.

Kanzaki Kiyoshi. "Noguchi Yuka." In *Gendai Nihon fujin den.* Tokyo: Chūō kōronsha, 1940, 31–72.

Kashima Kōji. *Taishō no Shitayakko.* Tokyo: Seiabō, 1978.

Katano Misako. "Ryōsai kenboshugi no genryū." In *Onnatachi no kindai.* Ed. Kindai joseishi kenkyūkai. Tokyo: Aki shobō, 1978, 32–57.

Katoda Keiko. "Waga kuni ni okeru hinji kyōiku." *Shakai fukushi,* no. 23 (1982), 90–124.

Katz, Michael. *In the Shadow of the Poorhouse.* New York: Basic Books, 1986.

Kawahara, Toshiaki. *Hirohito and His Times: A Japanese Perspective.* New York: Kodansha International, 1990.

———. *Michiko Kōgō.* Tokyo: Kōdansha, 1990.

———. *Michiko sama to kōzokutachi.* Tokyo: Kōdansha, 1992.

Kawashima Takeyoshi. *Ideorogii toshite no kazoku seido.* Tokyo: Iwanami shoten, 1957.

Kelly, Joan. "Family and Society." In *Women, History, and Theory: The Essays of Joan Kelly.* 1980; rpt. Chicago: University of Chicago Press, 1981, 110–155.

———. "The Social Relations of the Sexes: Methodological Implications of Women's History." In *Women, History, and Theory: The Essays of Joan Kelly.* Chicago: University of Chicago Press, 1984.

Kelly, William W. *Deference and Defiance in Nineteenth-Century Japan.* Princeton, N.J.: Princeton University Press, 1985.

Kerber, Linda. *Women of the Republic: Intellect and Ideology in Revolutionary America.* Chapel Hill: University of North Carolina Press, 1981.

Kinmonth, Earl. *The Self-Made Man in Meiji Japanese Thought: From Samurai to Salary Man.* Berkeley: University of California Press, 1981.

Kinney, Anne Behnke, ed. *Chinese Views of Childhood.* Honolulu: University of Hawai'i Press, 1995.

Kinoshita, Naoe. *Pillar of Fire.* Trans. Kenneth Strong. London: Allen and Unwin, 1972.

Kinzley, W. Dean. "Japan's Discovery of Poverty: Changing Views of Poverty and Social Welfare in the Nineteenth Century." *Journal of Asian History* 22, no. 1 (1988), 1–24.

Kinzley, W. Dean. *Industrial Harmony in Modern Japan: The Invention of a Tradition.* London: Routledge, 1991.

Kobayashi Hatsue. *Onna sandai.* Tokyo: Asahi shimbunsha, 1974.

Kōbe shiritsu hoikuen renmei. *Kōbe no hoikuenshi.* Kobe: Kōbe shiritsu hoikuen renmei, 1979.

Kojima, Hideo. "Child-Rearing Concepts as a Belief-Value System of the Society and the Individual." In *Child Development and Education in Japan.* Ed. Harold Stevenson, Hiroshi Azuma, and Kenji Hakuta. New York: W. H. Freeman, 1986, 39–54.

Komano Yōko. "Ryōsai kenboshugi no seiritsu to sono henyō." In *Josei kaihō no shisō to kōdō, senzen hen.* Ed. Tanaka Sumiko. Tokyo: Jiji tsūshinsha, 1975, 134–146.

Kondo, Dorinne. *Crafting Selves: Power, Gender, and Discourses of Identity in a Japanese Workplace.* Chicago: University of Chicago Press, 1990.

Kosaka Masaaki. *Japanese Thought in the Meiji Era.* Trans. David Abosch. Tokyo: Pan-Pacific Press, 1958.

Koven, Seth, and Sonya Michel. "Womanly Duties: Maternalist Politics and the Origins of Welfare States in France, Germany, Great Britain, and the United States, 1880–1920." *American Historical Review* 95, no. 4 (1990), 1076–1114.

Koyama Shizuko. *Ryōsai kenbo to iu kihan.* Tokyo: Keisō shobō, 1991.

Koyama, Shizuko. "The 'Good Wife and Wise Mother' Ideology in Post–World War I Japan." *U.S.-Japan Women's Journal,* English Supplement no. 7 (December 1994), 31–52.

Kōzu Zenzaburō. *Kyōiku aishi.* Nagano-shi: Ginga shobō, 1974.

Kublin, Hyman. *Asian Revolutionary: The Life of Sen Katayama.* Princeton, N.J.: Princeton University Press, 1964.

Kyutoku, Shigemori. *Bogenbyō.* rpt. Tokyo: Sanmaku shuppan, 1991 ed. Tokyo: Kyōiku kenkūsha, 1979.

Landes, Joan. *Women and the Public Sphere in the Age of the French Revolution.* Ithaca, N.Y.: Cornell University Press, 1988.

Large, Stephen S. *The Yuaikai 1912–1919: The Rise of Labor in Japan.* Tokyo: Sophia University, 1972.

————. *Organized Labor and Socialist Politics in Interwar Japan.* Cambridge: Cambridge University Press, 1981.

Lebra, Takie Sugiyama. *Japanese Women: Constraint and Fulfillment.* Honolulu: University of Hawai'i Press, 1984.

Lebra, Takie Sugiyama. *Above the Clouds: Status Culture of the Modern Japanese Nobility.* Berkeley: University of California Press, 1993.

Lerner, Gerda. "Placing Women in History." In *The Majority Finds Its Past: Placing Women in History.* New York: Oxford University Press, 1979.

Leupp, Gary. *Servants, Shophands, and Laborers in the Cities of Tokugawa Japan.* Princeton, N.J.: Princeton University Press, 1992.

————. *Male Colors: The Construction of Homosexuality in Tokugawa Japan.* Berkeley: University of California Press, 1995.

Levy, Anita. *Other Women: The Writing of Class, Race, and Gender, 1832–1898.* Princeton, N.J.: Princeton University Press, 1991.

Lewis, Catherine C. "From Indulgence to Internalization: Social Control in the Early School Years." *Journal of Japanese Studies* 15, no. 1 (1989), 139–157.

Lewis, Michael Lawrence. *Rioters and Citizens: Mass Protest in Imperial Japan.* Berkeley: University of California Press, 1990.

Lock, Margaret. *Encounters with Aging: Mythologies of Menopause in Japan and North America.* Berkeley: University of California Press, 1993.

Long, Susan Orpett. *Family Change and the Life Course in Japan.* Ithaca, N.Y.: Cornell University East Asia Papers, no. 44, 1987.

Long, Susan Orpett. "Nurturing and Femininity: The Ideal of Caregiving in Postwar Japan." In *Re-imaging Japanese Women.* Ed. Anne E. Imamura. Berkeley: University of California Press, 1996, 156–176.

Lynch, Katherine. *Family, Class, and Ideology in Early Industrial France: Social Policy and the Working-Class Family.* Madison: University of Wisconsin Press, 1988.

Mackie, Vera C. *Creating Socialist Women in Japan: Gender, Labour, and Activism, 1900–1937.* New York: Cambridge University Press, 1997.

Marshall, Byron. *Capitalism and Nationalism in Prewar Japan: The Ideology of a Business Elite, 1868–1941.* Stanford: Stanford University Press, 1967.

———. *Learning to Be Modern: Japanese Political Discourse on Education.* Boulder, Colo.: Westview Press, 1994.

Marsland, Stephen E. *The Birth of the Japanese Labor Movement: Tanaka Fusatarō and the Rōdō Kumiai Kiseikai.* Honolulu: University of Hawai'i Press, 1989.

Matsukawa Yukiko. "Jūkyū seikimatsu Kariforunia no mushō yōchien undō to waga kuni e no eikyō, Morishima Mine to Kariforunia yōchien renshū gakkō o chūshin ni." *Yamaguchi joshi daigaku kenkyū hōkoku, Dai ichibu jinbun shakai kagaku,* no. 13 (1983), 28–29.

Matsuzaki Masako. "Tokunaga Yuki." *Shakai jigyō ni ikita joseitachi.* Ed. Gomi Yuriko. Tokyo: Domesu shuppan, 1973, 208–221.

Matthews, Glenna. *Just a Housewife.* New York: Oxford University Press, 1987.

———. *The Rise of Public Woman: Women's Power and Women's Place in the United States.* New York: Oxford University Press, 1992.

Matthews, Gordon. *What Makes Life Worth Living? How Japanese and Americans Make Sense of their Worlds.* Berkeley: University of California Press, 1996.

Mayer, Frederick. *A History of Educational Thought.* 2d ed. 1960; rpt. Columbus, Ohio: Charles E. Merrill, 1966.

McCarthy, Kathleen. *Women's Culture: American Philanthropy and Art, 1830–1930.* Chicago: University of Chicago Press, 1991.

McCormack, Gavan, and Yoshio Sugimoto, eds. *Democracy in Contermporary Japan.* Armonk, N.Y.: M. E. Sharpe, 1986.

McCullogh, Helen Craig, and William H. McCullough, trans. *A Tale of Flowering Fortunes.* Stanford: Stanford University Press, 1979.

McGill, Nettie. *Infant Welfare Work in Europe: An Account of Recent Experiences in Great Britain, Austria, Belgium, France, Germany, and Italy.* U.S. Children's Bureau Community Child-Welfare Series no. 1. Washington, D.C.: Government Printing Office, 1921.

Meyer, Philippe. *The Child and the State.* Trans. Judith Ennew and Janet Lloyd. Cambridge: Cambridge University Press, 1982.

Mitsuda Kyōko. "Kindaiteki boseikan no henyō to tenkei." In *Bosei o tou,* vol. 2. Ed. Wakita Haruko. Kyoto: Jinbun shoin, 1985, 100–129.

Miyake, Akimasa. "Female Workers of the Urban Lower Class." In *Technology, Change and Female Labour in Japan.* Ed. Masanori Nakamura. New York: United Nations University Press, 1994, 97–131.

Miyake, Yoshiko. "Doubling Expectations: Motherhood and Women's Factory Work under State Management in Japan in the 1930s and 1940s." In *Recreating Japanese Women, 1600–1945*. Ed. Gail Lee Bernstein. Berkeley: University of California Press, 1991, 267–295.

Molony, Barbara. "Activism among Women in the Taisho Cotton Industry." In *Recreating Japanese Women, 1600–1945*. Ed. Gail Lee Bernstein. Berkeley: University of California Press, 1991, 217–238.

Molony, Barbara, and Kathleen Molony. *Ichikawa Fusae: A Political Biography*. Stanford: Stanford University Press, forthcoming.

Monbushō. *Yōchien kyōiku kyūjūnen shi*. Tokyo: Hikari no kuni Shōwa shuppan, 1969.

Mouer, Elizabeth. "Women in Teaching." In *Women in Changing Japan*. Ed. Joyce Lebra, Joy Paulson, and Elizabeth Powers. Stanford: Stanford University Press, 1976, 157–170.

Muraoka Suehiro, ed. *Futaba Hoikuen hachijūgonen shi*. Tokyo: Meiji tosho sentaa, 1984.

Murayama Sadao. "Meiji zenki no yōji hoiku no gaikan." In *Nihon yōji hoikushi*, vol. 1. Ed. Nihon hoiku gakkai. Tokyo: Furēberu kan, 1968, 31–43.

Murayama Seiichi. "Fukyūki no yōchien no hoiku katei (Meiji 30nen–Meiji 31nen)." In *Nihon yōji hoikushi*, v. 2. Ed. Nihon hoiku gakkai. Tokyo: Fureeberu kan, 1968, 50–65.

Murayama Seiichi. "Taishō ki no hoiku yonkō no naiyō." In *Nihon yōji hoikushi*, v. 3. Ed. Nihon hoiku gakkai. Tokyo: Fureeberu kan, 1969, 76–99.

Muta, Kazue. "Images of the Family in Meiji Periodicals: The Paradox Underlying the Emergence of the 'Home.'" *U.S.-Japan Women's Journal English Supplement*, no. 7 (1994), 53–71.

Nagahara Kazuko. "Ryōsai kenboshugi kyōiku ni okeru '*ie*' to *shokugyō*." In *Nihon joseishi*, vol. 4 Kindai. Ed. Joseishi sōgō kenkyūkai. Tokyo: Tōkyō daigaku shuppankai, 1982, 149–184.

Nagy, Margit. "Middle-Class Working Women during the Interwar Years." In *Recreating Japanese Women, 1600–1945*. Ed. Gail Lee Bernstein. Berkeley: University of California Press, 1991, 199–216.

Nakagawa Kiyoshi. *Senzen Tōkyō no toshi kasō*. Tokyo: Kokusai rengō daigaku, 1982.

———. *Nihon no toshi kasō*. Tokyo: Keisō shobō, 1986.

Nakajima Kuni. "Boseiron no keitō." *Rekishi kōron* 5, no. 12 (December 1979), 61–68.

Nakamura, Masanori, ed. *Technology, Change and Female Labour in Japan*. New York: United Nations University Press, 1994.

———. *Kinship and Economic Organization in Japan*. London: Athlone Press, 1967.

Nakane, Chie. "An Interpretation of the Size and Structure of the Household in Japan over Three Centuries." In *Household and Family in Past Time*. Ed. Peter Laslett with Richard Wall. Cambridge: Cambridge University Press, 1972, 517–543.

Nakano, Makiko. *Makiko's Diary: A Merchant Wife in 1910 Kyoto.* Trans. Kazuko Smith. Stanford: Stanford University Press, 1995.

Namae, Takayuki. "Standards of Child Welfare Work in Japan." In *Standards of Child Welfare: A Report of the Children's Bureau Conferences May and June, 1919.* Conference Series no. 1. Ed. U.S. Department of Labor, Children's Bureau. Washington, D.C.: 1921; rpt. New York: Arno Press, 1974, 321–338.

Nardinelli, Clark. *Child Labor and the Industrial Revolution.* Bloomington: Indiana University Press, 1990.

Nasaw, David. *Children of the City: At Work and at Play.* New York: Oxford University Press, 1985.

Neary, Ian. *Political Protest and Social Control in Pre-War Japan: The Origins of Buraku Liberation.* Atlantic Highlands, N.J.: Humanities Press International, 1989.

Nicholson, Linda. *Gender and History.* New York: Columbia University Press, 1986.

Nihon kodomo no rekishi. 5 vols. Tokyo: Daiichi hōki. 1976–1977.

Niimura, Kazuo. *The Ashio Riot of 1907: A Social History of Mining in Japan.* Durham, N.C.: Duke University Press, 1997.

Nishikawa, Yūko. "The Changing Form of Dwellings and the Establishment of the *Katei* (Home) in Modern Japan." *U.S.-Japan Women's Journal English Supplement,* no. 8 (June 1995), 3–36.

Nishikawa, Yūko. "Japan's Entry into War and the Support of Women." *U.S.-Japan Women's Journal English Supplement,* no. 12 (1996), 48–83.

Nishimura Kōichi. "Shokunin no ko—totei kara oyakata made." In *Bushi no ko, shōmin no ko, ge.* vol. 4, *Nihon kodomo no rekishi.* Ed. Ishikawa Matsutarō and Naoe Kōji. Tokyo: Daiichi hōki, 1977.

Nolte, Sharon. "Women, the State, and Repression in Imperial Japan." Michigan State University Working Papers on Women in International Development, no. 33 (Sept. 1983).

———. "Women's Rights and Society's Needs: Japan's 1931 Suffrage Bill." *Comparative Studies in Society and History* 28 (1986), 690–714.

Nolte, Sharon, and Sally Hastings. "The Meiji State's Policy toward Women, 1890–1910." In *Recreating Japanese Women, 1600–1945.* Ed. Gail Lee Bernstein. Berkeley: University of California Press, 1991, 151–174.

Norton, Mary Beth. *Liberty's Daughters: The Revolutionary Experience of American Women, 1750–1800.* Boston: Little, Brown, 1980.

O'Brien, Mary. *The Politics of Reproduction.* Boston: Routledge and Kegan Paul, 1981.

Ochiai, Emiko. *The Japanese Family System in Transition: A Sociological Analysis of Family Change in Japan.* Tokyo: LTCB International Library Foundation, 1996.

Offen, Karen. "Defining Feminism: A Comparative Historical Approach." *Signs: A Journal of Women, Culture, and Society* 14 (1988), 119–157.

Okada Masatoshi. *Nihon no hoiku seido.* Tokyo: Furēberu kan, 1970.

Ooms, Herman. *Tokugawa Village Practice: Class, Status, Power, Law.* Berkeley: University of California Press, 1996.

Ōsaka-shi minseikyoku. *Hoikujo no ayumi, 1909–1945.* Osaka: Ōsaka-shi minseikyoku, 1967.

Ōsugi, Sakae. The *Autobiography of Ōsugi Sakae.* Trans. Byron Marshall. Berkeley: University of California Press, 1992.

Papanek, Hannah. "Development Planning for Women." In *Women and Development: The Complexities of Change.* Ed. Wellesley Editorial Committee. Chicago: University of Chicago Press, 1977.

Passin, Herbert. *Society and Education in Japan.* 1965; rpt. New York: Kodansha International, 1982.

Pateman, Carol. *The Disorder of Women.* Stanford: Stanford University Press, 1989.

Peak, Lois. *Learning to Go to School in Japan: The Transition from Home to Preschool Life.* Berkeley: University of California Press, 1991.

Pflugfelder, Gregory. "Politics and the Kitchen: The Women's Suffrage Movement in Provincial Japan." Paper presented at the Association for Asian Studies Annual Meeting, Chicago, Illinois, April 7, 1990.

Pflugfelder, Gregory M. *Cartographies of Desire: Male-Male Sexuality in Japanese Discourse, 1600–1950.* Berkeley: University of California Press, forthcoming.

Pitts, Jesse R. "Social Control." In *International Encyclopedia of the Social Sciences,* vol. 14. Ed. David Sills. New York: The Macmillan Co. and The Free Press, 382.

Piven, Frances, and Richard A. Cloward. *Regulating the Poor: The Functions of Public Welfare.* New York: Pantheon, 1971.

Pollock, Linda. *Forgotten Children: Parent-Child Relations from 1500 to 1900.* Cambridge: Cambridge University Press, 1983.

Poovey, Mary. *Uneven Developments: The Ideological Work of Gender in Mid-Victorian England.* Chicago: University of Chicago Press, 1988.

Powell, Brian. "Matsui Sumako: Actress and Woman." In *Modern Japan: Aspects of History, Literature, and Society.* Ed. William G. Beasley. Berkeley: University of California Press, 1975, 135–147.

Pyle, Kenneth. *The New Generation in Meiji Japan.* Stanford: Stanford University Press, 1969.

————. "The Technology of Nationalism: The Local Improvement Movement, 1900–1918." *Journal of Asian Studies* 33 (1973), 51–60.

————. "The Advantages of Followership: German Economics and Japanese Bureaucrats, 1890–1925." *Journal of Japanese Studies* 3 (1977), 421–430.

Ransel, David. *Mothers of Misery: Child Abandonment in Russia.* Princeton, N.J.: Princeton University Press, 1988.

Rapp, Rayna, Ellen Ross, and Renate Bridenthal, eds. "Examining Family History." In *Sex and Class in Women's History.* Ed. Judith L. Newton, Mary P. Ryan, and Judith R. Walkowitz. Boston: Routledge & Kegan Paul, 1983, 232–258.

Register, Cheri. "Motherhood at Center: Ellen Key's Social Vision." *Women's Studies International Forum* 5 (1982), 599–615.

Rendall, Jane. *The Origins of Modern Feminism.* New York: Schocken Books, 1984.

Roberts, Glenda. *Staying on the Line: Blue-Collar Women in Contemporary Japan.* Honolulu: University of Hawai'i Press, 1994.

Robertson, Jennifer. "Doing and Undoing 'Female' and 'Male' in Japan: The Takarazuka Revue." In *Japanese Social Organization.* Ed. Takie Sugiyama Lebra. Honolulu: University of Hawai'i Press, 1992.

Rodd, Laurel. "Yosano Akiko and the Taisho Debate over the 'New Woman.'" In *Recreating Japanese Women, 1600–1945.* Ed. Gail Lee Bernstein. Berkeley: University of California Press, 1991, 175–198.

Roden, Donald. *Schooldays in Imperial Japan: A Study in the Culture of A Student Elite.* Berkeley: University of California Press, 1980.

Rohlen, Thomas. *Japan's High Schools.* Berkeley: University of California Press, 1983.

Rose, Barbara. *Tsuda Umeko and Women's Education in Japan.* New Haven, Conn.: Yale University Press, 1992.

Rosenberger, Nancy. "Fragile Resistance, Signs of Status: Women between State and Media in Japan." In *Re-Imaging Japanese Women.* Ed. Anne E. Imamura. Berkeley: University of California Press, 1996, 12–45.

Rubinger, Richard. *Private Academies of Tokugawa Japan.* Princeton, N.J.: Princeton University Press, 1982.

Ryan, Mary P. *Women in Public: Between Banners and Ballots.* Baltimore, Md.: Johns Hopkins University Press, 1990.

Saari, John L. *Legacies of Childhood: Growing up Chinese in a Time of Crisis 1890–1920.* Cambridge, Mass.: Harvard University Press, 1990.

Saji Emiko. "Gunji engo to katei fujin—shoki Aikoku Fujinkai ron." In *Onnatachi no kindai.* Ed. Kindai joseishi kenkyūkai. Tokyo: Kashiwa shobō, 1978, 116–143.

Sakai, Atsuharu. "Kaibara Ekiken and 'Onna Daigaku.'" *Cultural Nippon* 7, no. 4 (Dec. 1939), 43–56.

Sand, Jordan. "At Home in the Meiji Period: Inventing Japanese Domesticity." In *Mirror of Modernity: Invented Traditions of Modern Japan.* Ed. Stephen Vlastos. Berkeley: University of California Press, 1998, 191–207.

Sano, Toshiyuki. "Methods of Social Control and Socialization in Japanese Day-Care Centers." *Journal of Japanese Studies* 15, no. 1 (1989), 125–138.

Sansom, George. *The Western World and Japan.* 1949; rpt. New York: Vintage, 1973.

Sato, Barbara Hamill. "Japanese Women and *Modanizumu:* The Emergence of a New Women's Culture in the 1920s." Unpublished book manuscript.

Sato, Barbara Hamill. "The Moga Sensation: Perceptions of the Modan Gāru in Japanese Intellectual Circles." *Gender and History* 5, no. 3 (1993), 363–381.

Scheiner, Irwin. *Christian Converts and Social Protest in Meiji Japan.* Berkeley: University of California Press, 1971.

Scott, Joan. *Gender and the Politics of History.* New York: Columbia University Press, 1988.

Shibusawa, Eiichi. *The Autobiography of Shibusawa Eiichi.* Trans. Teruko Craig. Tokyo: Tokyo University Press, 1994.

Shields, James J. *Japanese Schooling: Patterns of Socialization, Equality, and Political Control.* University Park: Pennsylvania State University Press, 1989.

Shively, Donald. "The Japanization of the Middle Meiji." In *Tradition and Modernization in Japanese Culture.* Ed. Donald Shively. Princeton, N.J.: Princeton University Press, 1971, 77–119.

Sievers, Sharon. *Flowers in Salt: The Beginnings of Feminist Consciousness in Modern Japan.* Stanford: Stanford University Press, 1983.

Simon, Carol. "A Long-Distance Ticket to Life." *Smithsonian* 17, no. 2 (Mar. 1987), 44–56.

Sklar, Katherine Kish. *Catherine Beecher: A Study in American Domesticity.* New Haven, Conn.: Yale University Press, 1977.

Smethurst, Richard J. *A Social Basis for Prewar Japanese Militarism: The Army and the Rural Community.* Berkeley: University of California Press, 1974.

Smethurst, Richard J. *Agricultural Development and Tenancy Disputes in Japan, 1870–1940.* Princeton, N.J.: Princeton University Press, 1986.

Smith, Bonnie G. *Ladies of the Leisure Class: The Bourgeoises of Northern France in the Nineteenth Century.* Princeton, N.J.: Princeton University Press, 1981.

Smith, Robert J. "Making Village Women into 'Good Wives and Wise Mothers.'" *Journal of Family History* 8 (1983), 70–84.

Smith, Robert J., and Ella Lury Wiswell. *The Women of Suye Mura.* Chicago: University of Chicago Press, 1982.

———. *Agrarian Origins of Modern Japan.* Stanford: Stanford University Press, 1959.

Smith, Thomas C. "Right to Benevolence: Dignity and Japanese Workers, 1890–1920." Comparative Studies in Society and History 26 (1984), 587–613.

Smith-Rosenberg, Carroll. "The Female World of Love and Ritual: Relations between Women in Nineteenth-Century America." *Signs: Journal of Women in Culture and*

Society 1, no. 1 (1975); rpt. in *Disorderly Conduct,* Carroll Smith-Rosenberg. New York: Oxford University Press, 1985, 53–76.

Snyder, Agnes. *Dauntless Women in Early Childhood Education, 1856–1931.* Washington, D.C.: Association for Childhood Education International, 1972.

Stansell, Christine. *City of Women.* Urbana: University of Illinois Press, 1987.

Strasser, Susan. *Never Done: A History of American Housework.* New York: Pantheon, 1982.

Sugimoto, Etsu Inagaki. *A Daughter of the Samurai.* New York: Doubleday Doran, 1928.

Sugō Hiroshi. *Komori gakkō.* Tokyo: Popurasha, 1980.

Sussman, Warren. *Selling Mothers' Milk: The Wet-Nursing Business in France, 1715–1914.* Urbana: University of Illinois Press, 1982.

Suwa Yoshihide. *Hoiku no shisō: katei kyōiku to yō, ho kyōiku no kōzō.* Nagoya: Fūbaisha, 1976.

Tachi Kaoru. "Ryōsai kenbo." In *Kōza joseigaku* v. 1, *Onna no imēji.* Ed. Joseigaku kenkyūkai. Tokyo: Keisō shobō, 1984, 184–209.

Taeuber, Irene. *The Population of Japan.* Princeton, N.J.: Princeton University Press, 1958.

Taira, Koji. "Public Assistance in Japan: Development Trends." *Journal of Asian Studies* 26, no. 1 (1967), 100–130.

Takahashi, Mutsuko. *The Emergence of Welfare Society in Japan.* Brookfield, Vermont: Ashgate Publishing Co., 1997.

Takahashi, Nobuko. "Child-Care Programs in Japan." In *Child Care, Who Cares?* Ed. Pamela Roby. New York: Basic Books, 1973, 400–407.

Takai Toshio. *Watashi no jokō aishi.* Tokyo: Sōdo bunka, 1980.

Tamanoi, Mariko. "Songs as Weapons: The Culture and History of *Komori* (Nursemaids) in Modern Japan." *Journal of Asian Studies* 50, no. 4 (1991), 793–817.

———. *Under the Shadow of Nationalism: Politics and Poetics of Rural Japanese Women.* Honolulu: University of Hawai'i Press, 1998.

Tanaka Katsubumi. "Ie de hataraku kodomo." *Fukoku kyōheika no kodomo.* Vol. 5 of Nihon kodomo no rekishi. Ed. Naka Arata. Tokyo: Daiichi hōki, 1978.

Tanaka, Stefan. *Japan's Orient: Rendering Pasts into History.* Berkeley: University of California Press, 1993.

Tatara, Toshio. "1400 Years of Japanese Social Work from Its Origins through the Japanese Occupation, 552–1952." Bryn Mawr College, 1975.

Tobin, Joseph J., David Y. H. Wu, and Dana H. Davidson. *Preschool in Three Cultures: Japan, China, and the United States.* New Haven, Conn.: Yale University Press, 1989.

Tomizawa, Yoshiko. "From Child-Care to Local Politics." In *Voices from the Japanese Women's Movement.* Ed. AMPO: Japan Asia Quarterly Review. Armonk, N.Y.: M. E. Sharpe, 1996, 196–200.

Tsukamoto Tetsu, Ōtsuka Tatsuo, Urabe Hiroshi, and Kōkō Seiichi, eds. *Shakai fukushi jigyō jiten.* Kyoto: Minerurva shobō, 1966.

Tsurumi, E. Patricia. *Japanese Colonial Education in Taiwan.* Cambridge, Mass.: Harvard University Press, 1977.

———. *Factory Girls: Women in the Thread Mills of Meiji Japan.* Princeton, N.J.: Princeton University Press, 1990.

Ueno Chizuko, "'Kokumin kokka' to 'jiendaa': 'Josei no kokuminka' o megutte." *Gendai shisō* 24, no. 12 (Oct. 1995), 8–45.

Uno, Kathleen. "Day Care and Family Life in Late Meiji–Taisho Japan." *Transactions of the Asiatic Society of Japan.* 3d series, vol. 19 (1984), 30.

———. "'Good Wives and Wise Mothers' in Early Twentieth-Century Japan." Paper presented at a joint meeting of the Pacific Coast Branch of the American Historical Association and the Western Conference of Women Historians, August 1988.

———. "Japan." In *Children in Historical and Comparative Perspective: An International Handbook and Research Guide.* Ed. Joseph M. Hawes and N. Ray Hiner. Westport, Conn.: Greenwood Press, 1991, 389–419.

———. "Women and Changes in the Household Division of Labor." In *Recreating Japanese Women, 1600–1945.* Ed. Gail Lee Bernstein. Berkeley: University of California Press, 1991, 17–41.

———. "One Day at a Time: Work and Domestic Activities of Urban Lower-Class Women in Early Twentieth-Century Japan." In *Japanese Women Working.* Ed. Janet Hunter. London: Routledge, 1993, 37–68.

———. The Death of 'Good Wife, Wise Mother'?" In *Postwar Japan as History.* Ed. Andrew Gordon. Berkeley: University of California Press, 1993, 293–322.

———. "Origins of 'Good Wife, Wise Mother.'" In *Japanische Frauengeschichte(n).* Ed. Erich Pauer and Regine Mathias. Marburg, Germany: Förderverein Marburger Japan-Reihe, 1995, 31–46.

———. "Questioning Patrilineality: On Western Studies of the Japanese *Ie.*" *positions: East Asia cultures critique,* no. 3 (March 1996), 569–594.

Urabe Hiroshi. *Nihon hoiku undō shōshi.* Nagoya: Fūbaisha, 1969.

Urabe Hiroshi and Urabe Takeyo. *Michizure: Atarashii hoiku o motomete.* Tokyo: Sōdo bunka, 1982.

Urabe Hiroshi, Shishido Takeo, and Murayama Yūichi. *Hoiku no rekishi.* Tokyo: Aoki shoten, 1981.

U.S. Department of Labor, Children's Bureau. *Standards of Child Welfare: A Report of the Children's Bureau Conferences May and June, 1919.* Conference Series no. 1. Washington, D.C.: 1921; rpt. New York: Arno Press, 1974.

Uto Eiko. "Tomita Ei." In *Shakai jigyō ni ikita joseitachi.* Ed. Gomi Yuriko. Tokyo: Domesu shuppan, 1973, 236–259.

Vogel, Ezra. *Japan's New Middle Class.* Berkeley: University of California Press, 1963.

Vogel, Suzanne. "Professional Housewife: The Career of Urban Middle Class Japanese Women." *The Japan Interpreter* 12, no. 1 (Winter 1978), 17–43.

Wagatsuma, Hiroshi. "Some Aspects of the Contemporary Japanese Family: Once Confucian, Now Fatherless?" In *The Family.* Ed. Alice Rossi, Jerome Kagan, and Tamara Hareven. New York: Norton, 1977, 181–211.

Waltner, Ann. *Getting an Heir: Adoption and the Construction of Kinship in Late Imperial China.* Honolulu: University of Hawai'i Press, 1990.

Waswo, Ann. *Japanese Landlords: Decline of a Rural Elite.* Berkeley: University of California Press, 1977.

Watanabe, Tsuneo. *The Love of the Samurai: A Thousand Years of Japanese Homosexuality.* Trans. D. R. Roberts. London: GMP Publishers, 1989.

Weber, Eugen. *Peasants into Frenchmen: The Modernization of Rural France, 1870–1914.* Stanford: Stanford University Press, 1976.

Weiner, Michael. *Race and Migration in Imperial Japan.* New York: Routledge, 1994.

White, Merry. "The Virtue of Japanese Mothers." *Daedalus* 116, no. 3 (Summer 1987), 149–164.

———. *The Japanese Educational Challenge: A Committment to Children.* New York: The Free Press, 1987.

———. *The Japanese Overseas: Can They Go Home Again?* New York: The Free Press, 1988.

———. *The Material Child.* New York: The Free Press, 1993.

Wilson, Elizabeth. *Women and the Welfare State.* London and New York: Tavistock Publications, 1977.

Wilson, George O. *Patriots and Redeemers in Japan: Motives in the Meiji Restoration.* Chicago: University of Chicago Press, 1992.

Yamakawa, Kikue. *Women of the Mito Domain: Recollections of Samurai Family Life.* Trans. Kate Wildman Nakai. Tokyo: University of Tokyo Press, 1992.

Yamazaki, Tomoko. *The Story of Yamada Waka: From Prostitute to Feminist Pioneer.* Trans. Wakako Hironaka and Ann Kostant. Tokyo: Kodansha International, 1985.

Yamazumi Masami and Nakae Kazue. *Kosodate no sho,* vols. 1–2. Tokyo: Heibonsha, 1976, 1977.

Yanagita, Kunio. *Japanese Manners and Customs in the Meiji Period.* Trans. Charles S. Terry. Tokyo: Ōbunsha, 1957.

Yokoe, Katsumi. "Historical Trends in Home Discipline." In *Families East and West: Socialization Process and Kinship Ties.* Ed. Reuben Hill and Rene Konig. The Hague, Netherlands: Mouton, 1970, 175–186.

Yoshida Kyūichi. *Shakai jigyō riron no rekishi.* Tokyo: Ichiryūsha, 1974.

———. *Gendai shakai jigyōshi kenkyū.* Tokyo: Keisō shobō, 1979.

Zaretsky, Eli. "The Place of the Family in the Origins of the Welfare State." In *Rethinking the Family: Some Feminist Questions.* Ed. Barrie Thorne. New York: Longman, 1982, 188–224.

Zenkoku hoiku dantai renrakukai and Hoiku kenkyūjo, eds. *Hoiku hakusho.* Tokyo: Sōdo bunka, 1992.

Index

About the Author

Kathleen Uno teaches Japanese and comparative women's history at Temple University, where she is currently engaged in developing Asian American courses and curriculum. Professor Uno is also coeditor of the forthcoming *Gendering Modern Japanese History,* which examines changes in the aspects of the masculine and the feminine and their shifting mutual relationships in modern and postwar Japan. Her current research interests include further investigation of children's history and the evolution of "good wife, wise mother" (*ryōsai kenbo*) in Japan since the mid-nineteenth century.